Lecture Notes in Business Information Processing 292

Series Editors

Wil M.P. van der Aalst
Eindhoven Technical University, Eindhoven, The Netherlands
John Mylopoulos
University of Trento, Trento, Italy
Michael Rosemann
Queensland University of Technology, Brisbane, QLD, Australia
Michael J. Shaw
University of Illinois, Urbana-Champaign, IL, USA
Clemens Szyperski
Microsoft Research, Redmond, WA, USA

More information about this series at http://www.springer.com/series/7911

Valérie Monfort · Karl-Heinz Krempels
Tim A. Majchrzak · Paolo Traverso (Eds.)

Web Information Systems and Technologies

12th International Conference, WEBIST 2016
Rome, Italy, April 23–25, 2016
Revised Selected Papers

Editors
Valérie Monfort
University of Paris
Paris
France

Karl-Heinz Krempels
Department of Information Systems
   and Databases
RWTH Aachen University
Aachen
Germany

Tim A. Majchrzak
Faculty of Social Sciences
University of Agder
Kristiansand
Norway

Paolo Traverso
Center for Information Technology
FBK-ICT IRST
Trento
Italy

ISSN 1865-1348   ISSN 1865-1356 (electronic)
Lecture Notes in Business Information Processing
ISBN 978-3-319-66467-5   ISBN 978-3-319-66468-2 (eBook)
DOI 10.1007/978-3-319-66468-2

Library of Congress Control Number: 2017952865

Printed on acid-free paper

This Springer imprint is published by Springer Nature
The registered company is Springer International Publishing AG
The registered company address is: Gewerbestrasse 11, 6330 Cham, Switzerland

Preface

The present book includes extended and revised versions of a set of selected papers from the 12th International Conference on Web Information Systems and Technologies (WEBIST 2016), held in Rome, Italy, April 23–25, 2016.

WEBIST 2016 received 123 paper submissions from 35 countries, of which 7% are included in this book. The papers were selected by the event chairs and their selection is based on a number of criteria that include the classifications and comments provided by the Program Committee members, the session chairs' assessment of the presentation and discussion quality, and also the program chairs' global view of all papers included in the technical program. The authors of selected papers were then invited to submit a revised and extended version of their papers. Extended papers have at least 30% innovative material and ought to be revised based on the discussions at the conference.

The purpose of the 12th International Conference on Web Information Systems and Technologies (WEBIST) was to bring together researchers, engineers and practitioners interested in the technological advances and business applications of web-based information systems. The conference had five main tracks, covering different aspects of Web Information Systems, including Internet Technology, Web Interfaces and Applications, Society, e-Communities, e-Business, Web Intelligence and Mobile Information Systems.

The papers selected to be included in this book contribute to the understanding of relevant trends of current research on Web Information Systems and Technologies, comprising:

- recommender systems,
- sentiment analysis,
- ranking, and
- Web applications and Web architecture.

We would like to thank all the authors for their contributions and also the reviewers, who helped in ensuring the quality of this publication.

April 2017

Valérie Monfort
Karl-Heinz Krempels
Tim A. Majchrzak
Paolo Traverso

Organization

Conference Co-chairs

Valérie Monfort   LAMIH Valenciennes UMR CNRS 8201, France
Karl-Heinz Krempels   RWTH Aachen University, Germany

Program Co-chairs

Tim A. Majchrzak   University of Agder, Norway
Paolo Traverso   Center for Information Technology - IRST (FBK-ICT),
         Italy

Program Committee

Jose Luis Herrero Agustin   University of Extremadura, Spain
Guglielmo De Angelis   CNR - IASI, Italy
Margherita Antona   Foundation for Research and Technology - Hellas
         (FORTH), Greece
Valeria De Antonellis   University of Brescia, Italy
Giuliano Armano   University of Cagliari, Italy
Elarbi Badidi   United Arab Emirates University, UAE
Werner Beuschel   Technische Hochschule Brandenburg, Germany
Christoph Bussler   Oracle Corporation, USA
Maria Claudia Buzzi   CNR, Italy
Elena Calude   Massey University, Institute of Natural
         and Mathematical Sciences, New Zealand
Pasquina Campanella   University of Bari "Aldo Moro", Italy
Cinzia Cappiello   Politecnico di Milano, Italy
Luigi Di Caro   University of Turin, Italy
Nunzio Casalino   LUISS Guido Carli, Italy
Sven Casteleyn   Universitat Jaume I, Spain
Mario Cataldi   Université Paris 8, France
Shiping Chen   CSIRO, Australia
Dickson Chiu   The University of Hong Kong, Hong Kong, China
Mihaela Cocea   University of Portsmouth, UK
Martine De Cock   Ghent University, Belgium
Christine Collet   Grenoble Institute of Technology, France
Marco Comuzzi   City University London, UK
Isabelle Comyn-Wattiau   Cnam & Essec, France
Emmanuel Coquery   Université Claude Bernard Lyon 1, France
Daniel Cunliffe   University of South Wales, UK
Steven Demurjian   University of Connecticut, USA

Enrico Denti	Università di Bologna, Italy
Stefan Dessloch	Kaiserslautern University of Technology, Germany
Qian Dong	Sun Yet-Sen University, China
Brian Donnellan	Maynooth University, Ireland
Atilla Elci	Aksaray University, Turkey
Larbi Esmahi	Athabasca University, Canada
Davide Eynard	University of Lugano, Switzerland
Alexander Felfernig	Technische Universität Graz, Austria
Anna Fensel	STI Innsbruck, University of Innsbruck, Austria
Dieter A. Fensel	University of Innsbruck, Austria
Joao Carlos Amaro Ferreira	ISEL, Portugal
Josep-Lluis Ferrer-Gomila	Balearic Islands University, Spain
Karla Donato Fook	IFMA - Maranhão Federal Institute for Education, Science and Technology, Brazil
Geoffrey Charles Fox	Indiana University, USA
Pasi Fränti	University of Eastern Finland, Finland
Xiang Fu	Hofstra University, USA
Ombretta Gaggi	Università di Padova, Italy
John Garofalakis	University of Patras, Greece
Panagiotis Germanakos	University of Cyprus, Cyprus
Massimiliano Giacomin	Università degli Studi di Brescia, Italy
Henrique Gil	Escola Superior de Educação do Instituto Politécnico de Castelo Branco, Portugal
José Antonio Gil	Universitat Politècnica de València, Spain
Nuno Pina Gonçalves	Superior School of Technology, Polithecnical Institute of Setúbal, Portugal
Anna Goy	University of Turin, Italy
Ratvinder Grewal	Laurentian University, Canada
Naijie Gu	University of Science and Technology of China, China
Angela Guercio	Kent State University, USA
Francesco Guerra	University of Modena and Reggio Emilia, Italy
Shanmugasundaram Hariharan	Vel Tech Multi Tech, Avadi, Chennai, India
Ioannis Hatzilygeroudis	University of Patras, Greece
A. Henten	Aalborg University, Denmark
Jane Hunter	University of Queensland, Australia
Kai Jakobs	RWTH Aachen University, Germany
Monique Janneck	Luebeck University of Applied Sciences, Germany
Ivan Jelinek	Czech Technical University in Prague, Czech Republic
Yuh-Jzer Joung	National Taiwan University, Taiwan
Georgia Kapitsaki	University of Cyprus, Cyprus
George Karabatis	Umbc, USA
Sokratis Katsikas	Norwegian University of Science and Technology, Norway

Takahiro Kawamura	Toshiba Corp., Japan
Matthias Klusch	German Research Center for Artificial Intelligence (DFKI) GmbH, Germany
Waldemar W. Koczkodaj	Laurentian University, Canada
Hiroshi Koide	Kyushu Institute of Technology, Japan
Fotis Kokkoras	TEI of Thessaly, Greece
Tsvi Kuflik	The University of Haifa, Israel
Kin Fun Li	University of Victoria, Canada
Weigang Li	University of Brasilia, Brazil
Dongxi Liu	CSIRO, Australia
Leszek Maciaszek	Wroclaw University of Economics, Poland and Macquarie University, Sydney, Australia
Michael Mackay	Liverpool John Moores University, UK
Tim A. Majchrzak	University of Agder, Norway
Dwight Makaroff	University of Saskatchewan, Canada
Zaki Malik	Wayne State University, USA
Massimo Marchiori	University of Padua, Italy
Andrea Marrella	Università degli Studi di Roma La Sapienza, Italy
Kazutaka Maruyama	Meisei University, Japan
Ingo Melzer	Daimler AG, Germany
Weiyi Meng	Binghamton University, USA
Abdelkrim Meziane	CERIST Alger, Algeria
Tommi Mikkonen	Institute of Software Systems, Tampere University of Technology, Finland
Alex Norta	Tallinn University of Technology, Estonia
Dusica Novakovic	London Metropolitan University, UK
Declan O'Sullivan	University of Dublin Trinity College, Ireland
Kyparisia Papanikolaou	ASPETE, Greece
Kalpdrum Passi	Laurentian University, Canada
David Paul	The University of New England, Australia
Cesare Pautasso	University of Lugano, Switzerland
Toon De Pessemier	Ghent University - iMinds, Belgium
Luis Ferreira Pires	University of Twente, The Netherlands
Marco Pistore	Fondazione Bruno Kessler, Italy
Pierluigi Plebani	Politecnico Di Milano, Italy
Simona Popa	Universidad Católica San Antonio de Murcia, Spain
Jim Prentzas	Democritus University of Thrace, Greece
Birgit Pröll	Johannes Kepler University Linz, Austria
Thomas Risse	L3S Research Center, Germany
Davide Rossi	University of Bologna, Italy
Gustavo Rossi	Lifia, Argentina
Davide Di Ruscio	University of L'Aquila, Italy
Maytham Safar	Kuwait University, Kuwait
Yacine Sam	University of Tours, France
Manuel J. Sanchez-Franco	University of Seville, Spain
Comai Sara	Politecnico di Milano, Italy

Claudio Schifanella	Università degli Studi di Torino, Italy
Wieland Schwinger	Johannes Kepler University, Austria
Jochen Seitz	Technische Universität Ilmenau, Germany
Mohamed Sellami	RDI Group, LISITE LAB, ISEP Paris, France
Weiming Shen	NRC Canada, Canada
Marianna Sigala	School of Management, University of South Australia Business School, Australia
Marten van Sinderen	University of Twente, The Netherlands
Anna Stavrianou	Laboratoire LIG Grenoble, France
York Sure-Vetter	Karlsruhe Institute of Technology (KIT), Germany
Dirk Thissen	RWTH Aachen University, Germany
Paolo Traverso	Center for Information Technology - IRST (FBK-ICT), Italy
Raquel Trillo-Lado	University of Zaragoza, Spain
Th. Tsiatsos	Aristotle University of Thessaloniki, Greece
Jari Veijalainen	University of Jyväskylä, Finland
Maria Esther Vidal	Universidad Simon Bolivar, Venezuela
Petri Vuorimaa	Aalto University, Finland
Olga Vybornova	Université Catholique de Louvain, Belgium
Mohd Helmy Abd Wahab	Universiti Tun Hussein Onn Malaysia, Malaysia
Jason Whalley	Northumbria University, UK
Maarten Wijnants	Hasselt University, Belgium
Manuel Wimmer	Technische Universität Wien, Austria
Amal Zouaq	University of Ottawa, Canada

Additional Reviewers

Maribel Acosta	Karlsruhe Institute of Technology, Germany
Hassan Adelyar	Kabul University, Afghanistan
Nabeela Altrabsheh	University of Portsmouth, UK
Baseer Baheer	Tallinn University, Estonia
Marios Belk	University of Cyprus, Cyprus
Michael Färber	Karlsruhe Institute of Technology (KIT), Germany
Golnoosh Farnadi	Ghent University, The Netherlands
Christian Junker	STI Innsbruck, Austria
Diego Magro	University of Turin, Italy
Alexander Nikolaev	University at Buffalo (SUNY), USA
Anis Ben Othman	Tallinn University of Technology, Estonia
Karima Quayumi	Tallinn University, Estonia
Alexander Semenov	University of Jyvaskyla, Finland
Steffen Thoma	KIT, Germany
Amaury Trujillo	CNR, Italy
Shuaiqiang Wang	University of Jyväskylä, Finland

Invited Speakers

Frank Leymann	University of Stuttgart, Germany
Jérôme Euzenat	Inria and Univ. Grenoble Alpes, France
Mohammed Atiquzzaman	University of Oklahoma, USA
Leon Rothkrantz	Delft University of Technology, The Netherlands

Contents

A Query and Product Suggestion Method for Price Comparison Search Engines

Lucia Noce[(✉)], Ignazio Gallo, Alessandro Zamberletti, and Alessandro Calefati

Department of Theoretical and Applied Science,
University of Insubria, Via Mazzini, 5, 21100 Varese, Italy
{lucia.noce,ignazio.gallo}@uninsubria.it

Abstract. In this paper we propose a query suggestion method for price comparison search engines. Query suggestion techniques are used for generating alternative queries to facilitate web users in information seeking; in this specific domain, suggestions provided to web users need to be properly generated taking into account that the suggested products must be still available for sale. We propose a novel approach based on a slightly variant of classical query-URL graphs: the query-product click-through bipartite graph. Information extracted both from search engine logs and specific domain features are exploited to build the graph, and one of the advantages of this model is that such a graph can be used to suggest not only related queries but also related products. Concepts used in the proposed method are not restricted to our context but are used in many other major e-commerce and search engine websites, we tested the model on several challenging datasets, and also compared with a recent query suggestion approach specifically designed for price comparison engines. Our solution outperforms the competing approach, achieving higher results in terms of relevance of the provided suggestions and coverage rates on top-8 suggestions.

1 Introduction

Query suggestion plays an important role in helping users to find what they are looking for when querying web search engines. It is a particularly interesting research topic because the usability, popularity and success of web search engines are strongly related to the effectiveness of the helping tools provided to users while performing textual queries: the larger the amount of users that issue queries leading to optimal/desirable results, the higher is the usability of the web search engine and consequently the larger is the amount of users that will keep using that web search engine for other future queries.

Although many effective and sophisticated query suggestion algorithms that have been proposed in literature are currently employed by web search engines to improve user search experience [6], precisely understanding in a limited amount of time the needs of service users from textual queries is still a challenging task that has yet to find an optimal solution. In fact, achieving satisfying query suggestion accuracies for textual queries is a non-trivial task because most user-made textual

© Springer International Publishing AG 2017
V. Monfort et al. (Eds.): WEBIST 2016, LNBIP 292, pp. 1–14, 2017.
DOI: 10.1007/978-3-319-66468-2_1

queries are typically very short and contain ambiguous words, and it is therefore difficult to provide good query suggestions without using complex pipelines.

Most query suggestion algorithms in literature focus on improving user search experience by suggesting related queries from a given textual query, trying to guide users in finding what they are looking for. The list of suggestions is usually created by mining related queries from web search engine logs and session information, trying to gather previous users knowledge. Depending on the chosen approach, query suggestion techniques can be grouped into two categories [11]: session-based methods and click-through-based methods. The first approach uses the consecutiveness of the queries to model user behavior within each user session, while the second one focuses on the relationship between the submitted queries and the URLs clicked by the user. Both session-based methods and click-through-based methods are being used by many commercial web search engine, *e.g.* Google, Ask and Yahoo!, to provide correlated queries to improve usability.

Despite most of the query suggestion works in literature were developed for web search engines, query suggestion is also important for e-commerce platforms and price comparison search engines [4]. In this work we present a click-through-based query suggestion system specifically designed for price comparison websites, we tested the methodology using data gathered for two websites: ShoppyDoo [13] and TrovaPrezzi [17]. The system provides query suggestions on the basis of all the specific product information available in this context, *e.g.* the category of the product that the user is browsing while issuing the query and the clicked product. To this end, instead of using the URLs clicked by users, our click-though based method exploits the information from clicked products.

Query suggestion in price comparison websites is an even more challenging task because, for example, it may be disadvantageous to suggest a query for which there are no available product offers.

2   Related Works

Query suggestion is an interesting research topic widely investigated in researches on Internet search domain [5, 7, 15]. Algorithms for query suggestion can be classified as either session-based [2, 8, 12, 20, 21] or click-through-based [9, 10, 14].

Session-based methods assume that users submit queries in a *sequential manner*. The basic assumption is that when a badly written textual query is executed by a user, there will always be a correct version of the wrong textual query previously executed by the same user that follows the wrong one. The sequence of queries is usually obtained by exploiting user sessions, and it is used to extract the user's intentions. Among session-based query suggestion methods, the works that are closely related to our are the ones of [2, 8, 12, 20].

In their work about query refinement Lau *et al.* [8] assert that, after a failed search, most users refine their original query either by adding more details or by executing a new one. Another study by Ozmutlu and Spink [12] demonstrates that in 88.6% of cases a query session relates to a just a single topic, supporting the thesis that query sessions are useful to extract information that can be used for query suggestion purposes.

Following this approach, Boldi *et al.* [2] propose a system that uses query-flow graphs built from query session logs. In the query-flow graph, there exists an edge from a query q_1 to a query q_2 if and only if both queries belong to the same session. Edges and vertexes can be weighted. These weights represent the frequency of a query and the popularity of a transition for a vertex and for an edge respectively. Edges are also labelled with some extra information describing the nature of the transition (*e.g.* specialization, probability that user moves from q_1 to q_2, *etc.*). In their experimental evaluation, Boldi *et al.* show that adding weights and labels to query-flow graphs allows the creation of a session-based query suggestion algorithm which achieves the same results of click-through-based models.

A session-based query suggestion method specifically designed for price comparison engines has been proposed by Zanon *et al.* [20]. The model performs query suggestion system using the same query-flow graphs proposed by Boldi *et al.* [2]. Zanon *et al.* adapt the model of Boldi *et al.* to their context exploiting the fact that in price comparison engines offers are grouped into categories. Their model reach a quality of 70% and a coverage of 37% for top-8 suggestions.

Click-through-based methods exploit the information of the URL that a user clicks after having submitted a query. These category of approaches assume that two queries are similar if they share a consistent number of clicked URLs.

Baeza-Yates *et al.* [1] exploit click-through data in their query recommendation method. The presented methodology is based on a clustering process over data extracted from the query log, where suggested queries are proposed according to a rank score evaluated in terms of similarity and support of the queries.

Following Baeza-Yates *et al.* work, a query suggestion method for e-commerce was proposed by Hasan *et al.* [4]. Authors discuss about the challenges related to their context and underline that, due to the nature of the data belonging to e-commerce websites, it could be difficult to adapt session-based query suggestion approaches to e-commerce systems. Instead, a common approach in this field is to use graph representation for underlining queries and URLs relationship through a click-through bipartite graph. Click-through bipartite, represents an implicit judgment given by users of the relationships between queries. It has been proven that this type of graph is a very precious source of information for measuring similarities among its components [19].

Many click-through-based approaches exploit bipartite graph, *e.g.* Ma *et al.* [9] proposed a ranking method that is able to diversify query suggestion results, employing Markov random walk process and hitting time analysis; Song *et al.* use bipartite graph to analyze both clicked URLs and skipped URLs to recommend related queries [14]; Cao *et al.* [3] exploit click-through data and group similar queries into *concepts*, providing query suggestions based on these *concepts*.

3   Proposed Method

Query suggestion in price comparison websites is very similar to the query suggestion in e-commerce websites, because in both scenarios users search for products they want to buy and therefore it is reasonable to say that they issue to the two different search engine the same type of queries. Following the discussion of Hasan *et al.* [4] about e-commerce websites, the proposed method is a click-through-based query suggestion approach.

Our model exploits the two main entities of the website for which it has been designed for [13]: products and categories. We also applied the proposed method on a different price comparison search engine website [17], which adopts the same structure. These concepts are not restricted to our context but are used in many other major e-commerce and search engine websites.

More in details, the result of a generic query in our context is a list of commercial products sold by several retailers and sorted by descending price. Each item of the list is an offer. All the offers belong to a specific category, according to the type of the objects searched by the user. Offers may also be linked to products. Products represent aggregations of items/offers, and all the offers inherent to a specific item are collected under the related product.

In general, a click-through-based query suggestion algorithm is composed of two phases: (i) an offline module which manages the data and builds the model, (ii) and an online procedure which supplies the query suggestions. Our solution extracts information from web server logs. Starting from those logs, the offline phase of our method can be summarized in the following steps:

- Data Extraction: is the pre-processing phase, the web server log is parsed. Queries and related information are extracted, cleaned and normalized;
- Session creation: the sessions are created as associations between queries and clicked products;
- Building phase: creation of the click-through bipartite graph by exploiting the notion of product;

On the other hand, the subsequent online phase gathers query suggestions from the model and returns a fixed number of ranked related queries and products.

In Fig. 1, both the offline and the online phases of the proposed approach are visually summarized. In the following sections all their major details are reported.

3.1   Data Extraction

The first step consists of the extraction of data from the web server log. Those logs contains rough data that has to be cleaned before being used for query suggestion.

Different cleaning stages are performed to gather only log lines containing the information we want to exploit. First we performed bot filtering to retrieve only log search lines that lead to a user click. Within a log line we extract only the fields of interest: the textual query, the id of the category for which the query has been performed, and the clicked product. Synonym mapping for queries like "mtb" and "mountain bike" and spelling correction for cases such as

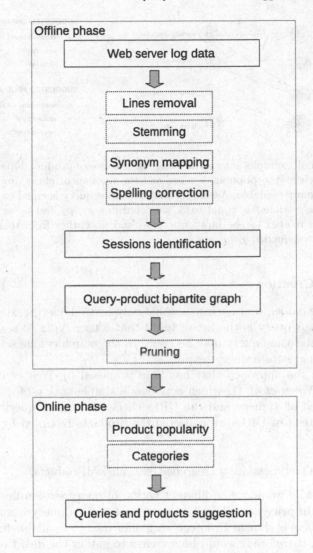

Fig. 1. Visual summarization of the proposed pipeline. From top to bottom: starting from raw log data, all the information needed to determine query sessions are extracted; the query-product bipartite graph is built and suggestions are provided by exploiting both the product categories and the product popularities extra-fields.

"dylandog" corrects into "dylan dog" are also performed. We also use stemming to detect equivalent queries, *e.g.* "woman bike" is equivalent to "women bikes", "samsung galaxy S6" represents the same query as "S6 samsung galaxy". Since the website is in italian, all the reported examples have been translated for better understanding.

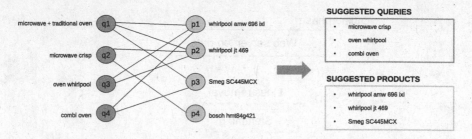

Fig. 2. This visual example shows the usage of the query-product bipartite graph. Some details, such as the popularity score and the number of clicks, are omitted to make the image more readable. Assuming that the input query is equal to q_1 and that N (number of suggestions) is equal to 3, we determine p_1, p_2 and p_3 as the 3 most popular products related to the input query q_1, and we gather from them the three most clicked related queries q_2, q_3 and q_4.

3.2   Session Creation

For building the model, we take into account only textual queries extracted from web server logs. A query is the list of terms that a user types to search for the item he needs, the same query may be issued to the search engine several times, each submission creates a query session.

We followed the approach that has been proposed by Wen *et al.* [18] and used by Baeza-Yates *et al.* [1] which considers a simple notion of query session that is composed of a query and the URLs clicked within its query results. In our method instead of URLs we collected the products returned by the query, as follows:

$$QuerySession = (searchedText, clickedProducts)$$

The reason why we adopt a different notion of query session lies our application context. In price comparison engines, each time a query is submitted, a list of related offers is shown. However, each offer may be available for a limited amount of time, therefore it would be senseless to gather the direct offers URLs which may have been already destroyed. Creating query suggestions dealing to unavailable offers is improper and unattractive for users, and may cause a loss of clients for the website.

The taxonomy of our price comparison website allows us to exploit the notion of product. Not every offer is related to a product, but statistical studies made by the website administrator shows that the majority (97%) of the offers dealing to a user click are related to a product. Starting from this assertion we consider only offers related to products and sessions storing products related to the submitted queries. This not only allows us to provide a more reliable query suggestion system, but also permits to supply product suggestions to users.

3.3 Building Phase

We build the proposed model using the notion of query session previously described. This way we create a different version of the well-known query-URL bipartite graph in which, instead of URLs, we use clicked products.

A query-product bipartite graph consists of two disjoint sets of nodes corresponding to queries and products respectively. Intuitively, in a click-through graph vertexes on one side correspond to queries, while vertexes on the other side represents products. An edge connecting a query q to a product p exists whenever p was clicked starting from q.

A visual example of such query-product bipartite graph is given in Fig. 2. The set of nodes in the left part are queries and the ones in the right part are products. An edge between a query q and an URL u indicates a user click of u when issuing q (for simplicity click numbers are omitted from the graph).

The query-product bipartite graph gathers a large amount of potential information that can be used for query suggestion, query clustering, query reformulation and so on.

In our method we consider two kind of graphs depending on whether a user uses a category when searching for a product or not. In our price comparison website, users are allowed to submit queries within a specified category, and they expect to receive product results from that same category. Showing query suggestions outside the selected category may be annoying for the users; as such so build two different kind of graphs. The first one does not exploit the concept of category and therefore it can be used to provide query suggestion results from all the website categories. On the other hand, query suggestion results from the second graph are restricted to a specific category selected by the user. By query suggestion results we intend both queries and products.

A final pruning phase is necessary to avoid the suggestion of queries that may have a negative impact on the user experience. We start removing products that are only related to one query, and then we remove queries that are only connected to one product.

Both the two versions of the query-product bipartite graph were tested and evaluated both in terms of time needed to complete their building phase, and in term of accuracy for the provided query suggestion results. All the experiments and results are reported and discussed in Sect. 4.

3.4 Online Query Suggestion

The online phase of our method exploits two basic concepts related to the taxonomy of the price comparison engine we used in this work: categories and popularity. As previously described, for query suggestion, we take into account only offers that belong to a product.

For each product the website administrator has provided us a numeric value which indicates the popularity of an offer. This value is computed considering both the whole server traffic and the available offers in a certain period of time, and it is periodically updated.

Given a user query q, if it belongs to the query set of the bipartite graph, we automatically obtain the list of the related queries and of the related products. The retrieved product list is then sorted by ascending popularity value, and the top k products are collected. Starting from this list of top k products, another list of related queries is produced and sorted by the number of clicks stored in the product-query bipartite graph edges. The top k retrieved queries are selected and provided as results.

On the other hand if a query q does not belong to the query-product bipartite graph we use the similarity measure described by Zanon *et al.* [20] to retrieve the more similar query q' among the bipartite graph. This measure exploits the concept of categories and the Jaccard similarity coefficient proposed by Tan *et al.* [16]. Once q' is found the system acts as previously described.

4 Experiments

We conducted several experiments to measure the effectiveness of our proposed method. Both query and product suggestions were evaluated with and without category information.

We built the query-product bipartite graph using data coming from 2 different search engine websites: ShoopyDoo and TrovaPrezzi. These two websites use the same notion of categories and products and share the same database of such entities; the main difference between the two platforms is the amount of traffic. The traffic recorded on the TrovaPrezzi website is significantly greater than the ShoppyDoo one. All the reported data are updated at June 2016. For both the price comparison search engines the total number of product is 321718, within them the number of products with almost one available offer associated is 66144, while the number of categories is 569.

To make results comparable, we built the two query-product bipartite graphs collecting the same three months query logs for both websites. In particular the selected months were March, April and May of the current year (2016). To build the ShoppyDoo query-product bipartite graph we collected a total of 292638 query/clicked product associations and we built a final version graph containing 41677 unique queries, 37348 unique products.

The final version of the query-product bipartite graph we built starting from TrovaPrezzi user query logs, is composed of 592851 unique queries and 72306 unique products, we started from a total of 8558097 of query/product associations.

In Table 1 we report both the time needed by our model to complete the graph building phase using one, two and three months of query logs for both platforms; and the details of the product-query bipartite graph in terms of number of queries and products before and after the pruning phase. Due to the larger size of the query log files, the time needed to build the TrovaPrezzi graph is obviously higher than the ShoppyDoo case.

The number of products collected in both the two graphs reflects the current availability of products with an associated and purchasable offer.

Table 1. ShoppyDoo and TrovaPrezzi building phase details. For each query log size (1, 2 or 3 months), the first line contains the size of the pruned bipartite-graph, while the second line reports the initial numbers of queries and products. Bold values denoted the final model used during the experimental phase.

# months	ShoppyDoo			TrovaPrezzi		
	Time (s)	# queries	# products	Time (s)	# queries	# products
3	**31.29**	**41677**	**37348**	**947.42**	**592851**	**72306**
		54334	40614		650814	78561
2	16.45	32578	25874	445.23	462490	67137
		38471	32540		498240	75521
1	5.32	20167	12587	175.53	407031	63290
		28541	25897		437951	69929

All the experiments with ShooppyDoo data have been performed on an Intel Core i5 @ 3.4 GHz with 12 GB of RAM, while the experiments with TrovaPrezzi data have been performed on an Intel Xeon E5-1620 v3 @ 3.50 GHz with 64 GB of RAM; the software has been developed using Java for the pre-processing phase, and MATLAB for the building and experimental phases.

4.1   Dataset

We created a test dataset following the manner adopted by Song *et al.* [14,15].

Three sets of 500 queries each are randomly selected from ShoopyDoo and TrovaPrezzi query log files. For both websites, the first set contains 500 queries not related to any category, the second contains 500 queries related to one of the categories (suggestions also belong to the same category), while the third contains a balanced equal number of queries related to 5 selected categories (more details are reported in Sect. 4 and in Tables 2). For each sampled query our algorithm generates top-8 suggestions for both queries and products.

Table 2. The five different categories adopted during the experimental phase have substantially different characteristics: the "Food Supplements" category is the smallest one and less products are associated to it; the "Tires" is the most popular one. The cardinality of each category deeply affects the quality of the query/product suggestions provided by our model, as reported in Tables 3 and 4. Data are updated at June 2016.

Category	Tot # products	# products with offers	# offers
Mobile phone	5492	864	8799
Oven	5162	1370	16445
Fridge	8705	2055	26798
Food supplements	175	160	3059
Tires	3101	2646	30043

Three judges were asked to evaluate the quality of our query suggestion model. In order to avoid a positional bias, we mix the provided suggestions during the evaluation phase. More in details, we have provided them the initial query along with 8 queries suggestions and 8 product suggestions. We have also provided some extra information, such as the category for which the query was originally executed to let them better understand the context and the meaning of the query. Judges could choose between three different values: relevant, irrelevant or no opinion (difficult to decide) for both types of suggestions.

For each query we have obtained two final rates, one for query suggestion and one for product suggestion. Those rates have been calculated using the majority vote among the three judges evaluations.

4.2   Evaluation Measure

We evaluate the quality of the two types of suggestions provided by the model using Precision at rank N (P@N) and Mean Average Precision (MAP).
The precision at rank N, $P(N)$, for a specific query is defined as the percentage of relevant queries:

$$P(N) = \frac{\# \text{ relevant queries}}{N} \tag{1}$$

$P@N$ is defined as the aggregated precision for all queries:

$$P@N = \frac{\sum P(N)}{\# \text{ total queries}} \tag{2}$$

MAP is the average of Average Precision for all queries. For each query q_i:

$$AverageP(q_i) = \frac{\sum_j P(j) \cdot rel(j)}{\# \text{ relevant queries}} \tag{3}$$

where the precision at rank j, $P(j)$ is defined as in Eq. 1, and $rel(j)$ is equal to 1 when the item at rank j is relevant, 0 otherwise. The mean average precision for a set of queries Q is the mean of the average precision scores for each query q_i:

$$MAP = \frac{\sum_{i=1}^{Q} AverageP(q_i)}{Q} \tag{4}$$

We also adopt a coverage metric to indicate for how many input queries the algorithm returns at least a minimum amount of query/product suggestions. We calculated coverage rate considering a minimum of 3, 5 and 8 queries.

4.3   Results

Evaluation metrics are calculated on three different types of dataset built as described in Sect. 4.1 for both ShoppyDoo and TrovaPrezzi. For either the two websites, the first dataset, called "uncategorized", contains queries not related to any category; second dataset, called "categorized", contains queries and query results within a randomly chosen category; the third dataset was formed by extracting queries from 5 different categories: *mobile phones, ovens, fridges, food supplements* and *tires*. For this third dataset we refer to the associated set of queries using their category name.

The category datasets are extracted from categories that present substantially different characteristics and cardinalities. Table 2 shows, for each category, the total number of products belonging to the category, the number of products which have some matched offers, and the number of offers that are matched to products.

Note that we did not chose only the most popular categories, but we also took into account categories having a low number of products (such as *food supplements*) in order to evaluate how the model deals with those less populated categories.

Coverage rate values reported in Tables 3 and 4 reflect the differences among the categories: the more populated categories reach higher results for both query and product suggestions. The exploitation of the category rank values in the "categorized" dataset enables the model to propose more results for both query and product suggestions, where the highest coverage values are achieved for the product suggestion task. Some differences between the two websites are underlined by the reported results: the query-product graph constructed starting from the TrovaPrezzi engine presents an high number of queries related to products, this cause a low query suggestion coverage, on the other hand, the product suggestion coverage is significantly higher (93.6% on the top-8) than the other search engine.

Table 3. Query suggestion coverage rates calculated on all the 7 test dataset and for both ShoopyDoo and TrovaPrezzi. The model provides better suggestions for the more populated categories (e.g. Oven) than it does for the less populated one (e.g. Mobile Phone). Also, the exploitation of the category popularity value enables to reach higher results within the "categorized" dataset compared to the "uncategorized" one.

Dataset	ShoppyDoo			TrovaPrezzi		
	3 sugg.	5 sugg.	8 sugg.	3 sugg.	5 sugg.	8 sugg.
Uncategorized	73.36 %	63.48 %	56.40 %	61.76 %	44.4 %	35.5 %
Categorized	**79.53** %	**78.94** %	**75.53** %	**63.87**%	**47.32** %	**36.2** %
Mobile phone	91.3 %	89.7 %	83.2%	73.2 %	61.87 %	55.23 %
Oven	93.6 %	85.7 %	83.3 %	74.67 %	60.23 %	53.11 %
Fridge	95.76 %	90.4 %	89.9 %	78.9 %	63.1 %	56.8 %
Food supplements	69.54 %	63.04 %	52.9 %	44.36 %	41.48 %	39.5 %
Tires	89.34 %	75.54 %	71.56 %	57.8 %	52.7 %	48.09 %

Table 4. Product suggestion coverage rates. The suggested products reach an high coverage rate among all the different test datasets. The lowest values are achieved applying the model to the less populated category, and the category values exploited on the "categorized" dataset helps the model in reaching the highest results.

Dataset	ShoppyDoo			TrovaPrezzi		
	3 sugg.	5 sugg.	8 sugg.	3 sugg.	5 sugg.	8 sugg.
Uncategorized	72.54 %	64.53%	45.7 %	96.2 %	94.4 %	90.4 %
Categorized	**88.53%**	**83.77%**	**81.44%**	**96.4 %**	**94.8 %**	**93.6%**
Mobile phone	72.10%	63.22%	54.78 %	88.45 %	86.15%	83.53 %
Oven	79.24%	75.47 %	70.58 %	91.68 %	90.05%	88.32 %
Fridge	84.23%	79.13%	75.88 %	92.08 %	91.25%	89.87 %
Food supplements	66.56 %	51.87 %	38.32 %	73.68 %	63.15%	54.68 %
Tires	77.17 %	73.76 %	70.33 %	87.32 %	85.15%	81.45 %

Tables 5 and 6 summarize the obtained results for the query suggestion model and the product suggestion model respectively. Results are shown in term of MAP and $P@N$, while varying N from 1 to 8.

From our experimental evaluation results we can conclude that our model proposes reliable suggestions on the top-8 result not only using the "categorized" dataset (76% query, 72% product for ShooppyDoo and 68% query, 88% product for TrovaPrezzi), but also using the "uncategorized" dataset (74% query, 70% product for ShooppyDoo and 66% query, 85% product for TrovaPrezzi) and for both the two different constructed bipartite graph. When referring to top-5 results, precision increases.

Due to the similarity of the context of our work and the one from Zanon et al. [20] and despite the fact that we used a different dataset, we propose a weak but still significant comparison between our results and those achieved by their model. Unlike all the other works in literature, Zanon et al. [20] evaluate their query suggestion model on two price comparison engines, reaching a coverage rate equals to 37% on the top-8 suggestion and an overall quality equals to 70%.

Our model overcomes those results, achieving significantly higher coverage rate: 75% on the "uncategorized" dataset and 56% on the "categorized" dataset for ShoopyDoo, and reaches comparable results for the TrovaPrezzi engine. The quality of our query/product suggestion method is also higher than theirs for top-8 results.

This confirms that a click-through based model better fits query suggestions task in price comparison and more in general in e-commerce website, as asserted in [4].

Table 5. Overall scores for the query suggestions task expressed in terms of MAP and P@N, considering the top-3, top-5 and top-8 suggestions.

Dataset	ShoppyDoo					TrovaPrezzi				
	MAP	P@1	P@3	P@5	P@8	MAP	P@1	P@3	P@5	P@8
Uncategorized	0.76	0.92	0.86	0.78	0.74	0.70	0.75	0.72	0.70	0.66
Categorized	0.80	0.93	0.90	0.80	0.76	0.73	0.79	0.71	0.70	0.68

Table 6. Overall scores for the product suggestions task expressed in terms of MAP and P@N, considering the top-3, top-5 and top-8 suggestions.

Dataset	ShoppyDoo					TrovaPrezzi				
	MAP	P@1	P@3	P@5	P@8	MAP	P@1	P@3	P@5	P@8
Uncategorized	0.78	0.95	0.83	0.76	0.70	0.86	0.94	0.92	0.90	0.85
Categorized	0.81	0.96	0.86	0.81	0.72	0.89	0.97	0.95	0.92	0.88

5   Conclusion

A novel click-through-based query suggestion model, specifically designed for price comparison websites, has been presented. One strength of the proposed query and product suggestion method is that it takes advantages of most of the relevant informations available for this category of websites: product offers and product categories.

We introduced a different version of the well know click-through bipartite graph, our model is built exploiting the associations between user queries and clicked products instead of using the association between queries and URLs clicked by users as in traditional click-through-based query suggestion approaches.

Since in most price comparison websites, product offers are clustered into products, our customized click-through bipartite graph allows the model to provide query and product suggestions using products rather than direct URLs of product offers which could be unavailable when suggestions are generated.

We evaluated the system using log data extracted from two different price comparison websites. Coverage rates and quality of results for both types of generated suggestions (query and products), were calculated demonstrating that the system reaches high precision values and satisfying coverage rates, outperforming also the results of a competing recently published approach, specifically designed for the same task.

References

1. Baeza-Yates, R., Hurtado, C., Mendoza, M.: Query recommendation using query logs in search engines. In: Proceedings of the 2004 International Conference on Current Trends in Database Technology (2004)

2. Boldi, P., Bonchi, F., Castillo, C., Donato, D., Vigna, S.: Query suggestions using query-flow graphs. In: Proceedings of the 2009 Workshop on Web Search Click Data (2009)
3. Cao, H., Jiang, D., Pei, J., He, Q., Liao, Z., Chen, E., Li, H.: Context-aware query suggestion by mining click-through and session data. In: Proceedings of the 14th ACM SIGKDD International Conference on Knowledge Discovery and Data Mining (2008)
4. Al Hasan, M., Parikh, N., Singh, G., Sundaresan, N.: Query suggestion for e-commerce sites. In: Proceedings of the Fourth ACM International Conference on Web Search and Data Mining (2011)
5. Jiang, D., Leung, K.W.-T., Vosecky, J., Ng, W.: Personalized query suggestion with diversity awareness. In: IEEE 30th International Conference on Data Engineering, Chicago, ICDE 2014, IL, USA, 31 March–4 April 2014 (2014)
6. Kato, M.P., Sakai, T., Tanaka, K.: When do people use query suggestion? A query suggestion log analysis. Inf. Retr. **16**(6), 725–746 (2013)
7. Kim, Y., Croft, W.B.: Diversifying query suggestions based on query documents. In: Proceedings of the 37th International ACM SIGIR Conference on Research & #38; Development in Information Retrieval (2014)
8. Lau, T., Horvitz, E.: Patterns of search: analyzing and modeling web query refinement. In: Proceedings of the Seventh International Conference on User Modeling (1999)
9. Ma, H., Lyu, M.R., King, I.: Diversifying query suggestion results. In: Proceedings of the Twenty-Fourth AAAI Conference on Artificial Intelligence (2010)
10. Mei, Q., Zhou, D., Church, K.: Query suggestion using hitting time. In: Proceedings of the 17th ACM Conference on Information and Knowledge Management (2008)
11. Meng, L.: A survey on query suggestion. Int. J. Hybrid Inf. Technol. **7**(6), 43–56 (2014)
12. Ozmutlu, H.C., Ozmutlu, S., Spink, A.: Multitasking web searching and implications for design. In: Proceedings of the American Society for Information Science and Technology (2003)
13. ShoppyDoo (2015). http://www.shoppydoo.it/
14. Song, Y., He, L.-W.: Optimal rare query suggestion with implicit user feedback. In: Proceedings of the 19th International Conference on World Wide Web (2010)
15. Song, Y., Zhou, D., He, L.-W.: Query suggestion by constructing term-transition graphs. In: Proceedings of the Fifth ACM International Conference on Web Search and Data Mining (2012)
16. Tan, P.-N., Steinbach, M., Kumar, V.: Introduction to Data Mining, 1st edn. Addison-Wesley Longman Publishing Co., Inc., Boston (2005)
17. TrovaPrezzi (2016). http://www.trovaprezzi.it/
18. Wen, J.-R., Nie, J.-Y., Zhang, H.-J.: Clustering user queries of a search engine. In: Proceedings of the 10th International Conference on World Wide Web (2001)
19. Wu, W., Li, H., Xu, J.: Learning Query and document similarities from click-through Bipartite Graph with Metadata. In: Proceedings of the Sixth ACM International Conference on Web Search and Data Mining (2013)
20. Zanon, R., Albertini, S., Carullo, M., Gallo, I.: A new query suggestion algorithm for taxonomy-based search engines. In: Proceedings of the International Conference on Knowledge Discovery and Information Retrieval (2012)
21. Zhang, Z., Nasraoui, O.: Mining search engine query logs for social filtering-based query recommendation. Appl. Soft Comput. **8**(4), 1326–1334 (2008)

Customizable Web Services Matching and Ranking Tool: Implementation and Evaluation

Fatma Ezzahra Gmati[1], Nadia Yacoubi Ayadi[1], Afef Bahri[2],
Salem Chakhar[3(✉)], and Alessio Ishizaka[3]

[1] RIADI Research Laboratory, National School of Computer Sciences,
University of Manouba, Manouba, Tunisia
fatma.ezzahra.gmati@gmail.com, nadia.yacoubi.ayadi@gmail.com
[2] MIRACL Laboratory, High School of Computing and Multimedia,
University of Sfax, Sfax, Tunisia
afef.bahri@gmail.com
[3] Portsmouth Business School and Centre for Operational Research and Logistics,
University of Portsmouth, Portsmouth, UK
{salem.chakhar,alessio.ishizaka}@port.ac.uk

Abstract. The matchmaking is a crucial operation in Web service discovery and selection. The objective of the matchmaking is to discover and select the most appropriate Web service among the different available candidates. Different matchmaking frameworks are now available in the literature but most of them present at least one of the following shortcomings: (i) use of strict syntactic matching; (ii) use of capability-based matching; (iii) lack of customization support; and (iv) lack of accurate ranking of matching Web services. The objective of this paper is thus to present the design, implementation and evaluation of the Parameterized Matching-Ranking Framework (PMRF). The PMRF uses semantic matchmaking, accepts capability and property attributes, supports different levels of customization and generates a ranked list of Web services. Accordingly, it fully overcomes the first, third and fourth shortcomings enumerated earlier and partially addresses the second one. The PMRF is composed of two layers. The role of the first layer is to parse the input data and parameters and then transfer it to the second layer, which represents the matching and ranking engine. The comparison of PMRF to iSeM-logic-based and SPARQLent, using the OWLS-TC4 datasets, shows that the algorithms supported by PMRF outperform those proposed in iSeM-logic-based and SPARQLent.

Keywords: Web service · Semantic similarity · Matchmaking · Ranking · Implementation · Performance evaluation

1 Introduction

Service Oriented Computing (SOC) is a distributed computing paradigm that utilizes services as the basic constructs to support the development of distributed

© Springer International Publishing AG 2017
V. Monfort et al. (Eds.): WEBIST 2016, LNBIP 292, pp. 15–36, 2017.
DOI: 10.1007/978-3-319-66468-2_2

applications, especially in heterogeneous environments. The Service-Oriented Architecture (SOA) is an element of SOC that enables service discovery, integration and use. Web services are the most successful realization of SOA paradigm [1] that are commonly used in the areas of business-to-business integration, distributed computing and enterprise application integration [2]. A fundamental challenge of SOA paradigm, especially Web services, is service discovery, which is the process of retrieving the service most similar to the user query based on the description of functional and/or non-functional semantics [3]. An important aspect of services discovery is service matchmaking. Web service matchmaking is the method that is used to determine which of available services satisfy at best the requirements of the user while taking into account the user request and the capabilities of available services.

Web services are generally described only syntactically through WSDL and UDDI for service discovery. The UDDI in combination with WDSL provides a basic mechanism for service discovery, but lacks support for automated discovery [1]. The most used automatic service discovery approach relies on the idea of interface matching, which is based on defining the requested service through its expected input-output interface and comparing this expected interface with the input-output interfaces of available services to find matching services. However, the matchmaking based only on service profile is not sufficient, especially in the case of composite services [3]. A possible improvement to overcome such a problem is the use of the information about precondition and effects in order to capture some constraints about the entry and exit points of a service [1].

To support automatic Web service discovery and composition, a number of different semantic languages—such as OWL-S, WSMO and WSDL-S—that allow describing the functionality of services in a machine interpretable form have been proposed. The semantic Web service is a new technology and most of existing Web services still use traditional matching approaches. Accordingly, most of existing matching frameworks still suffer from at least one of the following shortcomings: (i) use of strict syntactic matching, which generally leads to low recall and precision rates [1,3,4]; (ii) use of capability-based matching, which is proven [3,5] to be inadequate in practice; (iii) lack of customization support [6,7]; and (iv) lack of accurate ranking of Web services, especially within semantic-based matching [1,4].

The objective of this paper is hence to present the Parameterized Matching-Ranking Framework (PMRF), which uses semantic matchmaking, accepts capability and property attributes, supports different levels of customization and generates a ranked list of Web services. The PMRF fully overcomes the first, third and fourth shortcomings enumerated earlier and partially addresses the second one. The comparison of PMRF to iSeM-logic-based [8] and SPARQLent [9], using the OWLS-TC4 datasets, shows that the algorithms supported by PMRF behave globally well in comparison to iSeM-logic-based and SPARQLent.

The paper is organized as follows. Section 2 discusses some related work. Section 3 presents the architecture of the PMRF. Section 4 deals with system implementation. Section 5 studies the performance of the PMRF. Section 6 provides the comparative study. Section 7 concludes the paper.

2   Related Work

The first and traditional matchmaking frameworks are based on strict syntactic matching. Such syntactic matching approaches only perform service discovery and service matching based on particular interface or keyword queries from the user, which generally leads to low recall and low precision of the retrieved services [1,3,4]. In order to overcome the shortcomings of strict syntactic matching approaches, some advanced techniques and algorithms have been used such as genetic algorithmic and utility function. Alternatively, many authors propose to include the concept of semantics to deal with these shortcomings. The semantic Web service is a new and active research area. In the rest of this section, we briefly discuss some recent semantic matchmaking frameworks. More detailed reviews on semantic matchmaking approaches are available in, e.g., [10–14].

A matchmaking approach that uses the internal process models of services as primary source of knowledge has been proposed in [1]. The basic idea of this approach is to transform the service matchmaking into model checking in which services are represented as system models and service request as set of formal properties. By using the model checking as a reasoning mechanism, the authors in [1] designed three methods supporting both exact and partial matching.

A framework for content-based semantic Web service discovery that allows users to submit unstructured free text as input has been proposed in [15]. In this framework, a collection of nouns are extracted from the input text and then used for service discovery, after a disambiguation process that makes use of the WordNet lexical database for determining the meaning of the nouns. The proposal of [15] focuses specifically on OWL-S and does not provide a means for ranking the results.

In [16], the authors propose a fuzzy matchmaking approach for semantic Web services to support an automated and veracious service discovery process in collaborative manufacturing environments. The authors first introduce a theoretical framework for fuzzy matchmaking, and a semantic annotation specification of how the needed information of web service attributes can be captured as semantic annotation for WSDL interfaces, operations, faults, and XML Schema. Then, they propose a fuzzy matchmaking algorithm for calculating the fuzzy similarity degree of web services. The developed system has been used in material selection services in the area of collaborative manufacturing.

The author in [6] presents a parameterized and highly customizable semantic matchmaking framework that supports three types of matching: functional attribute level, functional service-level and non-functional. However, the paper addresses only functional matching where a series of algorithms that support a customizable matching process have been proposed. The authors in [17] extend the work of [6] by supporting non-functional matching.

The BAX-SET PLUS, proposed in [18], is a multi-agent taxonomy-based method for categorization, search, and retrieval, of semantic Web services.

The taxonomic navigation model includes a knowledge module represented by a taxonomic model, an OWL-S extension implemented and a semantic search module for a semantic Web services repository. In this model, user-selected concepts from a taxonomy are matched against concepts contained in OWL-S service descriptions.

The Semantic Web service discovery framework (SWSD) proposed in [4] comprises a keyword-based discovery process for searching Web services that are described using a semantic language. The framework relies on natural language processing techniques in order to establish a match between a user search query and a semantic Web service description. For matching keywords with semantic Web service descriptions given in WSMO, techniques like part-of-speech tagging, lemmatization, and word sense disambiguation are used. After determining the senses of relevant words gathered from Web service descriptions and the user query, a matching process takes place. In [4], the authors propose three methods for matching sets of words or senses.

The authors in [19] design and develop a semantic framework capable of matching security capabilities of providers and security requirements of customers. The matching process is composed of two steps. The aim of the first step is to assign a match level to each requirement-capability pair using the well-known concepts of exact, subsume, plugin, and no match introduced by [20]. In the second step, the overall match between the two policies is evaluated in order to identify the capability that matches at best for each requirement. The overall match is then defined to be the minimum among the individual match levels evaluated in the first step for each requirement-capability pair.

The Tomaco [7] is a semantic web service matching algorithm for SAWSDL. The system supports logic-based and syntactic strategies along with hybrid composite strategy. The logic-based strategy in Tomaco considers four matching cases (namely Exact, Desired, LessDesired and Fail) to determine the values of matching degree. The authors in [7] also introduce the Tomaco web application, which aims to promote wide-spread adoption of Semantic Web Services while targeting the lack of user-friendly applications in this field through a variety of configurable matching algorithms.

To improve matching effectiveness, the authors in [21] introduce first a new semantic similarity measure combining functional and process similarities. Then, a service discovery mechanism that utilises the new semantic similarity measure for service matching is proposed. The matchmaking framework is composed of two phases. The first phase uses functional attributes in order to group published Web services into services clusters. The second phase looks to identify the best matching Web services within these matching clusters.

3   System Architecture

In this section, we first introduce the conceptual and functional architectures of the PMRF. Then, we present the different supported matching and ranking algorithms.

3.1   Conceptual Architecture

Figure 1 provides the conceptual architecture of the PMRF. The inputs of the system are the specifications of the requested Web service and the different parameters. The output is a ranked list of Web services. The PMRF is composed of two layers. The role of the first layer is to parse the input data and parameters and then transfer it to the second layer, which represents the matching and ranking engine. The Matching Module filters Web service offers that match with the user specifications. The result is then passed to the Ranking Module that produces a ranked list of Web services. The assembler guarantees a coherent interaction between the different modules in the second layer.

The three main components of the second layer are:

- **Matching Module:** This component contains the different matching algorithms: basic, partially parameterized and fully parameterized matching algorithms (see Sect. 3.3).
- **Similarity Computing Module:** This component supports the different similarity measure computing approaches: Efficient similarity with MinEdge, Accurate similarity with MinEdge, Accurate similarity with MaxEdge and Accurate similarity with MaxMinEdge (see Sect. 3.4).
- **Ranking Module:** This component is the repository of score computing and ranking algorithms, namely score-based, rule-based and tree-based ranking algorithms (see Sect. 3.5).

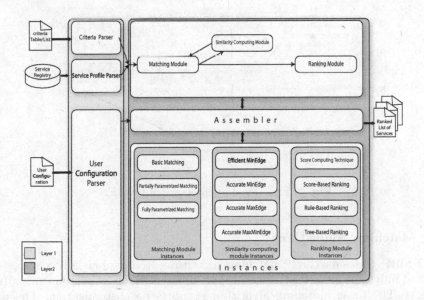

Fig. 1. Conceptual architecture of PMRF.

3.2 Functional Architecture

The functional architecture of the PMRF is given in Fig. 2. It shows graphically the different steps from receiving the user query (specifications of the requested Web service and the different parameters) until the delivery of the final results (ranked list of Web services) to the user.

We can distinguish the following main operations:

– The PMRF (1) receives the user query including the specifications of the desired Web service and the required parameters;
– The Matching Module (2) scans the Registry in order to identify the Web services matching the user query;
– During the matching process, the Matching Module (3) uses the Similarity Computing Module to calculate the similarity degrees;
– The Matching Module (4) delivers the Web services matching the user query to the Ranking Module;
– The Ranking Module (5) receives the matching Web services and processes them for ranking;
– During the ranking operation, the Ranking Module (6) uses the Scoring Technique to compute the scores of the Web services;
– The Ranking Module (7) generates a ranked list of Web services, which is then delivered by the PMRF to the user.

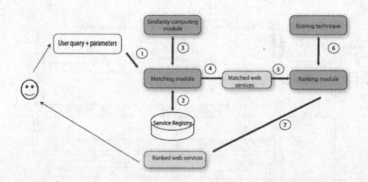

Fig. 2. Functional architecture of PMRF.

3.3 Matching Algorithms

The PMRF contains three matching algorithms (basic, partially parameterized and fully parameterized) that support different levels of customization (see Table 1). The basic matching algorithm supports no customization. The partially parameterized matching algorithm allows the user to specify the set of attributes to be used in the matching. Within the fully parameterized matching algorithm, three customizations are taken into account. A first customization consists in allowing the user to specify the list of attributes to consider. A second customization consists in allowing the user to specify the order in which the attributes are considered. A third customization is to allow the user to specify a desired similarity measure for each attribute. In the rest of this section, we present the third algorithm.

Table 1. Customization levels for matching algorithms.

Matching algorithm	List of attributes	Order of attributes	Desired similarity
Basic			
Partially parameterized	✓		
Fully parameterized	✓	✓	✓

In order to support all the above-cited customizations of the fully parameterized matching, we used the concept of Criteria Table (see [6]) that serves as a parameter to the matching process. A Criteria Table, C, is a relation consisting of two attributes, $C.T$ and $C.M$. The $C.T$ describes the service attribute to be compared, and $C.M$ gives the *least preferred similarity measure* for that attribute. Let $C.T_i$ and $C.M_i$ denote the service attribute value and the desired measure in the ith tuple of the relation. The $C.N$ denotes the number of tuples in C.

Let R be the service that is requested, A be the service that is advertised and C a criteria table. A sufficient match exists between R and A if for *every* attribute in $C.T$ there exists an identical attribute of R and A and the values of the attributes satisfy the desired similarity measure specified in $C.M$. Formally,

$$\forall_i \exists_{j,k} (C.T_i = R.T_j = A.T_k) \wedge \mu(R.T_j, A.T_k) \succeq C.M_i$$
$$\Rightarrow \text{SuffMatch}(R, A) \quad 1 \leq i \leq C.N. \tag{1}$$

The computing of the similarity degrees $\mu(\cdot, \cdot)$ is addressed in Sect. 3.4. The fully parameterized matching process is formalized in Algorithm 1, which follows directly from Sentence (1). Algorithm 1 proceeds as follows. First, it loops over the attributes in the Criteria Table C and for each attribute it identifies the corresponding attribute in the requested service R and the potentially advisable service under consideration A. The corresponding attributes are appended into two different lists rAttrSet (requested Web service) and aAttrSet (advisable Web service). This operation is implemented by sentences 1 to 10 in Algorithm 1. Second, it loops over the Criteria Table and for each attribute it computes the similarity degree between the corresponding attributes in rAttrSet and aAttrSet. This operation is implemented by sentences 11 to 14 in Algorithm 1. The output of Algorithm 1 is either success (if for every attribute in C there is a similar attribute in the advertised service A with a sufficient similarity degree) or fail (otherwise).

The Criteria Table C used as parameter to Algorithm 1 permits the user to control the matched attributes, the order in which attributes are compared, as well as the minimal desired similarity for each attribute. The structure of partially matching algorithm is similar to Algorithm 1 but it takes as input an unordered collection of attributes with no desired similarities. The basic matching algorithm do no support any customization and the only possible inputs are the specification of the requested R and advertised A services. Different versions and extensions of this algorithm are available in [6,17,22].

Algorithm 1. Fully Parameterized Matching.

Input : R, // Requested service.
         A, // Advertised service.
         C, // Criteria Table.
Output: Boolean, // fail/success.

1 **while** $(i \leq C.N)$ **do**
2   **while** $(j \leq R.N)$ **do**
3   **if** $(R.T_j = C.T_i)$ **then**
4   Append $R.T_j$ to rAttrSet;
5          $j \longleftarrow j+1$;
6   **while** $(k \leq A.N)$ **do**
7   **if** $(A.T_k = C.T_i)$ **then**
8   Append $A.T_k$ to aAttrSet;
9          $k \longleftarrow k+1$;
10     $i \longleftarrow i+1$;
11 **while** $(t \leq C.N)$ **do**
12   **if** $(\mu(\text{rAttrSet}[t], \text{aAttrSet}[t]) \prec C.M_t)$ **then**
13   return fail;
14     $t \longleftarrow t+1$;
15 return success;

3.4 Computing Similarity Degrees

To compute the similarity degree, we extended the solution of [23] where the authors define four degrees of match, namely Exact, Plugin, Subsumes and Fail as default. During the matching process, the inputs and outputs of the requested Web service are matched with the inputs and outputs of the advertised Web service by constructing a bipartite graph where: (i) the vertices in the left side correspond to advertised services; (ii) the vertices in the right side correspond to the requested service; and (iii) the edges correspond to the semantic relationships between the concepts in left and right sides of the graph. Then, they assign weights to each edge as follows: Exact: w_1, Plugin: w_2, Subsumes: w_3, Fail: w_4; with $w_4 \succ w_3 \succ w_2 \succ w_1$. Finally, they apply the Hungarian algorithm to identify the complete matching that minimizes the maximum weight in the graph. The final returned similarity degree is the one corresponding to the maximum weight in the graph. Then, the selected assignment is the one representing a strict injective mapping such that the maximal weight is minimized.

The algorithms used in PMRF to compute the similarity degree between services extend the works of [23] with respect to two aspects: (i) the way the degree of match between two concepts is computed, and (ii) the optimality criterion used to compute the overall similarity degree. Concerning the computation of the degree of match, two versions are included in PMRF: efficient and accurate. In the efficient version, the degree of match is computed as in Algorithm 2 where: (i) $\equiv$: equivalence relationship; (ii) $\sqsubset_1$: direct child/parent relationship; (iii) and $\sqsupset_1$: direct parent/child relationship. In this first version, only direct related concepts are considered for Plugin and Subsume similarity measures. This will affect the precision of the algorithm since it uses a small set of possible concepts but necessarily improves the query response time (since there is no need to use inference).

Algorithm 2. Degree of Match (Efficient Version).

```
Input   : K_R, // first concept.
          K_A, // second concept.
Output:   degree of match
1 if (K_R ≡ K_A) then
2 |   return Exact;

3 else
4 |   if (K_R ⊏_1 K_A) then
5 |   |   return Plugin ;

6 |   else
7 |   |   if (K_R ⊐_1 K_A) then
8 |   |   |   return Subsumes;

9 |   |   else
10|   |   |   return Fail ;
```

Algorithm 3. Degree of Match (Accurate Version).

```
Input   : K_R, // first concept.
          K_A, // second concept.
Output:   degree of match//
1 if (K_R ≡ K_A) then
2 |   return Exact;

3 else
4 |   if (K_R ⊏_1 K_A) then
5 |   |   return Plugin;

6 |   else
7 |   |   if (K_R ⊐_1 K_A) then
8 |   |   |   return Subsume;

9 |   |   else
10|   |   |   if (K_R ⊏ K_A) then
11|   |   |   |   return Extended-Plugin;

12|   |   |   else
13|   |   |   |   if (K_R ⊐ K_A) then
14|   |   |   |   |   return Extended-Subsume;

15|   |   |   |   else
16|   |   |   |   |   return Fail;
```

In the accurate version, we defined six similarity degrees: Exact, Plugin, Subsume, Extended-Plugin, Extended-Subsume and Fail. The degree of match in this version is calculated according to Algorithm 3 where: (i) $\equiv$: equivalence relationship; (ii) $\sqsubset_1$: direct child/parent relationship; (iii) $\sqsupset_1$: direct parent/child relationship; (iv) $\sqsubset$: indirect child/parent relationship; and (v) $\sqsupset$: indirect parent/child relationship. In Algorithm 3, indirect concepts are considered through Extended-Plugin and Extended-Subsume similarity measures.

The second extension of [23]'s work concerns the the optimality criterion used to compute the overall similarity value. The optimality criterion used in [23] is designed to minimize the false positives and the false negatives. In fact, minimizing the maximal weight would minimize the edges labeled Fail. However, the choice of $\max(w_i)$ as a final return value is restrictive and the risk of false negatives in the final result is higher. To avoid this problem, we propose to consider both $\max(w_i)$ and $\min(w_i)$ as pertinent values in the matching. A further discussion of similarity degree computing is available in [24].

3.5   Ranking Algorithms

The PMRF supports three ranking algorithms: score-based, rule-based and tree-based. The first algorithm relies on the scores only. The second algorithm defines and uses a series of rules to rank Web services. It permits to solve the ties problem encountered by the score-based ranking algorithm. The tree-based algorithm, which is based on the use of a tree data structure, permits to solve the problem of ties of the first algorithm. In addition, it is computationally better than the rule-based ranking algorithm. The score-based ranking is given in Algorithm 4. The rule-based and tree-based ranking algorithms are available in [22, 24], respectively. The main input of the score-based ranking algorithm is a list mServices of matching Web services. The function ComputeNormScores in Algorithm 4 permits to calculate the normalized scores of Web services. It implements the idea we proposed in [22]. The score-based ranking algorithm uses then an *insertion sort* procedure (implemented by lines 3–7 in Algorithm 4) to rank the Web services based on their normalized scores.

The list mServices used as input to Algorithm 4 has the following generic definition:

$$(A_i, \mu(A_i.T_1, R.T_1), \cdots, \mu(A_i.T_N, R.T_N)),$$

where: A_i is an advertised service, R is the requested service, N the total number of attributes and for $j \in \{1, \cdots, N\}$, $\mu(A_i.T_j, R.T_j)$ is the similarity measure between the requested Web service and the advertised Web service on the jth attribute A_j.

The list mServices will be first updated by function ComputeNormScores and it will have the following new generic definition:

$$(A_i, \mu(A_i.T_1, R.T_1), \cdots, \mu(A_i.T_N, R.T_N), \rho'(A_i)),$$

where: A_i, R, N and $\mu(A_i.T_j, R.T_j)$ $(j = 1, \cdots, N)$ are as above; and $\rho'(A_i)$ is the normalized score of advertised Web service A_i.

Algorithm 4. Score-Based Ranking.

```
Input   : mServices,// List of matching Web services.
          N,// Number of attributes.
Output: mServices,// Ranked list of Web services.
1 mServices ← ComputeNormScores(mServices, N);
2 r ← length(mServices );
3 for (i = 1 to r − 1) do
4       j ← i;
5       while (j ≥ 0 ∧ mServices[j − 1, N + 2] > mServices[j, N + 2]) do
6            swap mServices[j, N + 2] and mServices[j − 1, N + 2];
7            j ← j − 1;

8 return mServices ;
```

Based on the discussion in Sect. 3.4, we designed two versions for computing similarity degrees. Accordingly, two versions can be distinguished for the definition of the list mServices at the input level, along with the way the similarity degrees are computed. The first version is as follows:

$$(A_i, \mu_{\max}(A_i.T_1, R.T_1), \cdots, \mu_{\max}(A_i.T_N, R.T_N)),$$

where: A_i, R and N are as above; and $\mu_{\max}(A_i.T_j, R.T_j)$ $(j = 1, \cdots, N)$ is the similarity measure between the requested Web service and the advertised Web service on the jth attribute A_j computed by selecting the edge with the **maximum weight** in the matching graph.

The second version of mServices is as follows:

$$(A_i, \mu_{\min}(A_i.T_1, R.T_1), \cdots, \mu_{\min}(A_i.T_N, R.T_N)),$$

where A_i, R and N are as above; and $\mu_{\min}(A_i.T_j, R.T_j)$ $(j = 1, \cdots, N)$ is the similarity measure between the requested Web service and the advertised Web service on the jth attribute A_j computed by selecting the edge with the **minimum weight** in the matching graph.

To obtain the final rank, we need to use these two versions separately and then combine the obtained rankings. However, a problem of ties may occur since several Web services may have the same scores with both versions. The tree-based ranking algorithm [24] permits to solve this problem.

4   System Implementation

In this section, we first present the different tools and the strategy used to develop PMRF. Then, we present the customization support interface. Finally, we comment on the user/provider acceptability issues.

4.1   Implementation Tools and Strategy

To develop the PMRF, we have used the following tools: (i) Eclipse IDE as the developing platform, (ii) OWLS-API to parse the OWLS service descriptions, and (iii) OWL-API and the Pellet-reasoner to perform the inference for computing the similarity degrees. In order to minimize resources consumption (especially memory), we used the following procedure for implementing the inference operation: (1) A local Ontology is created at the start of the matchmaking process. The incremental classifier class, taken from the Pellet reasoner library, is associated to this Ontology. (2) The service parser based on the OWLs-API retrieves the Uniform Resource Identifier (URI) of the attributes values of each service and the concepts related to these URIs are added incrementally to the local Ontology and the classifier is updated accordingly. (3) In order to infer the semantic relations between concepts, the similarity measure module uses the knowledge base constructed by the incremental classifier. Figure 3 provides an extract from the class Matchmaker. In this figure, we can see the input and output functions. The latter contains the call for the matching and ranking operations.

```
27   public class Matchmaker implements IMatchmakerPlugin {
28
29          PelletReasoner reasoner=new PelletReasoner();
30          ServiceTuple query;
31          ArrayList<ServiceTuple> offers=new ArrayList<ServiceTuple>();
32
33
34⊖         public Matchmaker()
35          {}
36
37⊖         @Override
38          public void input(URL arg0) {
39              try {
40                      ServiceTuple service=new ServiceTuple(arg0,reasoner);
41                      offers.add(service);
42                      System.out.println("helloooo");
43              } catch (Exception e) {
44                      e.printStackTrace();
45              }
46          }
47⊖         @Override
48          public Hashtable<URL, Vector<URL>> query(URL arg0)
49          {
50          Hashtable<URL,Vector<URL>> finalOutput=new Hashtable<URL,Vector<URL>>();
51          try
52          {
53              query=new ServiceTuple(arg0,reasoner);
54              /*
55               * =============================================================
56               * We first perform the matching
57               * =============================================================
58               */
59              Group initialGroup=new Group();
60              for(ServiceTuple serviceAd:offers)
61              {
62                  match(query,serviceAd,reasoner);
63                  initialGroup.addAService(serviceAd);
64              }
65              /*
66               * =============================================================
67               * We secondly perform the ranking
68               * =============================================================
69               */
70              Node<Group>  root= new Node<Group>();
71              root.setData(initialGroup);
```

Fig. 3. Extract from the Class Matchmaker.

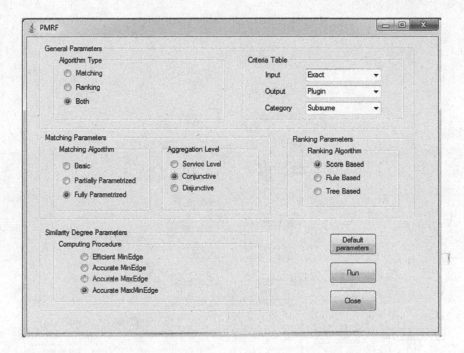

Fig. 4. Parametrization interface.

4.2 Customization Support

The parametrization interface of the PMRF is given in Fig. 4. The PMRF permits the user to choose the type of algorithm to use and to specify the criteria table to consider during the matching. The PMRF offers three matching algorithms (basic, partially parameterized and fully parameterized) and three ranking algorithms (score-based, rule-base and tree-based). In addition, the PMRF supports different aggregation levels: attribute level and service level. The attribute-level matching involves capability and property attributes and consider each attribute independently of the others. In this type of matching, the PMRF offers two types of aggregation, namely conjunctive and disjunctive, where the individual (for each attribute) similarity degrees are combined using either AND or OR logical operators. The service-level matching considers capability and property attributes but the matching operation involves attributes both independently and jointly.

The PMRF also allows the user to select the procedure to use for computing the similarity degrees. Four procedures are supported by the system: efficient similarity with MinEdge, accurate similarity with MinEdge, accurate similarity with MaxEdge and accurate similarity with MaxMinEdge.

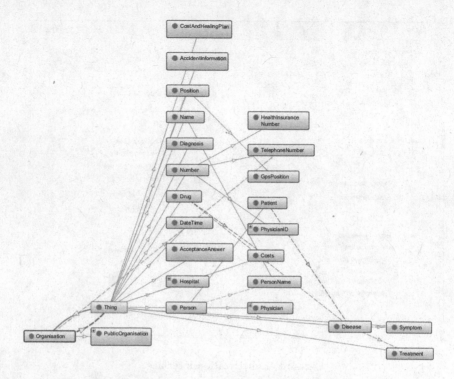

Fig. 5. Ontology example about Health Insurance.

4.3   User/Provider Acceptability Issues

One important characteristic of the proposed framework is its configurability by allowing the user to specify a set of parameters and apply different algorithms supporting different levels of customization. This, however, leads to the problem of user/provider acceptability and ability to specify the required parameters, especially the criteria Table. Indeed, the specification of these parameters may require some cognitive effort from the user/provider.

A possible solution to reduce this effort is to use a predefined Criteria Table. This solution can be further enhanced by including in the framework some appropriate Artificial Intelligence techniques to learn from the previous choices of the user.

Another possible solution to reduce the cognitive effort consists in exploiting the context of the user queries. First, the description of elementary services can be textually analysed and based on the query domain, the system uses either the efficient or the accurate versions of the similarity measure computing algorithm. Second, a global time limit to the matchmaking process can be used to orient the system towards the version that should be used. Third, the context of the query in the workflow can be used to determine the level of customization needed and also in the generation of a suitable Criteria Table.

A more advanced solution consists in combining all the idea cited above.

5   Performance Evaluation

In this section, we evaluate the performance of the different algorithms supported by the PMRF.

5.1   Evaluation Framework

To evaluate the performance of the PMRF, we used the Semantic Matchmaker Evaluation Environment (SME2) [25], which is an open source tool for testing different semantic matchmakers in a consistent way. The SME2 uses OWLS-TC collections to provide the matchmakers with Web service descriptions, and to compare their answers to the relevance sets of the various queries. The SME2 provides several metrics to evaluate the performance and effectiveness of a Web service matchmaker. The metrics that have been considered in this paper are: precision and recall, average precision, query response time and memory consumption. The definitions of these metrics are given in [25].

Experimentations have been conducted on a Dell Inspiron 15 3735 Laptop with an Intel Core i5 processor (1.6 GHz) and 2 GB of memory. The test collection OWLS-TC4 that has been used consists of 1083 Web service offers described in OWL-S 1.1 and 42 queries. Figure 5 provides an Ontology example (concerning health insurance) that has been used for the experimentations.

5.2   Performance Evaluation Analysis

To study the performance of the different modules supported by the PMRF, we implemented seven plugins (see Table 2) to be used with the SME2 tool. Each of these plugins represents a different combination of the matching, similarity computing and ranking algorithms. Figure 6 shows the main function of the SME2 plugin associated with Configuration 5.

The difference between configurations 1 and 2 is the similarity measure module instance: configuration 1 employs the **Accurate MinEdge** instance while the second employs the **Efficient MinEdge** instance. Figure 7(a) shows the

Table 2. Configurations used for comparison.

Configuration number	Similarity measure	Matching algorithm	Ranking algorithm
1	Accurate MinEdge	Basic	Basic
2	Efficient MinEdge	Basic	Basic
3	Accurate MaxEdge	Basic	Basic
4	Accurate MinEdge	Fully parameterized	Basic
5	Accurate MaxMinEdge	Basic	RankMinMax
6	Accurate MinEdge	Basic	Rule based
7	Efficient MinEdge	Basic	Rule based

```java
public Hashtable<URL, Vector<URL>> query(URL arg0)
    {
    Hashtable<URL,Vector<URL>> finalOutput=new Hashtable<URL,Vector<URL>>();
    try
    {
        query=new ServiceTuple(arg0,reasoner);
        /*
         * **************************************************************************
         * We first perform the matching
         * In the same time we create the initial group
         * the initial group represents the data of the root node
         * It contains all services
         * **************************************************************************
         */
        Group initialGroup=new Group();
        for(ServiceTuple serviceAd:offers)
        {
            match(query,serviceAd,reasoner);
            initialGroup.addAService(serviceAd);
        }
        /*
         * **************************************************************************
         * We secondly perform the ranking
         * **************************************************************************
         */
        /*
         * We Create the node we fill it with the initial group and set it as a root for
         the tree
         */
        Node<Group>  root = new Node<Group>();
        root.setData(initialGroup);

        Tree tree=new Tree();
        tree.setRootElement(root);
        /*
         * We instantiate a sorting instance, it is the class that will perform all the
         ranking procedures
         */
        Sorting sort =new Sorting();
        /*
         * We generate the tree
         */
        ArrayList<Node<Group>> firstLevelChildren= sort.rankMinMaxArb(root,2);
        root.setChildren(firstLevelChildren);

        for(Node<Group> firstLevelChild: firstLevelChildren)
        {
            if(!firstLevelChild.getData().hasSingleService())
            {
                ArrayList<Node<Group>> secondLevelChildren=
                sort.rankMinMaxArb(firstLevelChild,1);
                firstLevelChild.setChildren(secondLevelChildren);
                for(Node<Group> secondLevelChild: secondLevelChildren)
                {
                    if(!secondLevelChild.getData().hasSingleService())
                    {
                        ArrayList<Node<Group>> thirdLevelChildren =
                        sort.rankMinMaxArb(secondLevelChild,3);
                        secondLevelChild.setChildren(thirdLevelChildren);
                    }
                }
            }
        }
        /*
         * We generate the final ranked list of services
         */
        List<Node<Group>> rankedServices=new ArrayList<Node<Group>>();
        tree.walk(root, rankedServices);
        /*
         * We assign the ranked services into the final data structure
         */
        Vector<URL> output=new Vector<URL>();
        for(Node<Group> node:rankedServices)
        {
            output.add(node.getData().getSingleService().serviceDocument);
        }
        finalOutput.put(arg0, output);

    }
    catch (Exception e) {
        e.printStackTrace();
    }
    return finalOutput;
    }
```

Fig. 6. Main function of the SME plugin associated with configuration 5.

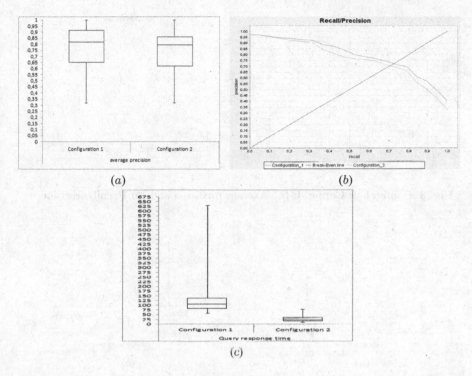

Fig. 7. Config. 1 *vs.* Config. 2: (*a*) Average precision, (*b*) Recall/precision and (*c*) Query response time.

Average Precision and Fig. 7(*b*) illustrates the Recall/Precision plot of configurations 1 and 2.

We can see that configuration 1 outperforms configuration 2 for these two metrics. This is due to the use of logical inference, that obviously enhances the precision of the first configuration. In Fig. 7(*c*), however, configuration 2 is shown to be remarkably faster than configuration 1. This is due to the inference process used in configuration 1 that consumes considerable resources.

The configurations 1 and 4 use different matching module instances. The first configuration is based on the basic matching algorithm while the second uses the fully parameterized matching. Figure 8(*a*) shows the Average Precision metric results. It is easy to see that configuration 4 outperforms configuration 1. This is due to the fact that the Criteria Table restricts the results to the most relevant Web services, which will have the best ranking leading to a higher Average Precision. Figure 8(*b*) illustrates the Recall/Precision plot. It shows that configuration 4 has a low recall rate. The overly restrictive Criteria Table explains these results, since it fails to return some relevant services.

The difference between configurations 5 and 6 is the ranking module instance and the similarity computing procedure. The first uses the tree-based ranking algorithm while the second employs the rule-based ranking algorithm. Figure 9(*a*) shows that configuration 5 has a slightly better Average Precision

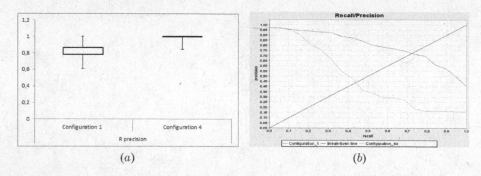

Fig. 8. Config. 1 *vs* Config. 4: (*a*) Average precision and (*b*) Recall/precision.

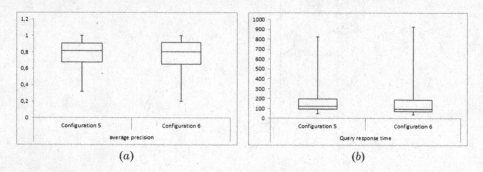

Fig. 9. Config. 5 *vs* Config. 6: (*a*) Average precision and (*b*) Query response time.

than configuration 6 while Fig. 9(*b*) shows that configuration 6 is obviously faster than configuration 5.

6   Comparative Study

We compared the results of the PMRF matchmaker with SPARQLent [9] and iSeM [8] frameworks. Configuration 7 Table 2 was chosen to perform this comparison. The SPARQLent is a logic-based matchmaker based on the OWL-DL reasoner Pellet to provide exact and relaxed Web services matchmaking. The iSeM is an hybrid matchmaker offering different filter matchings: logic-based, approximate reasoning based on logical concept abduction for matching Inputs and Outputs. We considered only the I-O logic-based in this comparative study. We note that SPARQLent and iSeM consider preconditions and effects of Web services, which are not considered in our work.

The Average Precision is given in Fig. 10(*a*). This figure shows that the PMRF has a more accurate Average Precision than iSeM logic-based and SPARQLent, leading to a better ranking precision than the two other frameworks. In addition, the generated ranking is more fine-grained than SPARQLent and iSeM. This is due to the score-based ranking that gives a more coarse evaluation than a degree aggregation. Indeed, SPARQLent and iSeM approaches adopt

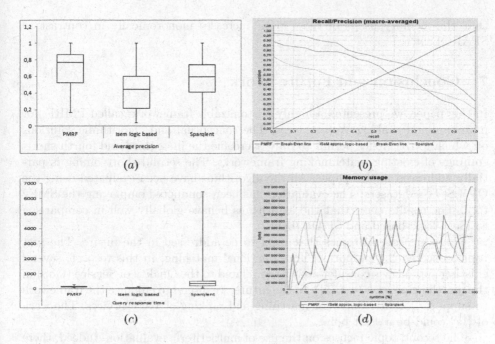

Fig. 10. Comparative study: (a) Average precision, (b) Recall/precision, (c) Query response time and (d) Memory usage.

a subsumption-based ranking strategy as described in [20], which gives equal weights to all similarity degrees.

Figure 10(b) presents the Recall/Precision of the PMRF, iSeM logic-based and SPARQLent. This figure shows that PMRF recall is significantly better than both iSeM logic-based and SPARQLent. This means that our approach is able to reduce the amount of false positives (see [23] for a discussion on the false positives problem).

The comparison of the Query Response Time of the PMRF, logic-based iSeM and SPARQLent is shown in Fig. 10(c). The experimental results show that the PMRF is faster than SPARQLent (760 ms for SPARQLent versus 128 ms for PMRF) and slightly less faster than logic-based iSeM (65 ms for iSeM). We note that SPARQLent has especially high query response time if the query include preconditions/effects. The SPARQLent is also based on an OWL DL reasoner, which has an expensive processing. PMRF and iSeM have close query response time because both consider direct parent/child relations in a subsumption graph, which reduces significantly the query processing. The PMRF highest query response time limit is 248 ms.

Figure 10(d) shows the Memory Usage for PMRF, iSeM logic-based and SPARQLent. It is easy to see that PMRF consumes less memory than iSeM logic-based and SPARQLent. This can be explained by the fact that the PMRF does not require a reasoner (in the case of Configuration 7) neither a SPARQL queries in order to compute similarities between concepts. We note, however, that the memory usage of the PMRF increases monotonically in contrast to SPARQLent.

7 Conclusion and Future Work

In this paper, we presented a highly customizable framework, called PMRF, for matching and ranking Web services. The conceptual and algorithmic solutions on which PMRF relies permit to fully overcome the first, third and fourth short-comings of existing matchmaking frameworks. The second shortcoming is partially addressed in this paper. All the algorithms have been evaluated using the OWLS-TC4 datasets. The evaluation has been conducted employing the SME2 tool. The results show that the algorithms behave globally well in comparison to iSeM-logic-based and SPARQLent.

There are several topics that need to be addressed in the future. The first topic concerns the support of non-functional matching. In this respect, several existing approaches consider attributes related to the Quality of Service (QoS) in the matching process (e.g. [5]). In the future, we intend to enhance the framework to support QoS attributes for matching and ranking of Web services. The work of [17] could be a start point.

The second topic focuses on the use of multicriteria evaluation. Indeed, there are few proposals that explicitly use multicriteria evaluation to support matching and ranking of Web services (e.g. [26]). In the future, we intend to use a well-known and more advanced multicriteria method, namely the Dominance-based Rough Set Approach (DRSA), which is particularity suitable for including the QoS attributes in the matching process.

The last topic relates to the support of the imprecision and uncertainty in matching and ranking of Web services. In this paper, we assumed that the data and user parameters are crisply defined. In the future, we intend to enhance the proposed framework by conceiving and developing algorithms and tools that support the imprecision and uncertainty aspects in Web services matching and ranking.

References

1. Günay, A., Yolum, P.: Service matchmaking revisited: an approach based on model checking. Web Semant. Sci. Serv. Agents World Wide Web **8**, 292–309 (2010)
2. Narock, T., Yoon, V., March, S.: A provenance-based approach to semantic web service description and discovery. Decis. Support Syst. **64**, 90–99 (2014)
3. Khater, M., Habibeche, S., Malki, M.: Behaviour approach for composite OWL-S services discovery. Int. J. Bus. Inf. Syst. **25**, 55–70 (2017)
4. Sangers, J., Frasincar, F., Hogenboom, F., Chepegin, V.: Semantic web service discovery using natural language processing techniques. Expert Syst. Appl. **40**, 4660–4671 (2013)
5. Alnahdi, A., Liu, S.H., Melton, A.: Enhanced web service matchmaking: a quality of service approach. In: 2015 IEEE World Congress on Services, New York, USA, pp. 341–348 (2015)

6. Chakhar, S.: Parameterized attribute and service levels semantic matchmaking framework for service composition. In: Fifth International Conference on Advances in Databases, Knowledge, and Data Applications (DBKDA 2013), Seville, Spain, pp. 159–165 (2013)
7. Stavropoulos, T., Andreadis, S., Bassiliades, N., Vrakas, D., Vlahavas, I.: The tomaco hybrid matching framework for SAWSDL semantic web services. IEEE Trans. Serv. Comput. **9**, 954–967 (2016)
8. Klusch, M., Kapahnke, P.: The iSeM matchmaker: a flexible approach for adaptive hybrid semantic service selection. Web Semant. Sci. Serv. Agents World Wide Web **15**, 1–14 (2012)
9. Sbodio, M., Martin, D., Moulin, C.: Discovering semantic web services using SPARQL and intelligent agents. Web Semant. Sci. Serv. Agents World Wide Web **8**, 310–328 (2010)
10. Elsayed, D., Salah, A.: Semantic web service discovery: a systematic survey. In: The 11th International Computer Engineering Conference (ICENCO 2015), pp. 131–136 (2015)
11. Nacer, H., Aissani, D.: Semantic web services: standards, applications, challenges and solutions. J. Netw. Comput. Appl. **44**, 134–151 (2014)
12. Priyadharshini, G., Gunasri, R., Saravana, B.: A survey on semantic web service discovery methods. Int. J. Comput. Appl. **82**, 8–11 (2013)
13. Toch, E., Reinhartz-Berger, I., Dori, D.: Humans, semantic services and similarity: a user study of semantic web services matching and composition. Web Semant. Sci. Serv. Agents World Wide Web **9**, 16–28 (2011)
14. Tosi, D., Morasca, S.: Supporting the semi-automatic semantic annotation of web services: a systematic literature review. Inf. Softw. Technol. **61**, 16–32 (2015)
15. Paulraj, D., Swamynathan, S.: Content based service discovery in semantic web services using wordnet. In: Thilagam, P.S., Pais, A.R., Chandrasekaran, K., Balakrishnan, N. (eds.) ADCONS 2011. LNCS, vol. 7135, pp. 48–56. Springer, Heidelberg (2012). doi:10.1007/978-3-642-29280-4_6
16. Liu, M., Shen, W., Hao, Q., Yan, J., Bai, L.: A fuzzy matchmaking approach for semantic web services with application to collaborative material selection. Comput. Ind. **63**, 193–209 (2012)
17. Chakhar, S., Ishizaka, A., Labib, A.: Semantic matching-based selection and qos-aware classification of web services. In: Monfort, V., Krempels, K.-H. (eds.) WEBIST 2014. LNBIP, vol. 226, pp. 96–112. Springer, Cham (2015). doi:10.1007/978-3-319-27030-2_7
18. Luna, J.A.G., Pardo, I.D.T., Builes, J.A.J.: BAX-SET PLUS: a taxonomic navigation model to categorize, search and retrieve semantic web services. In: Gaol, F. (ed.) Recent Progress in Data Engineering and Internet Technology. Lecture Notes in Electrical Engineering, vol. 156. Springer, Heidelberg (2013). doi:10.1007/978-3-642-28807-4_50
19. Di Modica, G., Tomarchio, O.: Matchmaking semantic security policies in heterogeneous clouds. Future Gener. Comput. Syst. **55**, 176–185 (2016)
20. Paolucci, M., Kawamura, T., Payne, T.R., Sycara, K.: Semantic matching of web services capabilities. In: Horrocks, I., Hendler, J. (eds.) ISWC 2002. LNCS, vol. 2342, pp. 333–347. Springer, Heidelberg (2002). doi:10.1007/3-540-48005-6_26
21. Chen, F., Li, M., Wu, H., Xie, L.: Web service discovery among large service pools utilising semantic similarity and clustering. Enterpr. Inf. Syst. **11**, 452–469 (2017)

22. Gmati, F.E., Yacoubi-Ayadi, N., Chakhar, S.: Parameterized algorithms for matching and ranking web services. In: Meersman, R., Panetto, H., Dillon, T., Missikoff, M., Liu, L., Pastor, O., Cuzzocrea, A., Sellis, T. (eds.) OTM 2014. LNCS, vol. 8841, pp. 784–791. Springer, Heidelberg (2014). doi:10.1007/978-3-662-45563-0_50

23. Bellur, U., Kulkarni, R.: Improved matchmaking algorithm for semantic Web services based on bipartite graph matching. In: IEEE International Conference on Web Services, Salt Lake City, Utah, USA, pp. 86–93 (2007)

24. Gmati, F.E., Yacoubi Ayadi, N., Bahri, A., Chakhar, S., Ishizaka, A.: A tree-based algorithm for ranking web services. In: Monfort, V., Krempels, K.H. (eds.) The 11th International Conference on Web Information Systems and Technologies (WEBIST 2015), Lisbon, Portugal, 20–22 May 2015, pp. 170–178. SciTePress (2015)

25. Klusch, M., Dudev, M., Misutka, J., Kapahnke, P., Vasileski, M.: SME^2 Version 2.2. User Manual. The German Research Center for Artificial Intelligence (DFKI), Germany (2010)

26. Chakhar, S., Haddad, S., Mokdad, L., Mousseau, V., Youcef, S.: Multicriteria evaluation-based framework for composite web service selection. In: Bisdorff, R., Dias, L.C., Meyer, P., Mousseau, V., Pirlot, M. (eds.) Evaluation and Decision Models with Multiple Criteria. IHIS, pp. 167–200. Springer, Heidelberg (2015). doi:10.1007/978-3-662-46816-6_6

How Reliable Is Sentiment Analysis?
A Multi-domain Empirical Investigation

Tao Ding$^{(\boxtimes)}$ and Shimei Pan$^{(\boxtimes)}$

University of Maryland, Baltimore County, Baltimore, MD 21250, USA
{taoding01,shimei}@umbc.edu

Abstract. Sentiment analysis (also known as opinion mining) is frequently used in monitoring public opinions on the internet. For example, it can help marketers evaluate the success of an ad campaign. It can also be used to assess public opinions during a political campaign. As a result, many businesses and organizations are exploring the potential value of employing sentiment analysis as a part of their business and social intelligence strategies. However, the technology isn't fully mature yet. As a result, if not used carefully, the results from sentiment analysis can be misleading. In this paper, we present an empirical investigation of the effectiveness of using current sentiment analysis tools to assess people's opinions in five different domains. The results were very uneven, from decent (e.g., hotel reviews) to poor (e.g., comments on public policies). We also proposed several *effectiveness indicators* that can be used to signal the appropriateness of using these tools in specific domains.

Keywords: Content analysis · Sentiment analysis · Performance measure

1 Introduction

With the rise of the World Wide Web, people are expressing their opinions and thoughts online using review sites, blogs, forums, and social networking sites. They collectively represent a rich source of information on different topics. Being able to capture the emotional responses of the public can help gain insight and make informed decisions. For example, it can help determine if a marketing initiative is driving the planned responses, or determine whether consumers prefer a new product just launched or not, or people's reaction to a political debate [5,20]. To meet this need, many open source and commercial sentiment analysis (SA) tools have been developed. With these tools, more and more businesses, organizations, and individuals can harness the power of sentiment analysis by applying these tools directly to their data. Moreover, the easy availability of massive amount of opinion-rich online data also fuels the wide adoption of SA tools. For example, open-source web crawlers can be used to collect the review data easily. Many social media sites also release their application programming interfaces (APIs), which makes data collection from social media convenient.

© Springer International Publishing AG 2017
V. Monfort et al. (Eds.): WEBIST 2016, LNBIP 292, pp. 37–57, 2017.
DOI: 10.1007/978-3-319-66468-2_3

Nowadays, SA has been widely used to gauge public opinions towards products [6], services [17], social events [23], political events [5], political candidates, and public policies [4,20].

However, due to the complexity in automated text analysis, today's sentiment analysis tools are far from perfect. For example, many of them are good at detecting useful mood signals (e.g., positive or negative sentiment) but inadequate in tracking and inferencing the relationships between different moods and different targets. As a result, if not used carefully, the results from sentiment analysis can be meaningless or even misleading. Since the typical users of SA are not researchers but business owners or individuals, they may not have the necessary knowledge to determine whether a SA tool is appropriate for their application domains or not.

In this paper, we present an empirical analysis of the effectiveness of using existing sentiment analysis tools for different applications. We have collected data from five different domains: movie reviews, hotel reviews, public comments on net neutrality, Tweets about political candidates, and public comments on Harvard University's admission policy. Based on these data, we study the relations between the results of sentiment analysis and the corresponding common perception of the public opinion. To help determine whether a SA tool is appropriate for one's data, we also proposed several *effectiveness indicators* that can be computed efficiently from given datasets.

The main contributions of our work include:

1. This is the first formal study known to us that analyzes the appropriateness of using sentiment analysis on diverse data sets. Our results can shed lights on the limitations of existing tools. Our results can also help raise the awareness of the potential pitfalls associated with the misuse of this technology.
2. We also propose a diverse set of *effectiveness indicators* that can be computed efficiently from given datasets to help people determine the appropriateness of using a sentiment analysis tool on given datasets.

In the following, we first review the current sentiment analysis methods and their applications, followed by a description of our datasets and the analyses we performed to assess the effectiveness of applying sentiment analysis on these datasets. Then we explain our effort in developing a few effectiveness indicators to help users determine whether a SA tool is appropriate for a given dataset. Finally, we conclude the paper by summarizing the main findings and pointing out a few future directions.

2 Related Works

Sentiment Analysis, also called opinion mining, in a broad sense is defined as the computational study of opinions, sentiments and emotions expressed in text [12]. According to [9], the task of sentiment analysis is to automatically extract a quintuple from text:

$$(e_i, a_{ij}, s_{ijkl}, h_k, t_l),$$

where e_i is a target object, a_{ij} is an aspect or attribute of e_i, s_{ijkl} is the sentiment value of aspect a_{ij} of entity e_i, h_k is the opinion holder, and t_l is the time when an opinion is expressed by a opinion holder. Once the sentiment quintuples are extracted from text, they can be aggregated and analyzed qualitatively or quantitatively to derive insights. Extracting the quintuples from unstructured text however is very challenging due to the complexity in natural language processing (NLP). For example, a positive or negative sentiment word may have opposite orientations in different application domains; Sarcasm is hard to detect; Coreference resolution, negation handling, and word sense disambiguation, a few well known but unsolved problems in NLP need for correct inference. Since many of the existing sentiment analysis tools did not solve these problems appropriately, they may work well in simple domains but not effective for more complex applications.

In terms of the methods used in typical sentiment analysis systems, they can be divided into lexicon-based and machine learning-based [10]. Since a purely lexicon-based approach is less common these days, here we focus on machine learning-based methods. Frequently, a machine learning-based system also incorporates lexical features from sentiment lexicons in its analysis.

Machine learning-based sentiment analysis can be further divided into supervised and unsupervised learning methods. The supervised methods make use of a large number of annotated training examples to build a sentiment classification model. Typical classification methods include Naive Bayes, Maximum Entropy classifiers and Support Vector Machines [13]. In general, for supervised sentiment analysis, if the target domain is similar to the source domain from which the training examples are collected, the prediction accuracy will be similar to the specified performance. In contrast, if the target domain is very different from the source domain, the sentiment analysis performance can deteriorate significantly. Among existing supervised sentiment analysis tools, some provide pre-trained models such as the Mashape Text-Processing API[1], others require users to provide labeled data and then train their own prediction models, such as Google Prediction API[2], NLTK text classification API[3].

Since annotating a large number of examples with sentiment labels can be very time consuming, there are also many unsupervised sentiment analysis systems that do not require annotated training data. They often rely on opinion bearing words to perform sentiment analysis [1,22]. Turney [19] proposed a method that classifies reviews by using two arbitrary seed words – poor and excellent, to calculate the semantic orientations of other words and phrases. Read [16] proposed a weakly-supervised technique, using a large collection of unlabeled text to determine sentiment. They used PMI [19], semantic spaces, and distributional similarity to measure similarity between words and polarity

---

[1] http://text-processing.com/docs/sentiment.html.
[2] https://cloud.google.com/prediction/docs.
[3] http://www.nltk.org/api/nltk.classify.html.

prototypes. The results were less dependent on the domain, topic and time-period represented by the testing data. In addition, Hu [7] investigated whether models of emotion signals can potentially help sentiment analysis.

So far, hundreds of commercial state-of-the-art tools are available for automatic sentiment analysis, such as Semantria[4], SentimentAnalyzer[5], SentiStrength[6], MLAnalyzer[7], TextProcessing[8]. These tools can be applied directly to unlabeled documents without the need for domain-specific model training. In our experiment, we used Semantria as an unsupervised sentiment analysis tool to evaluate its effectiveness on different domains. Since most supervised sentiment analysis tools did not provide the original training data, we choose TextProcessing as a supervised sentiment analysis tool in our experiment since the original training data is available, which are movie reviews created by Pang [11]. As a result, the similarity between trained domain and target domains can be computed.

Fewer open-source tools dedicated to sentiment analysis are available today. To compare the results among different supervised methods, we train our Naive Bayes classifier using the NLTK API. The training data are the same as those in TextProcessing. To compare unsupervised tools, we employed SANN[9] [14]. Table 1 summarizes the tools used in this investigation.

Table 1. Categorization of Selected tools.

Method	Tool
Supervised	NLTK API (Naive Bayes)
	TextProcessing
Unsupervised	SANN
	Semantria

3   Data Collection

To evaluate the impact of domain differences on sentiment analysis, we included five datasets:

1. **H**otel Reviews (Hotel): the dataset was originally used in [21]. We chose this dataset because reviews such as product reviews, hotel reviews and restaurant reviews are the most typical domains for sentiment analysis. In our study, we included 18726 reviews for 152 hotels, each includes the textual content, the author, and the overall rating that ranges from 1 star to 5 stars.

---

[4] https://semantria.com/.
[5] http://sentimentanalyzer.appspot.com/.
[6] http://sentistrength.wlv.ac.uk/.
[7] https://www.publicapis.com/mlanalyzer.
[8] http://text-processing.com/demo/sentiment/.
[9] https://github.com/nik0spapp/unsupervisedsentiment.

2. **Net Neutrality(NN):** The US Federal Communications Commission (FCC) [3] has published the public comments they received on the Open Internet/Network Neutrality bill. This bill considers the protection and Promotion of the principle of Open Internet to ensure that government and internet service providers should treat all data on the internet the same, not discriminating or charging differentially by user, content, site, platform, application, type of attached equipment, or mode of communication (FCC 14–28[10]). In our experiments, we included 26282 comments from this dataset. With this dataset, we want to evaluate the effectiveness of using sentiment analysis to assess public opinions towards a public policy.

3. **Tweet:** We collected a set of tweets related to the 2016 presidential campaign of Hillary Clinton. We used the search keywords "Hillary Clinton president" as the query to collect related tweets using the Twitter API. After filtering out redundant tweets, our dataset includes 7237 tweets. With this dataset, we want to investigate the effectiveness of using sentiment analysis to assess public opinions towards a political candidate based on social media posts since nowadays, social media-based opinion analysis becomes increasingly more popular.

4. **Harvard university Admission Policy (HAP):** In 2015, *Wall Street Journal* published an article on a lawsuit filed by a group of Asian-American organizations alleging that Asian-Americans face discriminatory standards for admission to Harvard University [2]. The complaint claimed that Harvard has set quotas to keep the number of Asian-American students admitted to the university much lower than their applications should warrant. We collected 924 public comments on this article. With this dataset, we want to study the effectiveness of using sentiment analysis to assess the public reaction toward a social event.

5. **Movie Review:** To investigate the impact of domain difference on the effectiveness on a supervised sentiment analyzer, we also include a dataset of movie reviews. The data source was the Internet Movie Database (IMDb). These reviews were originally used by Pang et al. (2002). They selected reviews where the author rating was expressed with stars. Ratings were automatically extracted and converted into one of three categories: positive, negative, or neutral. They only kept 1000 positive reviews and negative reviews for sentiment classification. Some existing sentiment analysis tool, such as TextProcessing, used these polarity data to train sentiment classifier. We compare the other four domains with the movie domain in our experiments to study the performance of supervised sentiment analysis tools.

Table 2 shows some statistics of these dataset.

---

[10] https://www.fcc.gov/rulemaking/most-active-proceedings.

Table 2. Dataset.

	# of doc	# of sentence	size of corpus
Hotel	18726	171231	867795
NN	26282	88039	4672959
Tweet	7237	10160	867795
HAP	924	3105	25198
Movie	2000	64720	636524

3.1   Annotation Task

To evaluate the effectiveness of each sentiment analysis tool on different domains, we obtained two types of ground truth (1) the *emotion or feeling* expressed in a sentence or a message (called *emotion ground truth*) (2) the *opinion* expressed in a message (called *opinion ground truth*). Here we differentiate *emotion/feeling* from *opinion*. Emotion or feeling, is an immediate, instinctive and direct response to experience while opinion is more complicated. It is a combination of our autonomic emotional responses, behavior as well as cultural or societal meaning towards a subject. We would like to investigate whether the emotions or feelings expressed in a text is easier to detect than opinions since emotion is more direct while opinion is often indirect and appeals to preconceived notions and cultural norms.

To obtain the *emotion* and *opinion* ground truth, we used Amazon's Mechanical Turk (AMT). Amazon Mechanical Turk is a crowdsourcing Internet marketplace that enables individuals and businesses (known as Requesters) to coordinate the use of a large number of workers (a.k.a Turkers) to perform tasks. In this case, we asked each Turker to read a post and decide the emotion and opinion expressed in the text. The emotion annotation is at both sentence and message level while the opinion annotation is only at the message level. For emotion annotation, each sentence or message is annotated with four labels: positive, negative, neutral and don't know. The opinion label is specific for each application. To ensure the quality of the ground truth data, each post is annotated by three different annotators. All the annotators also have to be pre-qualified based on the following criteria: they must have submitted over 5000 tasks on AMT with an acceptance rate of over 95%.

Specifically,

For opinion annotation for hotel reviews, we ask each participant to decide whether 1. the author likes the hotel; 2. the author dislikes the hotel; 3. the author is neutral; 4. the author's opinion is unclear.

One example from the hotel domain is the following:

Great Hotel Fantastic Hotel. Get the goldfish to keep you company. We still miss ours, Phil! Jeff at the concierge was a great help. Loved the crazy room— somehow the stripes work. Will definitely return. Breakfast at the restaurant was outstanding.

For emotion annotation, we first ask each participant to choose an emotion label for each sentence. After that, the participant also need to provide an overall emotion/feeling label for the entire post. Figure 1 shows the emotion annotation UI used in the AMT study. Overall 500 hotel reviews were selected randomly to be annotated on AMT.

For opinion annotation on the net neutrality public comment dataset, we asked each Turker whether 1. the author supports net neutrality; 2. the author is against net neutrality; 3. the author is neutral; 4. the author's opinion is unclear. Then, the Turker was also asked to annotate emotions at both the sentence and the message level. Overall, 500 comments from the net neutrality dataset are selected randomly to annotate. Here is an example from the net neutrality dataset:

The Internet was created with public funds for the use of the public and the government. No for-profit organization should have the right to control access from the people who need and use it.

To annotate the opinions expressed in Twitter posts, we asked each Turker to rate whether 1. the author supports Hillary Clinton 2. the author does not support Hillary Clinton, 3. the author is neutral or 4. the opinion of the author is unclear. Then, the Turker is also asked to complete the emotion annotation task. We randomly selected 1000 tweets to annotate. Here is an example of such a tweet:

I WILL NOT vote for Hillary Clinton for President WE DO NOT want Bill BACK in the White House y'all know what I mean.

The HAP comments are more complex. Many contain deeply embedded conversation threads (e.g., comments on comments). In this case, sufficient context is particularly important for Turkers to understand the opinion expressed by different people. For example, one comment: *@David Smith: I totally agree with you, the university should pay attention to that.* is a reply to a previous comment expressed by David Smith. The opinion expressed in this comment is ambiguous if we don't know the opinion of David Smith. To provide Turkers enough context to determine opinions expressed in a message, instead of providing a comment without context, we asked the Turkers to annotate an entire conversation thread. The following is a conversation thread from HAP:

Glenn Wilder : And of course the Dept Chair of African American Studies simply cannot be delivering lectures to a room full of Hispanics Asians and Caucasians. The class may actually have some value...but it would be lost on such a group. This alone justifies the need to balance out the student body.

Patrick O'Neil : @ Glenn Wilder This seems prejudicial! Why isn't there a Chair of Hispanic American studies and Asian American studies?

Preston Moore : @ Glenn Wilder Don't forget the Chair of the Women's Studies dept or Chair of East Asia Languages.

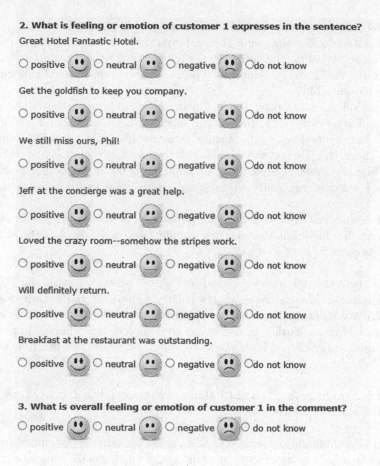

Fig. 1. An example of the AMT emotion annotation UI.

After reading each conversation thread, we ask each Turker to annotate the opinion and emotions expressed by each person involved in the conversation. For the above example, we ask each Turker to annotate whether Glenn Wilder thinks that the Harvard admission policy is 1. fair 2. unfair 3. neutral 4. I don't know the opinion of this person. We also ask each Turker to annotate Glen Wilder's emotions expressed in the post. We ask the Turker to do the same for Patrick O'Neil and Preston Moore. Figure 2 shows the distribution of sessions which includes different numbers of replies in each thread. The average number of replies in each thread in the dataset is 3.86, the median number of replies is 5.

In our dataset, the hotel reviews are highly focused and opinion rich with little irrelevant information, these reviews always talk about hotels or some aspects of a hotel, such as its location, cleanliness, service and price. Also, there is no interactions between reviewers, which means a reviewer cannot comment on another review.

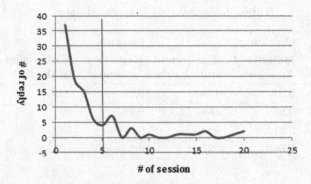

Fig. 2. Thread distributions in HAP.

Similar to the hotel reviews, the net neutrality dataset also does not contain any interactions between commenters. But unlike the hotel reviews which have clearly defined object-aspect relations between entities, the structure of the net neutrality comments is much more complex and there is no well-defined relations between the entities discussed in the comments (e.g., the policy itself, internet service providers, individual consumers, Netflix, pricing and innovation). Thus it can be very challenging to map different sentiments associated with different entities to an overall opinion about the net neutrality policy.

Comparing with the hotel reviews and net neutrality comments, the Twitter posts are much shorter - at most 140 characters. It involves a small number of interactions, such as retweet and reply. Since retweets normally do not change the sentiment and replies are relatively rare in our dataset, the impact of user interactions on Twitter sentiment analysis may not be as significant as that on HAP.

We did not perform additional annotations on the movie reviews since they are already annotated with sentiments and the dataset is mainly used to assess the appropriateness of employing supervised sentiment analysis for different domains.

3.2   Annotation Results

Since each data instance was annotated by three Turkers, we used the majority agreement as the ground truth labels. We also filtered out instances whose labels are "I do not know". Table 3 displays the average agreement with the ground truth annotation for each domain. The results show that other than the HAP domain, the agreement with the ground truth opinion and emotion annotations from all the domains are high (near or above 90%). The most challenging case is HAP, because of the structural complexity of its posts, the agreement is only around 67% for the ground truth opinion annotation and 74% for the ground truth emotion annotation. Overall, for human annotators, other than the HAP domain, it is relatively easy for them to identify and agree on the emotions and opinions expressed in the posts.

Table 3. Agreement of annotated data.

	Opinion		Emotion	
	Majority Agreement	# of ground truth labels	Majority Agreement	# of ground truth labels
NN	0.91	458	0.86	431
Hotel	0.96	483	0.98	490
Tweet	0.912	899	0.95	949
HAP	0.669	84	0.74	101

3.3   Correlation Between the Opinion and Emotion Ground Truth

We have annotated two sets of ground truth, one is the emotions, the other is the opinions. Since opinions are more indirect and may require a deep understanding of the relationships between targets of emotions and a specific topic, we performed correlation analysis to assess their relations. We performed a Pearson chi-square test [15] to determine if the opinion and emotion ground truth are independent or correlated. If the p-value is smaller than 0.05, we can reject the null hypothesis of independence, which means there is a significant correlation between these two variables. Moreover, to measure the strength of this correlation, we calculated Cramer's V. V may be viewed as the association between two variables as a percentage of their maximum possible variation. V can reach 1.0 when the two variables have equal marginals. A V value over 0.25, means the level of association is very strong. As shown in Table 4, other than net neutrality, the emotion and opinion ground truth are significantly correlated. However, based on the V values, the correlation on the HAP domain (0.357) is not as strong as those on the Hotel (0.98) and Twitter domain (0.93). Thus, for the net neutrality dataset, since the p-value is 0.24, we cannot reject the independence hull hypothesis. Thus, it is possible that the two sets of ground truth are independent. This result indicates that if a SA tool is only capable of picking up emotion signals but not good at figuring out the relationships between targets of emotions and the subject of the opinion, it may not perform well on opinion mining on the NN or the HAP domain.

Table 4. Correlation between the opinion and the emotion ground truth.

Domain	p-value	Cramer's V
NN	0.24	0.081
Hotel	<0.0001	0.98
Tweet	<0.0001	0.93
HAP	<0.0001	0.357

4   Empirical Study

To evaluate how different sentiment analysis tools perform on different datasets, we employed different tools. Among them, two are commercial state-of-the-art tools, two are open-source tools. Also, in terms of the learning methods, two of them use supervised sentiment classification and two of them use unsupervised sentiment analysis. All of them achieved over 75% prediction accuracy based on test data from their training domains.

4.1   Supervised Sentiment Analysis

Supervised methods consider sentiment classification as a standard classification problem in which labeled data are used to train a classifier. Many existing supervised sentiment analysis engines either provide pre-trained models or allow users to re-train their models using user-provided training data.

In our experiment, we used a commercial sentiment analyzer called TextProcessing which provides a pre-trained sentiment analysis model. The model was trained using annotated data from both the movie review domain and the Twitter domain. The movie review data come from [11] which are publicly available. It contains 1000 positive and 1000 negative reviews. The Twitter dataset is private and not available to us. Since TextProcessing is trained on two different domains, it is difficult for us to test the influence of domain difference on the analysis results. To overcome this, we also used a Naive Bayes-based text classifier to build a sentiment analyzer using the training examples from the movie review domain. To test the performance of our Naive Bayes sentiment analyzer, we randomly split the dataset into a training set (75%) and a testing set (25%). We repeat the process five times and the average prediction accuracy is 78%. The Naive Bayes sentiment analyzer used in the following experiments was trained using all 2000 annotated movie reviews. Because our training data have only two sentiment values: positive and negative; we only keep the positive and negative cases in our test data. Table 5 shows the statistics of the test datasets used to evaluate the performance of the two supervised SA tools on four different domains.

Table 5. Testing data of supervised tool.

Domain	Opinion		Emotion	
	Naive Bayes	TextProcessing	Naive Bayes	TextProcessing
NN	458	458	354	431
Hotel	483	483	474	490
Tweet	530	899	535	949
HAP	55	84	76	101

Figure 3 includes the prediction results based on the opinion ground truth. It shows that Naive Bayes analyzers performed the best on the hotel data.

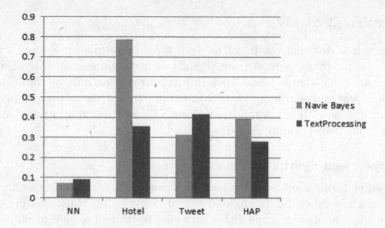

Fig. 3. Performance of supervised tools on opinion prediction.

The performance deteriorated significant on the HAP data. The Naive Bayes analyzer also performed significantly worse on the Twitter data. In contrast, the TextProcessing analyzer performed the best on the Twitter data. This may be due to the fact that a part of its training data came from Twitter. Surprisingly, both analyzers performed the worst on the Net Neutrality data since for humans, the HAP dataset is the most difficult one while the net neutrality data being relatively easy.

Figure 4 shows the evaluation results against the emotion ground truth. Again, the Naive Bayes classifier worked the best on the Hotel domain and the worst on the net neutrality domain. And the TextProcessing Analyzer worked the best on the HAP domain and the worst on the net neutrality domain.

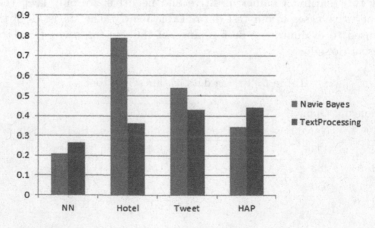

Fig. 4. Performance of supervised tools on emotion prediction.

When comparing their performance in predicting emotions and opinions, the TextProcessing analyzer performed much better in predicting emotions on NN and HAP domain. The Naive Bayes classifier captured emotion better on on NN and Twitter domain. The expression of emotion and opinion are very similar on the hotel, so the both analyzers performed similarly. Likewise, the TextProcessing worked similarly on the Twitter domain. It is worth noting that the Naive Bayers classifier performed better in prediction emotions on the Twitter domain. The Naive Bayers classifier trained with movie review data, the results shows the training set is more helpful to capture emotion signal instead of true opinion on different domain.   ✎

4.2 Unsupervised Sentiment Analysis

For unsupervised sentiment analysis, we employed Semantria, a commercial tool and SANN an open source sentiment analyzer. Both tools produce three sentiment labels: positive, negative and neutral.

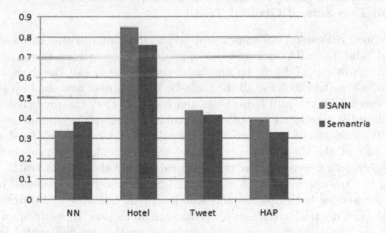

Fig. 5. Performance of unsupervised tools on opinion prediction.

Figure 5 shows the evaluation results against the opinion ground truth. The performance of SANN and Semantria are very similar - both of them achieved about 0.8 accuracy on the hotel data. Accuracy on tweet is both about 0.45. They performed the worst on the net neutrality and the HAP dataset with a prediction accuracy around 0.3.

Figure 6 shows the evaluation results against the emotion ground truth. Similarly, both SANN and Semantria performed the best on the hotel data. Twitter however seems to be the most challenging for both tools in emotion detection (accuracy is around 0.2).

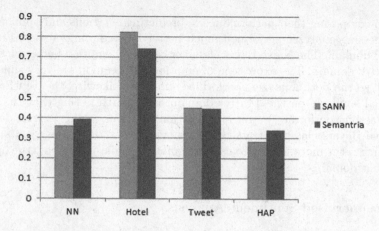

Fig. 6. Performance of unsupervised tools on emotion prediction.

4.3   Correlation Analysis Between Prediction Results and Two Sets of Ground Truth

We performed a Pearson chi-square test [15] to determine if two variables, the predicted value by a SA tool and the opinion/emotion ground truth, are correlated As shown in Table 6, on the hotel dataset, since all the p-values are significantly less than 0.05 for all the tools for both opinion and emotion prediction, we can reject the null hypothesis and conclude that the predicted values are significantly correlated to both the opinion and emotion ground truth. To measure the strength of this correlation, we calculated Cramer's V. As shown in Table 6, since all the Vs on the hotel dataset are greater than 0.25, this indicates a strong correlation between the predicted values and the ground truth. Moreover, the two unsupervised tools SANN and Semantria performed well on the Twitter dataset for both opinion and emotion prediction. They also performed well on the net neutrality dataset for sentiment prediction. In contrast, none of the tools performed well in predicting opinions on the net neutrality dataset. Most of the tools also performed badly on the HAP dataset for both opinion and emotion prediction.

5   Domain Analysis

As we have shown in the previous section, domain differences have significant impact on sentiment analysis performance. If applied properly (e.g., to hotel reviews), the sentiment results may provide useful insight. If not careful and apply them mindlessly, the results can be meaningless or even misleading. For example, if we plot the sentiment analysis results from Semantria on the Net Neutrality dataset, we would believe that the public opinions towards net neutrality is ambivalent: 27% negative, 29% positive and 44% neutral (See Fig. 7). In fact

Table 6. Pearson chi-square test and Crammer's V.

Method	Measure	NN		Hotel		Tweet		HAP	
		O	E	O	E	O	E	O	E
Navie Bayer	p-value	0.432	0.047	<0.0001	<0.0001	0.195	0.0985	0.21	0.618
	Crammer's V	0.035	0.105	0.262	0.27	0.082	0.001	0.144	0.058
Text Processing	p-value	0.678	0.007	<0.0001	<0.0001	0.01	0.0002	0.82	0.25
	Crammer's V	0.041	0.127	0.376	0.277	0.121	0.156	0.084	0.15
SANN	p-value	0.105	0.007	<0.0001	<0.0001	<0.0001	<0.0001	0.571	0.054
	Crammer's V	0.095	0.385	0.503	0.357	0.213	0.23	0.117	0.196
Semantria	p-value	0.326	<0.0001	<0.0001	<0.0001	<0.0001	<0.0001	0.531	0.47
	Crammer's V	0.067	0.233	0.587	0.409	0.166	0.213	0.122	0.122

Note: O is opinion, E is emotion

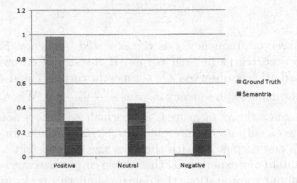

Fig. 7. Distribution of true opinion and Semantria's results on net neutrality.

the real public opinion based on the ground truth annotation is un-ambiguously supportive: 97% support, 3% against and 0% neutral.

In the following, we investigate whether it is possible to automatically compute a set of effectiveness indicators to guide us in assessing the appropriateness of applying a sentiment analysis tool to a given dataset. For unsupervised methods, the effectiveness of a sentiment analysis tool is mainly determined by the properties of the target domain(e.g., complexity). For supervised methods, in additional to domain complexity, we hypothesize that the effectiveness can also be affected by the differences between the source and the target domain. In the following, we empirically verify the usefulness of several effectiveness indicators including *domain similarity, data genre, structure complexity* and *vocabulary complexity*.

5.1 Domain Similarity

For a supervised Sentiment Analysis tool, the similarity between the target and the source domain may have significant impact on sentiment analysis results. Among the two supervised tools, the pre-trained TextProcessing model was trained on both movie reviews and Tweets while the Naive Bayes classifier was trained only on the movie review data. Since we don't have access to the Twitter training data used in TextProcessing, here we focus on the Naive Bayes Classifier. We computed two measures to assess the similarity: the *cosine similarity* and the χ^2 *similarity*. The *cosine similarity* is frequently used in information retrieval to measure the similarity between a search query and a document [18]. Here, we first construct two word vectors, one for all the movie reviews from the training data, one for all the text in a target domain (e.g., the hotel reviews). The length of a domain vector is the size of the entire vocabulary from all five domains. We then compute the cosine similarity between these two word vectors. We also computed the χ^2 *similarity* since it was shown to be the best one for assessing corpus similarity [8]:

$$\chi^2 = \sum \frac{(o - e)^2}{e}$$

Here, o is the observed frequency, e is the expected frequency. For each word, we calculate its occurrences in each corpus. If the size of corpus 1 and 2 are N_1, N_2, the word W has observed $O_{w,1}$ times in corpus 1 and $O_{w,2}$ times in corpus 2, then the expected frequency $e_w = \frac{N_1*(O_{w,1}+O_{w,2})}{N_1+N_2}$. When $N_1 = N_2$, the $e_w = \frac{O_{w,1}+O_{w,2}}{2}$. Since the χ^2 measure is not normalized, it does not permit direct comparison between corpora of different sizes [8]. As a result, for each domain, we constructed a new corpus, all with the same size by randomly sampling posts from each domain. In our experiment, the sample corpus size was set to be 25000 tokens. Based on our computation, the domain similarity ranks are:

$$HAP > HOTEL > NN > Tweet.$$

The most similar corpus to the movie corpus is HAP, while the Twitter corpus is the most different (Table 7).

Table 7. Corpus similarity between training dataset and testing dataset.

	$\cos(\theta)$	χ^2
NN	0.26	24000
Hotel	0.32	22427
Tweet	0.15	38034
HAP	0.45	21100

5.2 Genre

We also believe that the genre of text may impact the effectiveness of a sentiment analyzer. Here we categorize a text into three types: *review*, *comment* and *other*. Among them, reviews are often collected from dedicated review sites.

Each review contains explicit opinions about an obvious target. It has little irrelevant information. Also, there is a simple object-aspect relationship between the entities in a typical review (e.g., the screen of a digital camera). In our datasets, both the movie reviews and the hotel reviews belong to this category. Moreover, similar to reviews, comments are also opinion-rich. But the relationship between different entities in a comment is not well-defined. Also, due to the interactions between different commenters, correct sentiment analysis may require proper understanding of the conversation context, which makes comment-based sentiment analysis very challenging. In our datasets, both the FCC Net Neutrality dataset and the HAP dataset belong to this category. Finally, we categorize the Twitter data as *other* since they are collected based on keyword search and they can be almost anything. Simply speaking, the current sentiment analysis tools performed the best on reviews but poorly on comments or Tweets.

5.3 Structure Complexity

In sentiment analysis, complex domain often makes sentiment analysis difficult. Here, we first define a few measures on structure complexity. A straight-forward indicator of structure complexity is the average length of the posts in a domain. The ranking according to the length measure is:

$$Hotel > NN > HAP > Tweet$$

$$162.5 > 68.39 > 58.84 > 15.78.$$

Thus, hotel reviews tend to be much longer than the others. Due to the size constraints, Tweets are the shortest.

The second structure complexity indicator is the percentage of posts with external references. For example, in the following tweet: *Hillary Clinton: President Hopeful or Hopeless?* http://wp.me/p3UNuh-BC. Without opening the actual content using the URL, it is hard to know what the author's opinion is. The ranking according to the measure is:

$$Tweet > HAP > NN > Hotel$$

$$0.05 > 0.001 > 0.0001 > 0.$$

Thus, in these datasets, Tweets tend to have many embedded links while Hotel reviews are always self-contained without any external links.

The third structure complexity indicator is the average depth of a conversation thread, which is used to assess the complexity in user interactions. The ranking according to the average depth of a thread is:

$$HAP(4.8) > Tweet(1.37) > NN(1) = Hotel(1).$$

Based on this measure, HAP is the most complex domain with an average thread depth of about five. In contrast, both the NN and hotel reviews do not contain any user interacts.

Based on the performance of the tools, among the three structure complexity indicators, the post length seems to have little impact on the prediction accuracy while external links and tread depth can make opinion analysis more difficult.

5.4   Vocabulary Complexity

Entropy is a measurement of vocabulary's homogeneity. Given a sequence of words i.e. words $(w_i, w_2, w_3..., w_n)$, the entropy can be computed using:

$$H = - \sum_{W_i^n \in L} P(W_i) * \log P(W_i)$$

To normalize it, we calculated the relative entropy $H_{rel} = \frac{H}{H_{max}}$, where H_{max} is the max entropy which occurs when all the words have a uniform distribution, thus $p = 1/\|w\|$. To avoid the impact of corpus size, we construct four new corpora with equal size, each by randomly sampling posts from each of the four original corpora. As shown in Fig. 8, computed relative entropy is no longer sensitive to corpus size. When we varied the sample corpus size from 1000 to 25000, there is no significant difference in computed relative entropy.

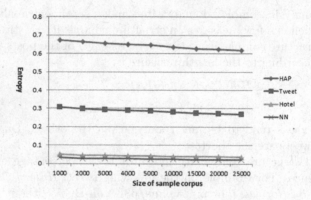

Fig. 8. Entropy of each corpus.

As shown in Fig. 8, the vocabulary complexity of HAP is much higher than the other three. It is also pretty high for the twitter domain. The values of hotel and NN are very close, both have low entropy. This is an indication that their vocabularies are relatively homogeneous.

5.5   Result Analysis

Based on our results, HAP should be the most difficult domain for sentiment analysis. Its genre is *comment*, one of the more complex genres for sentiment analysis. Its vocabulary complexity based on relative entropy is the highest. In terms of average thread depth, its structure complexity is the highest as well. This has been proven to be true for both humans (based on the ground truth annotation) and for computers (The prediction accuracy is about 0.3 for all the supervised and unsupervised tools we tested). In contrast, the hotel review domain should be relatively easy for sentiment analysis. Its genre is review, one of the easiest. It has little or no external references and user interactions. Moreover, its vocabulary complexity is one of the lowest, which makes it an ideal domain for sentiment analysis.

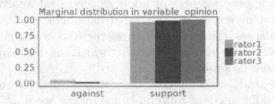

Fig. 9. Annotated opinion distribution on NN.

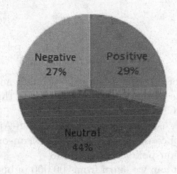

Fig. 10. Detected result distribution on NN.

It is worth noting that our sentiment analyzers performed poorly on NN. Based on our domain analysis, its vocabulary complexity is among the easiest (very close to the hotel domain), its average post length is much shorter than hotel reviews. It also does not have many external references and user interactions. It is a surprise to see that all the tools performed poorly on this dataset. By inspecting the ground truth data, we found that it is highly unbalanced. As shown in Fig. 9, over 95% people support net neutrality. In contrast, the output from Semantria has a very different distribution of sentiment (see Fig. 10). After inspecting the positive and negative comments predicted by Semantria, we found that the system is unable to map the sentiment expressed in the text to a opinions toward net neutrality since the relationships between them are very complex. For example, a person may express "Net Neutrality is great for innovation" or "Comcast is very greedy". Although the sentiment in the first message is "positive" while the second one is negative, the authors of both comments support net neutrality. To get it right, sophisticated inferences of the relationship between Comcast and net neutrality is needed. So far, most of the sentiment analysis tools are not capable of handling this type of inference.

6   Conclusion

Sentiment analysis has been used frequently by businesses, organizations and individuals to assess public opinions and gain insights. In this paper, we empirically analyze the appropriateness of applying sentiment analysis tools in five different domains. Our results demonstrated the importance of understanding the potential pitfalls associated with applying these tools in a given domain. We also proposed several *effectiveness indicators* which can be computed automatically to signal potential problems.

In our current study, we only compare datasets vertically which means all of them are from different data sources. In the future, we want to compare the domain horizontally, collecting data on different topics from the same source (e.g., on Twitter). We also noticed the importance in understanding the relationships between different entities in a domain and the target opinion. We plan to develop new measures that can capture the complexity of entity-opinion relationships in a domain.

References

1. Andreevskaia, A., Bergler, S.: Unsupervised sentiment analysis with emotional signals. In: 11th Conference of the European Chapter of the Association for Computational Linguistics, EACL 2006 (2006)
2. Belkin, D.: Harvard accused of bias against Asian-Americans. Wall Street J. (2015). http://www.wsj.com/articles/asian-american-organizations-seek-federal-probe-ofharvard-admission-policies-1431719348
3. Bob Lannon, A.P.: What can we learn from 800,000 public comments on the FCC's net neutrality plan? @ONLINE (2014)
4. Chung, W., Zeng, D.: Social-media-based public policy informatics: sentiment and network analyses of U.S. immigration and border security. J. Assoc. Inf. Sci. Technol. **67**(7), 1588–1606 (2015)
5. Diakopoulos, N.A., Shamma, D.A.: Characterizing debate performance via aggregated twitter sentiment. In: Proceedings of the SIGCHI Conference on Human Factors in Computing Systems, CHI 2010, pp. 1195–1198. ACM, New York (2010)
6. Ghose, A., Ipeirotis, P.G., Sundararajan, A.: Opinion mining using econometrics: a case study on reputation systems. In: Proceedings of the 44th Annual Meeting of the Association for Computational Linguistics (2007)
7. Hu, X., Tang, J., Gao, H., Liu, H.: Unsupervised sentiment analysis with emotional signals. In Proceedings of the 22nd International Conference on World Wide Web, WWW 2013, Republic and Canton of Geneva, Switzerland, pp. 607–618. International World Wide Web Conferences Steering Committee (2013)
8. Kilgarriff, A., Rose, T.: Measures for corpus similarity and homogeneity. In: 3rd Conference on Empirical Methods in Natural Language Processing (1998)
9. Liu, B.: Sentiment Analysis and Opinion Mining. Morgan and Claypool, New York (2012)
10. Maynard, D., Funk, A.: Automatic detection of political opinions in tweets. In: García-Castro, R., Fensel, D., Antoniou, G. (eds.) ESWC 2011. LNCS, vol. 7117, pp. 88–99. Springer, Heidelberg (2012). doi:10.1007/978-3-642-25953-1_8

11. Pang, B., Lee, L.: A sentimental education: sentiment analysis using subjectivity. In: Proceedings of ACL, pp. 271–278 (2004)
12. Pang, B., Lee, L.: Opinion mining and sentiment analysis. Found. Trends Inf. Retr. **2**(1–2), 1–135 (2008)
13. Pang, B., Lee, L., Vaithyanathan, S.: Thumbs up? Sentiment classification using machine learning techniques. In Proceedings of the ACL-02 Conference on Empirical Methods in Natural Language Processing, EMNLP 2002, Stroudsburg, PA, USA, vol. 10, pp. 79–86. Association for Computational Linguistics (2002)
14. Pappas, N., Katsimpras, G., Stamatatos, E.: Distinguishing the popularity between topics: a system for up-to-date opinion retrieval and mining in the web. In: 14th International Conference on Intelligent Text Processing and Computational Linguistics (2013)
15. Plackett, R.L.: Karl pearson and the chi-squared test. Int. Stat. Rev. **51**, 59–72 (1983)
16. Read, J., Carroll, J.: Weakly supervised techniques for domain-independent sentiment classification. In: Proceedings of the 1st International CIKM Workshop on Topic-Sentiment Analysis for Mass Opinion, TSA 2009, New York, NY, USA, pp. 45–52 (2009)
17. Shi, H.-X. and Li, X.-J.: A sentiment analysis model for hotel reviews based on supervised learning. In: 2011 International Conference on Machine Learning and Cybernetics (ICMLC), vol. 3, pp. 950–954 (2011)
18. Singhal, A.: Modern information retrieval: a brief overview. IEEE Data Eng. Bull. **24**(4), 35–43 (2001)
19. Turney, P.D.: Thumbs up or thumbs down? Semantic orientation applied to unsupervised classification of reviews. In: Proceedings of the 40th Annual Meeting on Association for Computational Linguistics, ACL 2002, Stroudsburg, PA, USA, pp. 417–424. Association for Computational Linguistics (2002)
20. Wang, H., Can, D., Kazemzadeh, A., Bar, F., Narayanan, S.: A system for real-time twitter sentiment analysis of 2012 U.S. presidential election cycle. In: Proceedings of the ACL 2012 System Demonstrations, ACL 2012, Stroudsburg, PA, USA, pp. 115–120. Association for Computational Linguistics (2012)
21. Wang, H., Lu, Y., Zhai, C.: Latent aspect rating analysis without aspect keyword supervision. In Proceedings of the 17th ACM SIGKDD International Conference on Knowledge Discovery and Data Mining, KDD 2011, New York, NY, USA, pp. 618–626 (2011)
22. Peng, W., Park, D.H.: Generate adjective sentiment dictionary for social media sentiment analysis using constrained nonnegative matrix factorization. In: The International AAAI Conference on Web and Social Media, ICWSM (2011)
23. Zhou, X., Tao, X., Yong, J., Yang, Z.: Sentiment analysis on tweets for social events. In: 2013 IEEE 17th International Conference on Computer Supported Cooperative Work in Design (CSCWD), pp. 557–562 (2013)

Modeling and Calculating Capabilities of Composite Web Applications for Assisted End User Development

Carsten Radeck[✉], Gregor Blichmann, and Klaus Meißner

Faculty of Computer Science, Technische Universität Dresden, Dresden, Germany
{carsten.radeck,gregor.blichmann,klaus.meissner}@tu-dresden.de

Abstract. Based on an increasing number of web resources and services, the mashup paradigm enables end users to create custom web applications consisting of several components in order to fulfill specific needs. End user development of such composite web applications poses tough challenges to composition platforms, especially with non-programmers as end users. For instance, communicating on a non-technical level is crucial. Furthermore, assistance is essential throughout the entire process, ranging from composition to usage of mashups. Amongst others, users should be supported by explaining inter-widget communication, by helping to understand a mashup's functionality and by identifying mashups providing desired functionality. However, prevalent mashup solutions provide no or limited concepts regarding these aspects. In this paper, we introduce our proposal for formalizing and calculating the functionality of mashup compositions based on capabilities and communication relations of mashup components as well as semantic domain knowledge. It serves as a foundation for our assisted, capability-centered end user development approach within the CRUISE platform. The latter features several assistance mechanisms, like presenting the functionality of mashups and recommending composition steps. We describe a prototypical implementation of the proposed algorithm and discuss its usage in our platform. Additionally, we evaluate our modeling and algorithmic concepts by means of example applications and an expert evaluation.

Keywords: Mashup · Capabilities · Functional semantics · End user development

1 Introduction

Powered by the growth of available web resources and application programming interfaces, the mashup paradigm enables loosely coupled components to be reused in a broad variety of application scenarios to fulfill the long tail of user needs. Recently, universal composition approaches allow for platform-independent modeling of composite web application (CWA) and uniformly describing and composing components spanning all application layers, ranging from data and logic services to user interface widgets.

© Springer International Publishing AG 2017
V. Monfort et al. (Eds.): WEBIST 2016, LNBIP 292, pp. 58–82, 2017.
DOI: 10.1007/978-3-319-66468-2_4

The mashup paradigm and end user development complement each other quite well. It is, however, still very cumbersome for end users to develop and even use CWA, especially in case of non-programmers. Challenging tasks in CWA development and usage, posing tough requirements to mashup platforms, are amongst others: (1) expressing goals or requirements towards the mashup in a non-technical manner, (2) understanding what single components are capable of and what functionality they provide in interplay, (3) being aware of inter-widget communication, as shown by [8], (4) adding or removing whole "functional blocks" rather than several technical elements like components and connections, and (5) understanding what functionality recommendations will provide in context of the current task.

The CRUISE platform adheres to universal composition and strives for enabling domain experts without programming knowledge to build and use situation-specific CWA. Non-programmers can extend and manipulate running CWAs in a WYSIWYG manner to get instant feedback on their actions. Thereby, they are guided by recommendations on composition steps [15]. Components are semantically annotated with the functionality they provide in terms of capabilities. Based on this, the capabilities of whole composition models are estimated automatically. This allows our mashup environment to offer several assistance features which we exemplify with the help of two **scenarios** now.

Scenario 1: Non-programmer Bob uses a mashup for travel planning recommended by a friend. It consists of two maps, a route calculator, a weather widget, a widget for searching points of interest and a hotel search widget. Since Bob is neither familiar with the overall application nor the components, he faces several problems understanding what functionality the mashup provides and what not. For instance, Bob is not sure why there are two maps and if the location in a map has effect in other components, and if so, which kind of effect. In addition, he is uncertain how to find hotels near the target location. While normally he would have to explore the application manually in a try & error style, the platform supports Bob in gaining insight. First, there is an overview panel displaying the mashup functionality, possibly composed of several sub-functionalities. It allows Bob to inspect what tasks he can solve with the CWA at hand and to get aware of the components that partake in those tasks. Thus, Bob understands that one map serves for selecting the start location, while the other one is used to select the target location for the route calculation. Further, Bob can start tutorials explaining necessary steps and interactions he has to perform, e.g., in order to see a list of routes. Bob activates a mode animating the actual data flow. This way, Bob gets aware of data transfer between map and weather widget, which are positioned far away from each other on the screen. In addition, Bob is assisted in identifying capabilities of a component and how these are reflected on the component user interface (UI). So, Bob understands that he can move a marker or type the location name in an input field of the map in order to select a location. After Bob uses the mashup for a while, the platform recommends useful functional extensions. All recommendations are presented by the functionality they would add to the mashup. For instance, Bob gets the recommendation to "search events" and explores its details. He accepts it, and his mashup is extended automatically.

Scenario 2: Alice is a knowledge-worker with good domain knowledge, but no programming skills, and requires an enterprise search CWA for finding experts within her company for a specific topic. The mashup platform formally models Alice's goals in form of domains concepts and activities or tasks to be performed on those. To this end, Alice is asked to answer questions and to define criteria, e.g. regarding her role, the problem domain and her aims, in a wizard-style dialog. Thereby, Alice gets advice on existing, similar, alternative and complementary concepts as well as tasks. During this iterative procedure, mashups that semantically match her requirements at least partially are identified based on a classification of the provided functionality and are previewed to her. Since a hierarchical functionality description is supported, mashups that offer "search experts" on highest level can be considered possible candidates even tough on lower levels of the functional description and especially comparing the underlying composition models there may be differences. Facilitating this, Alice can decide which optional functionalities she needs or does not need, implicitly selecting a candidate. After finishing a certain subtask in the selected CWA, she removes it from the application. Necessary changes according to the technical composition model are performed transparently. Finally, Alice shares another subtask with the responsible colleague Horst.

In order to implement the scenarios, to provide the mentioned features, and to tackle the challenges stated above, there are at least the following fundamental **requirements**:

– The functionality of composition fragments has to be described. The notion composition fragment refers to arbitrary partial composition models like components, patterns and whole applications. In order to allow for automation at least some formalism is required. To further ease communication with users, there should be a link between capabilities and actual UI-parts which serve to provide them.
– While capabilities of components can be statically defined, it is far from trivial to estimate the functionality of component interplay in an arbitrary composition fragment. For instance, functionality of an entire composition fragment is typically more than the sum of its parts. Further, it is domain-specific, requiring additional knowledge to be incorporated. Such a description should be derived semi-automatically, i.e., automatic estimation complemented with learning techniques and feedback for validation to increase quality of results.

Most prevalent mashup approaches support users with recommendations and graphical composition metaphors. However, assisting users to understand the mashup at hand or presenting recommendations by the functionality they provide is neglected so far. Estimating which functionality a user wants to achieve with his current mashup is out of scope, too. In order to allow for such features, basic concepts like a proper model and algorithms are currently missing. Thus, the **contributions** of this paper are twofold. First, we introduce a meta-model for light-weight functional semantics – *capabilities* – of composition fragments, which also allows to establish a link between semantic and UI layer. Second, we present, evaluate and show the practicability of an algorithm for automatically calculating a composition fragment's capabilities.

These concepts are the foundation for our capability-centered end user development (EUD) approach. Several development and assistance tools rely on knowledge about a composition fragment's capabilities, which result from component capabilities and inter-component communication, and their relation to component UIs, e.g., in order to calculate and present recommendations and to explain the application functionality.

In this article we update and extend our concepts presented at WEBIST 2016 [13]. The remaining paper is structured as follows. In Sect. 2 we discuss related work. Next, we briefly describe our overall approach for assisted CWA development and usage in Sect. 3. The semantic capability meta-model as a foundations of our concepts is subject of Sect. 4. Based on this, an algorithm for estimating a composition fragment's capabilities is introduced in Sect. 5. We evaluate our concepts in Sect. 6 then. Finally, Sect. 7 concludes the paper and outlines future work.

2 Related Work

In the mashup domain, recent approaches feature a tightly interwoven development and usage as a commonality with capability-centered mashup EUD. Within the OMELETTE project [7] a live development mashup environment has been created, which features a recommender system and an assistant for the user to express his goals. Patterns reflect composition knowledge and recommendations are based on patterns and are visualized by incorporated components and textual description which has to be provided manually. However, there is no model for functional semantics. Similarly, PEUDOM [10] allows to manipulate mashups during usage and offers a recommender system, but there is nothing similar to our capability meta-model and algorithm.

SMASHAKER [4] utilizes semantic component annotation and based on this offers a hybrid recommender system. As part of those annotations, a category provides high-level functional classification. In [5] this approach has been extended by semantic tags capturing functionality by referring to concepts in WordNet. Analogously, mashups are annotated with semantic tags. However, this approach is less expressive than capabilities since categories are predefined, semantic tags build up on a dedicated taxonomy and the relation between multiple semantic tags is undefined. Our model captures arbitrary domain-specific capabilities, which combine activity and entity and can be related to each other. Semantic tags are statically defined by designers. Though we follow a similar approach for component annotations, functional classification of mashups are automatically derived by our algorithm rather than asking mashup developers to do so, which seems to be a cumbersome task keeping our target group of developers in mind.

In NaturalMash [2] restricted natural language is used to describe and define mashup functionality and a link between text fragments and corresponding UI parts is provided, too. We utilize a formal, semantic model to describe functionality, which we also use to derive natural language sentences. For instance, we developed CapView [12], an overlay view that allows to explore and manipulate a mashup's functionality, and abstract the composition procedure to coupling capabilities. However, CapView does not support composite capabilities, for which we provide the foundation in this article.

DEMISA [18] proposes a top-down procedure to build CWA. Mashup developers first graphically define a semantic task model [17], which is transformed semi-automatically into a CWA then. Our capability meta-model is largely influenced by task models, but dedicated to CWA, e.g. by establishing links to the UI. Further, we also enable the bottom-up approach with our algorithm, i.e. from CWAs to capability models, making explicit modeling unnecessary.

Purpose tags which capture aspects of intent are proposed in [16]. They describe the context in which resources can be used, the goals or purpose a user had in mind. Capabilities have a similar aim, stating for which purpose composition fragments can be used. However, capabilities are more formalized by referring to concepts in domain ontologies. Further, purpose tags have to be provided manually, while we strive to automate this task for composition fragments. The authors of [9] introduce an approach for automatic generation of intent tags for textual resources. Intent tags are derived for each sentence and aggregated to annotations for the whole document. We utilize semantic knowledge to derive higher-level capabilities from given component capabilities. A tagging-based approach to annotate components and discover and compose them to applications is described in [6]. Tag taxonomies are utilized to avoid ambiguity and allow more flexible matching. However, the model is less formal and expressive. Further, the application functionality equals all annotations of a flow, while we estimate a hierarchical structure based on semantic domain knowledge.

An ontology-based model of mashups and their functionality is described in [3]. It shares some similarity with our capability meta-model. However, functionality is not semantically backed but rather free-text. Further, an algorithm to automatically instantiate such models from existing mashups is provided. It uses lexical analysis of functionality descriptions, but no hierarchical structuring and sub-sequencing takes place. Our approach allows to detect superordinate functional relations in CWA.

3   End User Development of Mashups—The CRUISE Approach

In this section we briefly outline our overall approach for EUD of CWA and relate the concepts we describe in this paper to it.

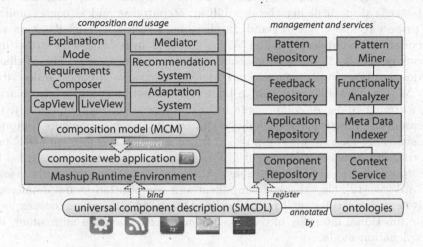

Fig. 1. Architectural overview of the CRUISE platform for EUD of CWA.

Adhering to universal composition, the CRUISE platform follows a model-driven composition approach to create and execute CWA. Thereby, components of the data, business logic and UI layer encapsulate arbitrary web resources and are black-boxes described by a uniform component model. The latter characterizes components by means of several abstractions: events and operations with typed parameters, typed properties, and capabilities. The Semantic Mashup Component Description Language (SMCDL) [11] serves as a declarative language implementing the component model. It features semantic annotations of domain ontology concepts to clarify the meaning of component interfaces and capabilities [12]. Based on the component model, the declarative Mashup Composition Model (MCM) describes all aspects of a CWA, like the components to be integrated and their configuration, screens respectively views with their layout and the transitions between them, and the event-based communication including mediation techniques to resolve interface heterogeneity.

A fundamental characteristic of our approach is that run time and development time of a CWA are strongly interwoven. End users – in our case domain experts which know their problem and possible solutions in terms of domain tasks to perform, but fail to map such solutions on mashup – can seemingly switch between editing and using an application. Thereby, they are not bothered with composition model or implementation details. Instead, communication with users takes place on capability level and necessary mappings of composition steps to composition model changes are handled transparently.

To facilitate EUD, a mashup runtime environment (MRE) is equipped with a set of tools and mechanisms, see Fig. 1. For instance, the recommendation system covers the whole recommendation loop, starting from identifying when recommendations may be necessary (triggers), querying recommendations from a pattern repository, and displaying candidate patterns to the end user [15]. The latter is done utilizing the capabilities of patterns and is contextualized with respect to the CWA at hand. Implicit and explicit user feedback on recommendations, components and CWA is gathered by a MRE and stored in a feedback repository in order to improve recommendation quality. The Mediator provides means to implement semantic data mediation techniques as described in MCM [14]. This allows to resolve a lot of incompatibility-issues at signature level, fostering re-use of components in unanticipated settings. Optionally, the user can define functional and quality requirements in a requirements composer when searching for suitable composition fragments. Furthermore, an MRE provides different views on the current CWA: In the live view, mainly intended for usage, only component UIs are visible to the user, while there are overlay views, like CapView [12], that display component and composition model details and mainly serve for development purposes. In addition, an MRE offers tools explaining the functional interplay of components in a textual and visual manner, like the explanation mode.

Components are registered at the component repository using SMCDL descriptors and can be queried. Analogously, composition models of CWAs are managed on server-side in a repository separated from concrete MREs. There are also modules attached to repositories that analyze the persisted items. For example, composition models are classified regarding the approximate capabilities they provide by the meta data indexer, which uses the functionality analyzer. The same holds for patterns which are detected by pattern miners using semantic technologies that exploit component interface annotations or using statistical analysis methods on composition models. In any case the pattern functionality in terms of capabilities is derived, too. Required models, algorithms and applications of such a functional classification are in scope of this paper.

The following platform features build up on the calculation of capabilities of composition fragments, i.e., CWA and patterns:

- Explaining a composition fragment's functionality, i.e., capabilities provided by single components and capabilities resulting from the interplay of components;
- Awareness mode highlighting inter-widget communication;
- Collecting a user's functional requirements towards composition fragments;
- Calculating composition fragment recommendations and presenting them to the user based on the functionality they provide;
- Performing composition steps on whole "functionality blocks" rather than single technical concepts like components and channels;

We argue that utilizing capabilities is beneficial for all those use cases and eases communication with the end user. In order to enable such features, it is obviously necessary to model and estimate capabilities of composition fragments. Thus, we introduce our solutions to this end in the following sections.

4   Modeling Capabilities of Composition Fragments

Based on our previous work [12] and research on task models, see [17] for an overview, we developed a meta-model for capabilities, which is shown in Fig. 2. The main idea and assumption is that components serve to solve tasks, and that a composition of components can fulfill more complex tasks accordingly. The proposed model is more lightweight than traditional task models, uses semantic annotations of ontology concepts and is dedicated to CWA since it is possible to establish links to UI elements.

Capabilities describe functional and, tough restricted, behavioral semantics of a composition fragment, i.e., what it is able to do or which functionality it provides, like displaying a location or searching hotels. To this end, capabilities essentially are tuples (*activity*, *entity*) – denoted `activity entity` from now on – and express which activity or task is performed on or with which domain object, e.g. `search hotel`. References to semantic concepts like classes, properties and individuals described in Web Ontology Language (OWL)[1] ontologies back the description with formal semantics providing domain-specific knowledge and allow for reasoning. There are optional attributes to address activity and entity more precisely: In case the entity is an OWL property e.g. `hasName`, *entity context* can define the domain, e.g. `person`; similarly, an *activity modifier* can clarify the activity without the need to blow up ontologies with individuals or sub concepts. For instance, `sort` with activity modifier `hasName` can be defined instead of declaring an individual `sortByName` in the ontology. Optionally, a capability belongs to a *domain* or a certain topic. In order to achieve a capability, it may be necessary for the user to partake and interact with the component UI or not. Therefore, UI and system capabilities are distinguished.

Our meta-model allows to build *composite capabilities* i.e. to establish hierarchical structures. The relation of children of a composite capability is expressed with the help of a *connective*. Currently, we support parallel and sequential relations. In case of sequences, capabilities are chained to define the order using *next* and *previous*. As an example, it is possible to describe the capability `search route` as a sequence of `select start`, `select destination`, `search route` and `display route`.

Relating capabilities with *requirements* allows to state that the provision of a capability depends on certain parameters and conditions of the user, usage or execution context. For instance, the capability `take picture` requires access to a camera within the runtime environment context.

A concept particular for UI capabilities are *view bindings*. They link the semantic layer and the user interface of the according component. Basically, a view binding describes interaction steps via atomic, parallel or sequential operations. These point to UI elements using a selector language, like CSS selectors, and define the interaction technique, like click and sweep. In case a capability

---

[1] http://www.w3.org/TR/owl2-overview/.

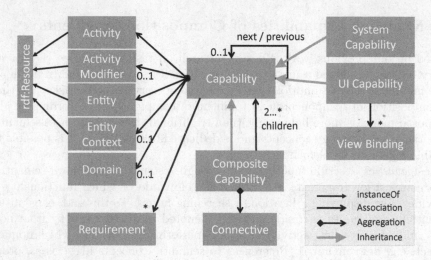

Fig. 2. Schematic overview of our capability meta-model.

has multiple view bindings, for instance, if it is possible to select a location via typing something in a text field or double clicking a map, they are considered alternative.

All composition fragments, i.e. components, CWA and patterns, can carry capabilities. Capabilities of components are statically annotated by component developers in the corresponding SMCDL descriptor. Listing 1 shows an excerpt from a map component's descriptor. Most concepts of the capability meta-model are reflected by XML elements and attributes. Thereby, capabilities can be located at two positions: at level of the whole component (see Listing 1 lines 2–15), where especially UI capabilities are annotated, and at interface level (lines 22–24), where only system capabilities occur that are exclusively achieved when invoking an operation or setting a component property. In order to reduce annotation effort for component developers, it is not necessary to declare composite capabilities in SMCDL. However, capabilities can and should be linked via `causes` and `causedBy` (see e.g. line 6) with other capabilities. This reflects causality and is a replacement that enables to derive composite capabilities afterwards. Single entries in `causes` and multiple ones connected via `and` map to a sequence, multiple `or`-ed entries are mapped to a parallel composite capability. Details on this step are provided in Sect. 5.2. Events and properties of a mashup component reference existing capabilities via *causedBy* (and *causes* in case of properties) rather than declaring new ones, see line 19.

```
1  <component id="..." name="Map">
2    <capability id="capDispLoc" activity="act:Display" entity="geo:Location">
3      <viewbinding>
4        <atomicoperation element="div[id$='_map']" />
5      </viewbinding>
6      <causedBy>capInpLoc or capSelLoc or capInpLocDet</causedBy>
7    </capability>
8    <capability id="capSelLoc" activity="act:Select" entity="geo:Location">
9      <viewbinding>
10       <atomicoperation element="input[id$='mapTextField']" interactionTech="
               i:TypeOperation" />
11     </viewbinding>
12     <viewbinding>
13       <atomicoperation element="div[id$='gMapCurrentLocationIcon']"
               interactionTech="i:DragNDrop" />
14     </viewbinding>
15   </capability> ...
16   <interface>
17     <event name="locationSelected">
18       <parameter name="loc" type="geo:Location" />
19       <causedBy>capSelLoc</causedBy>
20     </event>
21     <operation name="showLocation">
22       <capability entity="geo:Location" activity="act:Input" id="capInpLoc">
23         <causes>capDispLoc</causes>
24       </capability>
25       <parameter name="loc" type="geo:Location" />
26     </operation> ...
```

Listing 1. Excerpt of a map component's SMCDL descriptor.

While the implementation of our capability meta-model in SMCDL has its specificities, CWA and patterns are directly equipped with arbitrarily structured capabilities. Since components are the atomic building blocks, capabilities of patterns and mashups result of the statically declared capabilities of components and especially how these are connected via communication channels. Thus, capabilities of patterns and CWA are not predefined and consequently have to be derived for each composition fragment. Our solution for that is presented next.

5   Classification Algorithm

After specifying the capabilities meta-model in the previous section, we now go into details on our algorithm for estimating the capabilities of an arbitrary, valid composition fragment. First, basic definitions are introduced, before the algorithm is explained.

5.1   Foundations

As a prerequisite we briefly describe some basic concepts and foundations of the algorithm in this section.

A *capability graph* is a set of *capability nodes* and directed edges called *capability links*, see Fig. 3. It may be cyclic and represents the capabilities of a composition fragment since for each communication channel and *causes* or *causedBy* relation a capability link is created between nodes encapsulating the coupled capabilities. Each capability link comprises a start and a target capability node

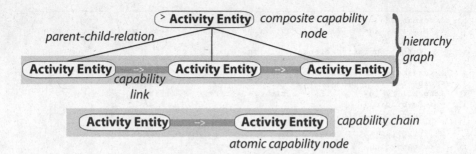

Fig. 3. Schematic example of a capability graph.

and stores selected composition model information, e.g. mediation techniques applied on a channel.

Besides the dataflow or causality-oriented graph built from atomic capabilities and links between them, there is an overlay structure, the *hierarchy graph*. It is created from deriving composite capabilities with the help of our algorithm.

In case a capability graph consists of multiple isolated subgraphs which are coherent in themselves, these are called *capability chains*.

As mentioned earlier, entities refer to OWL concepts. The latter can be related in different ways using OWL properties, like `subClassOf` and defining range and domain. When deriving a composite capability it is necessary to identify an entity as expressive as possible, which we call *dominant entity*. Thereby, we utilize inheritance (`subClassOf`, `subPropertyOf`) to identify coarse grained concepts subsuming other entities. Further, we assume that a class C_1 aggregates or subsumes C_2 if there are OWL properties with domain C_1 and range C_2. In more detail, a dominant entity is calculated by analyzing the semantic entity annotations of all direct child capabilities of the composite capability at stake, denoted as set E, as follows.

- For each concept $e \in E$, we first calculate set L_e of all concepts that are "subsumed" by e. Since e can be an ontology class, a property and an individual, a class c is determined ($c = e$ if e is a class; e `rdf:type` c in case e is an individual; e `rdfs:domain` c if e is an OWL property). Then, all subclasses of c and, if e is an OWL property, all concepts for which holds true q `rdfs:subPropertyOf` e are added to L_e. In addition, OWL properties with `rdfs:domain` c and their range concept become element of L_e. In this step we skip symmetric and inverse properties. Then, all concepts in L_e that are also in E are removed from E.
- In a next step, for each remaining $e \in E$ coarse-grained concepts U_e "subsuming" e are determined. As in the previous step, class c is defined. Then, all superclasses of c and, if e is an OWL property, all concepts with which it is related via `rdfs:subPropertyOf` are added to U_e. Furthermore, OWL properties, where c is `rdfs:range`, and their `rdfs:domain` are added to U_e. Again, we pay attention to symmetric and inverse properties.
- Finally, the set of dominant entities of E is defined as the intersection of all U_e.

A concept is dominant if it subsumes all $e \in E$. Such a concept does not have to be element of E. Lets consider a simple example: The entities `location` and `route` are given and the ontology states that each `route` has OWL ObjectProperties `hasStart` and `hasDestination`, both with range `location`. Then, `route` is the dominant entity.

5.2   Detailed Procedure

Basic ideas and assumptions of our algorithm can be summarized as follows. The core functionality of a CWA is achieved by components and their interplay based on capability links. Through transitive connections more complex functional relations are established within a CWA. Facilitating semantic information of capabilities, heuristics and learned data, composite capabilities can be estimated and describe functionality of whole composition fragments. Figure 4 shows the essential workflow of our algorithm, which is explained in detail in the following.

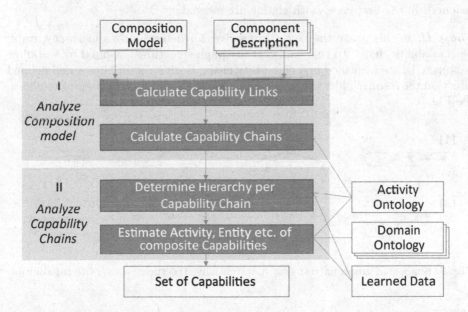

Fig. 4. Inputs, main steps and outputs of the algorithm.

Phase I. Given a composition model representing the composition fragment, a main goal of the first phase is to calculate capability links by analyzing MCM as well as SMCDLs of included components.

In a preparation step, information about components and their annotations are gathered, for instance, references in element *causes* are resolved to actual capabilities and for each component property, a capability with activity `set` and an entity according to the property type is created.

Then all communication channels in the composition model are considered. We assume that a channel has exactly one publisher and one subscriber interface element, and more complex communication patterns are build on top of such "atomic" channels. For all combinations of relevant capabilities of publisher and subscriber a capability link is created. Subsequently, those capability links are completed by following the intra-component relations *causes* and *causedBy* and creating additional capability links for each of them.

Optionally, if requested by the client or if there are no capability links so far, the capability graph is extended by intra-component capability nodes and links. Thereby, only capabilities that are not yet part of the capability graph and which can be performed by users, i.e. no capabilities at operation level and none exclusively caused by operation calls, are considered. As described above, capability links are established based on the relations *causes* and *causedBy*.

Capability chains, i.e. functionality blocks of a CWA, are identified then. Beginning at capability nodes with outgoing links only, capability links are followed until either another chain or a capability node without outgoing links is reached. In the first case, both chains are merged.

Phase II. In this phase the algorithm strives for determining a hierarchy graph per capability chain. To this end, certain graph structures, inspired by workflow patterns [1], are identified in a capability chain. Each structure has a well defined effect on the resulting hierarchy graph leading to the creation of composite nodes, see Fig. 5.

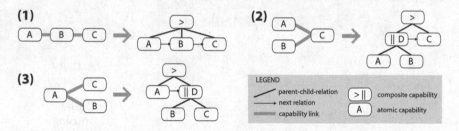

Fig. 5. Supported graph patterns for hierarchically structuring composite capabilities.

(1) **Sequence.** If there are two or more capability nodes connected in a line pattern and all nodes have max. 1 in and max. 1 outgoing link, they are assigned as children to a composite capability node with sequence connective.

(2) **Synchronization.** Converge several capability links in a capability node, the latter is a synchronization point. In the resulting overlay hierarchy, all sources (A and B in Fig. 5) are grouped to a parallel composite node (D), which is source in a sequence with the target node (C).

(3) **Parallel split.** In this case, a capability node has multiple outgoing capability links. The target nodes (B and C in Fig. 5) are assigned to a parallel composite node (D), which is in sequence with the source node (A), this time as target node.

These rules are applied to create composite capabilities forming the hierarchy graph whereby (2) and (3) are higher prioritized than (1).

As described in Sect. 3, the MCM allows to define different views on a CWA, which, for instance, is useful on mobile devices with limited screen size. Such screens respectively views affect the visibility of UI components and, from an end-user-perspective, consequently the accessibility of corresponding UI capabilities. Thus, rules (2) and (3) are adapted: In case the underlying components of D's child capability nodes do not occur in the same view, the connective of D is set to sequential, otherwise parallel. The order in a sequence corresponds to the view order. Figure 6 gives an example.

Next, sub sequencing takes place. In this central step, child nodes of sequence nodes are analyzed regarding their activity concept in order to detect potential subdivisions. According to a system-theoretical paradigm, we assume that functionality essentially consists of inputting something, transforming it and outputting a result. Based on this, we define the following rules determining potential borders between sub functionalities in a sequence of capability nodes. Further, we classify activities or actions according to the superclasses **input**, **transform**, **output** in our activity ontology [17]. Let act_i denote the superclass of the activity of the i-th capability in a sequence. Then a potential border is after capability i

- if $act_i =$ **output** and $act_{i+1} \neq$ **output** or
- if $act_i =$ **transform** and $act_{i+1} =$ **input**

In case all resulting sequences would have more than one child, the hierarchy graph is adapted accordingly. Please refer to Fig. 7 for an example, where the sequence in the upper part is analyzed accordingly, and the resulting structure is shown below. Potential borders are depicted in orange.

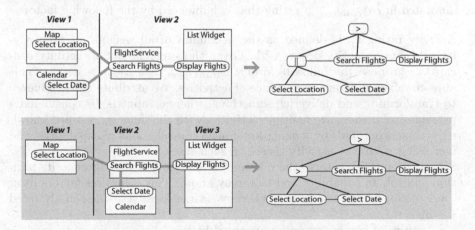

Fig. 6. Exemplified impact of different CWA view configurations on the resulting hierarchy graph.

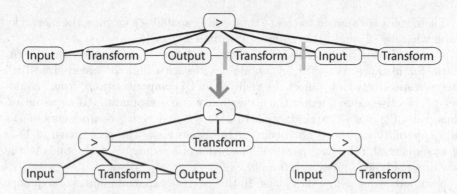

Fig. 7. Exemplified sub sequencing approach.

The intermediate result at this point is a hierarchy graph per capability chain whose composite capability nodes are not semantically annotated yet. All hierarchy graphs are assigned as children to the root node. Thus, semantic annotations are estimated next. To this end, composite capability nodes are arranged in layers according to the distance from the root. Then, the procedure begins on the lowest layer and performs for each composite capability node c_{comp} a number of steps. All child nodes $cap_{children}$ are analyzed to try to estimate the most likely capability for c_{comp}. External knowledge for this is provided by ontologies used to annotate activity and entity concepts, as well as learned data from previous runs in shape of confirmed capability and hierarchy graphs. First, a look-up for known solutions in learned data is performed by graph matching. If there exists an identical case, where connective, order and annotations of child nodes match with those of c_{comp}, annotations of c_{comp} are set accordingly. Otherwise the estimation proceeds and calculates for every entity concept, which is annotated in $cap_{children}$, a rating that is influenced by the following factors.

– Activity rating r_a is defined as the maximum of all weights w_a for activity concepts an entity occurs with. Given the superclass of an activity concept we propose the following order: $w_{transform} > w_{output} > w_{input}$. This aims to reflect different importance of activities. We attribute more influence to transforming and delivering something, whereas inputting is considered a prerequisite. If there are multiple activities with the same w_a, learned knowledge is incorporated, by looking for similar constellations of capabilities and increasing w_a of the activity chosen in such cases.
– Structural rating r_s states the relevance of an entity with respect to its position and role in capability and hierarchy graph. This comprises factors like:
  • Position within a sequence, whereby entities located at the end are rated higher.
  • Entities of composite nodes are rated higher.
  • Entities of capability nodes partaking in capability links derived from communication channels, are considered more important.

- Frequency rating r_f denotes the relative frequency of an entity with the set under investigation.
- Semantic rating r_{sem} expresses, if an entity is dominant regarding the set under investigation.

The overall rating $rating_{entity}$ for an entity is defined as

$$rating_{entity} = r_a + r_s + r_f + r_{sem}$$

If there are multiple entities with the same rating, we determine if one of them is the dominant entity with respect to that set, and increase the rating. Furthermore, we incorporate learned knowledge by looking for a capability node where the children are equipped with the same annotations. If such a similar case exists, we set that entity's rating to the highest value since we consider the data as validated.

Finally a composite capability cap_{result} is created with the best rated entity, the corresponding activity and its activity modifier. In addition, the *domain* of cap_{result} is derived. We use the ontology defining the entity concept of cap_{result} and expect it to provide rdfs:label annotations, which serve as a brief domain descriptor. In some cases we also set cap_{result}'s entity context: We check if the child capability node carrying the best rated entity is connected via a capability link to the previous node cap_p and if this link originates from a communication channel which uses projection for mediating source and target interface, e.g., Event $\rightarrow$ hasName. Then, the parent nodes entity context is set to the entity of cap_p. This enables to distinguish slightly different capabilities, like search article by name of an event or a location.

Additionally, a *confidence* value is calculated and attached to cap_{result}. It is proportional to the distance of the highest and second highest $rating_{entity}$. To increase the plausibility of the overall result, the hierarchy graphs root node is removed if its *confidence* value is below a threshold c_{min}, leading to several capability nodes as a result.

6 Evaluation

In this section, we go into detail on the prototype we developed and how we validated our capability meta-model and proposed algorithm.

6.1 Implementation and Usage Within the CRUISE Platform

We implemented the algorithm and a set of clients as part of the CRUISE platform. In the following, the conceptual architecture and selected implementation details are presented utilizing Fig. 8.

The algorithm is situated on server-side and implemented in Java. It is encapsulated in a dedicated package, to which the class **Functionality Analyzer** is

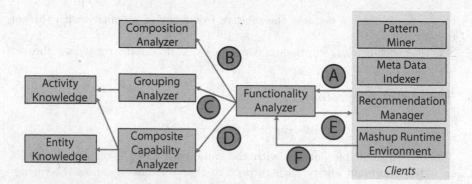

Fig. 8. Architectural overview of our prototype.

the central access point to. Therefore, several interfaces are provided, e.g., as SOAP web service using the Apache Axis2 framework[2].

The `Functionality Analyzer` orchestrates several other modules and performs pre-processing steps like format transformations in order to answer incoming requests (A). First (B), the `Composition Analyzer` is responsible for analyzing the given composition fragment in terms of a composition model and the SMCDL descriptors of components included in the composition fragment to be analyzed. The resulting capability links are handed over to the `Grouping Analyzer` in step (C) which derives capability chains and the capability hierarchy. The latter is enriched with semantic annotations by the `Composite Capability Analyzer` then (D). It utilizes semantic knowledge from the modules `Activity Knowledge` and `Entity Knowledge`. They manage the activity ontology respectively domain ontologies and provide access to reasoning facilities and to answer queries. For example, class `Entity Knowledge` provides a method that tries to derive the dominant entity from a given set of entity concepts. For such tasks, our prototype employs the framework Apache Jena[3] in both modules. We formalized most ontologies in OWL DL, since it is expressive enough and decidable. Finally, results are delivered to the client after some post-processing (E). User feedback on algorithm results is transfered from an MRE to the server side, see (F). This way, the database of learned data is updated by new confirmed solutions.

There are several clients, which depend on the `Functionality Analyzer`, to be considered. The `Recommendation Manager` requires the algorithm for calculating recommendations paying attention to capabilities required by the user or already part of a mashup. Further, within our repositories for applications and components, the `Meta Data Indexer` and `Pattern Miners` use the `Functionality Analyzer` to derive the capabilities of persisted mashups or newly identified composition patterns.

---

[2] http://axis.apache.org/.
[3] https://jena.apache.org/.

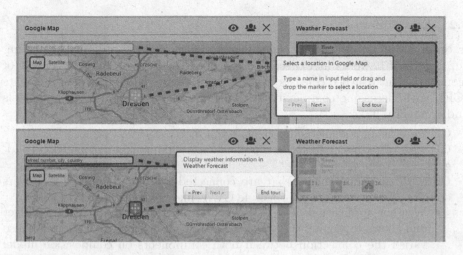

Fig. 9. The explanation mode for a rather simple CWA presenting a dynamically generated, interactive tutorial consisting of two steps.

An MRE provides several tools for understanding and developing mashups. For instance, results of the algorithm are used to present capabilities by generating short natural language sentences [12] when giving recommendations, e.g., in the CapView and a recommendation menu, and when composing functional requirements in a wizard. Furthermore, there is a widget visualizing the capability hierarchy of the current CWA, as illustrated on the left-hand side of Fig. 10. Additionally, we developed mechanisms for visually and textually explaining application and component capabilities to users. An interactive tutorial can be started e.g. from the aforementioned widget. We utilize capabilities and their view bindings to explain inter-widget communication and necessary interactions directly in component UIs, as exemplified in Fig. 9. To this end, we highlight view bindings by querying the CSS selectors and creating `div` elements, overlaying and framing the original elements. Capability links are represented by arrows using the JavaScript framework jsPlumb[4]. We re-use label generation facilities from our previous work [12] to display short textual explanations in bootstrap popovers[5] placed next to corresponding view binding frames or capability link arrows. Building up on those basic features, interactive tutorials are generated using the framework Bootstrap Tour[6] then. The user can step backwards and forwards within sequences of capabilities and corresponding interaction steps (atomic or composite operations), respectively.

As these use cases illustrate, the capability meta-model and the algorithm are beneficial for our EUD approach. Next, we validate the quality of the both concepts.

---

[4] https://jsplumbtoolkit.com.

[5] http://getbootstrap.com/javascript/#popovers.

[6] http://bootstraptour.com.

6.2   Experiments

In order to validate the prototypical implementation of the proposed algorithm, i.e., to test if it works as expected, we defined several test cases in context of scenario 1. Our test bed consists of the following types of composition fragments (CF), with increasing complexity in terms of number of components, channels and capability links:

- CF comprising a single component, e.g. a map.
- CF with two non-connected components, e.g. wikipedia and soundcloud widgets.
- CF with two components that are connected via one channel. This covers coupling patterns and rather simple CWA, like the following.
  - Weather application: This CWA comprises a map and a weather widget and allows to display the weather forecast for a selected location. We also varied the connection between both components on composition model level to test if the result is semantically the same. For instance, both components can be coupled via event and operation or via properties.
  - News application: It features a list of news and a picture display component. When a news entry is selected, its keywords or tags are transfered to the picture widget, which then queries suitable pictures and shows them.
- CF from different application domains with 3–8 components and 2–7 channels. Some examples are listed below. Again we tested structural variations if applicable.
  - Travel planner I: Consists of 7 components and 7 channels and provides capabilities to `Search Routes`, `Search Hotels` and `Display Weather`.
  - POI search application: 6 components linked via 4 channels enable users to `Search POIs`. When selecting a POI from a result list, its location is displayed on a map and an article in a wikipedia widget is searched.
  - Appointment scheduling: This CWA consists of 3 components and 2 channels. It serves for creating or updating appointments using a form-based editor and a map. All appointments are visualized in a calendar widget.
  - Hotel search consists of 3 components and 2 channels. It allows to `search hotels` for locations selected in a map.
  - Travel planner II: In contrast to the previous CFs, this CWA features two separate capability chains. It is depicted in Fig. 10 and allows to `search routes` (components ①, ②, ⑤, ⑦), to `display weather information` at the destination (② and ⑥) and to `search POIs` (③, ④, ⑧).

Based on the test bed described above, we were also interested in the performance of our research prototype to show the practicability and applicability. To this end, we measured the average calculation time needed by our algorithm to process increasingly complex composition fragments. For each data set we performed 100 runs in a single thread in order to lower the impact of outliers. The test system features an Intel i7-4900 with 2.8 GHz and 32 GB RAM. Table 1 shows the results in case of local calls.

The results indicate that calculation time increases proportional to the structural complexity of the inputted composition fragment. Even for rather complex

Fig. 10. Screenshot of a travel planning CWA in our test bed.

Table 1. Benchmark results. $T_\varnothing$ is the average computation time, including deserialization of given MCM ($\approx$100 ms) and component descriptors, and excluding network delay.

Test case	$N°$ components	$N°$ Channels	$N°$ Cap. links	$T_\varnothing$
News mashup	2	1	1	205 ms
Appointment management	4	2	2	303 ms
Hotel search	3	2	2	250 ms
Point-of-Interest search	6	4	7	422 ms
Travel planner II	8	7	12	526 ms

mashups, the calculation time is far below one second, which we consider good performance taking into account the prototypical character of our implementation. Further, none of our use cases poses hard time constraints with particularly low response time.

6.3 Expert Evaluation

Methodology. In order to validate both our capability meta-model and the estimation algorithm, we conducted an expert evaluation. Seven computer scientists or master students, which work in and have contributed to the area of mashups or service-oriented architectures, participated. All participants have profound knowledge about using and building component-based applications. We sketched nine mashups of our test bed with increasing complexity on paper, like the CWA depicted in Fig. 10. Thereby, components, their capabilities and capability links were schematically represented, see Fig. 11. The rational behind this rather abstract representation was to avoid expectations and assumptions of experts regarding the functionality which would influence the results. There should be a starting point comparable as possible for experts and our algorithm. Whether that worked as expected will be discussed later.

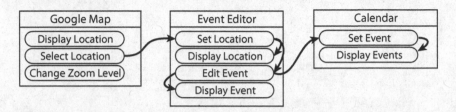

Fig. 11. Example of a schematic representation of a CWA shown to experts in our study.

If required by participants, a short introduction to our capability meta-model was given. Further, we showed live CWA in our platform on demand to avoid misinterpretations. Then, the experts were asked to answer the following questions for one CWA at a time by sketching capability graphs on paper. Explanations and thoughts were noted by the interviewer.

Q1. *How would you describe the overall functionality the CWA provides in terms of capabilities?*

Q2. *Would you decompose those capabilities? If yes, how?*

Our main goal was to show that the proposed capability meta-model is well suited to describe functionality and that our algorithm is able to automatically derive adequate capability hierarchies for composition fragments covering a broad variety of realistic cases. To this end, we then compared the capability models our experts would assign with the actual output of our algorithm.

Results and Discussion. Experts were in nearly all cases able to express what they wanted using our capability meta-model. Often they qualified activities or entities, e.g., "search article for location", which is mappable to *activity modifier* and *entity context*. Repeatedly the following suggestions were made. It is possible to use one capability, e.g. `select location`, as source for multiple capability links or to provide several sources in multiple components. Some experts remarked that in the latter case, a distinction of those capabilities should be possible, since there are several instances e.g. of location. We agree, and required information are only implicitly part of our model, given by ID and corresponding components of capabilities. Thus, it is mainly a matter of properly analyzing and presenting the model in a front end. Additionally, few experts suggested to allow optional capabilities.

Regarding *Q1* the results are promising. We calculated a matching degree for activities and entities. We considered semantically similar concepts as 50% match, e.g. `show` and `display`. In case, experts derived additional hierarchy levels, we matched the layer comparable to the algorithmic result. An entity match of 96.83% and an activity match of 80.16% lead to an overall accuracy of 88.49% in our test.

There was no consensus about if `transform` or `output` activities are more important. However, in all cases at least 5 of 7 experts decided for the first, which confirms our prioritization. In case there are multiple capabilities with the same type of activity in sequence, e.g., `search song` → `search article`, 6 of 7 experts prioritized entity `article` when deriving a parent capability. That is consistent with our heuristics, which pay attention to flow direction.

We did not incorporate learned data in order to validate the base concepts and heuristics of our algorithm. Due to this, in more complex scenarios, our algorithm was not able to derive a meaningful root capability like experts did. For instance, for the CWA in Fig. 10 our prototype calculates three composite capabilities. Though this is in line with what experts derived, 6 of 7 experts additionally defined `plan trip` or similar as additional parent capability. In the test case "appointment management", our prototype derives `edit` as activity of the root capability based on annotated concepts, while experts often used similar terms, like `manage` or `plan`, based on assumptions and additional knowledge. Deriving such capabilities is far from trivial, especially in a generic automatic way, in some cases even for experts. Combining community and semantic knowledge seems the most promising solution. However, semantics-based heuristics enable to avoid cold start problems in case there are no feedback, training or learned data available.

Regarding *Q2* results showed, that the capability graphs experts drew were in principle similar to our concept. However, it becomes evident that experts tend to subsume capabilities and leave them out. For instance, some experts stated, that it is clear to them that to `search` something implies to `input` search criteria first. Due to the multitude of use cases our algorithm keeps such capabilities. It is up to the concrete client to apply filters if necessary. In the most complex scenario, experts struggled to structure the hierarchy up to the leaves, while the upper hierarchy layers were without difficulty. This underpins the necessity of an automated approach. We observed, that experts created sub-sequences similarly to our concept, although not in every case our algorithm would do. However, this mainly leads to flatter hierarchies rather than different semantics. Regarding the importance of non-linked component capabilities opinions differed. Some experts ignored them, others subsumed or grouped them in a composite capability, e.g., with activity `display`.

In general, we noticed that experts were influenced by experiences with web applications and consequently assumed functionalities when reading component names, even if there was no adequate capability presented. The same holds for incomplete annotations like missing links, which were assumed by experts. This underpins the crucial role of careful semantic component annotations. Annotating is a potentially cumbersome and error prone task. Thus, component developers should be provided with proper tooling. Also the quality of ontologies used for annotation has a strong impact on the results. Therefore, well accepted ontologies should be utilized. However, we argue that mashup platforms benefit from semantic annotations—we have indicated some use cases throughout this paper. Further, based on our proposal, annotations of composition fragments can be derived without explicit modeling of developers or users.

7   Conclusion and Future Work

Development and usage of composite web applications are still cumbersome tasks for domain experts without programming knowledge. For example, understanding the functionality an unfamiliar CWA provides, may turn out to be difficult due to the composite nature of CWA. The model-driven mashup approach within our CRUISE platform strives for capability-centered EUD. Its core ingredients are tightly interwoven runtime and development time and capabilities as a semantic description of functionality of composition fragments. A palette of EUD tools and other platform features utilize capabilities, e.g., as a means to communicate with domain experts on an appropriate level of abstraction. This novel approach aims to overcome limitations of current mashup platforms. Knowledge about the capabilities of arbitrary (parts of) composition models is a central aspect, but proper models and algorithms for automatic calculation are missing so far. Even with semantically annotated components it is far from trivial to derive the functionality of a set of connected components, since functionality of an entire composition fragment is typically more than the sum of its parts. Thus, in this paper, we propose our capability meta-model which allows to describe functional semantics of composition fragments. Based on this, we introduce a novel algorithm for calculating capabilities of arbitrary composition fragments. It analyzes semantic annotations of components and the communication channels between them, and incorporates validated solutions known from previous runs. These concepts are utilized in our platform, e.g., to present recommendations and explain application functionality.

We validated the proposed capability meta-model and the algorithm by integrating them in the CRUISE platform, by utilizing the algorithm results in several front end EUD tools and with the help of an expert evaluation. The results are promising and indicate sufficient expressiveness of our capability meta-model and that our algorithm meets the expectations of experts.

Future work includes back end extensions, e.g. completion of causes relations, and front end concepts for capability-centered mashup EUD, like implementing and validating the requirements wizard. Finally, we strive for a user study evaluating our overall EUD approach and comparing it with related composition platforms.

Acknowledgements. The work of Carsten Radeck is funded by the European Union and the Free State of Saxony within the EFRE program. Gregor Blichmann is funded by the German Federal Ministry of Economic Affairs and Energy (ref. no. 01MU13001D).

References

1. van der Aalst, W., ter Hofstede, A., Kiepuszewski, B., Barros, A.: Workflow patterns. Distrib. Parallel Databases **14**(1), 5–51 (2003)
2. Aghaee, S., Pautasso, C.: End-user development of mashups with naturalmash. J. Vis. Lang. Comput. **25**(4), 414–432 (2014)
3. Bai, L., Ye, D., Wei, J.: A goal decomposition approach for automatic mashup development. In: van Sinderen, M., Johnson, P., Xu, X., Doumeingts, G. (eds.) Enterprise Interoperability. LNBIP, vol. 122, pp. 20–33. Springer, Berlin Heidelberg (2012). doi:10.1007/978-3-642-33068-1_4
4. Bianchini, D., De Antonellis, V., Melchiori, M.: A recommendation system for semantic mashup design. In: 2010 Workshop on Database and Expert Systems Applications (DEXA), pp. 159–163 (2010)
5. Bianchini, D., Antonellis, V., Melchiori, M.: A multi-perspective framework for web API search in enterprise mashup design. In: Salinesi, C., Norrie, M.C., Pastor, Ó. (eds.) CAiSE 2013. LNCS, vol. 7908, pp. 353–368. Springer, Heidelberg (2013). doi:10.1007/978-3-642-38709-8_23
6. Bouillet, E., Feblowitz, M., Liu, Z., Ranganathan, A., Riabov, A.: A tag-based approach for the design and composition of information processing applications. SIGPLAN Not. **43**(10), 585–602 (2008)
7. Chudnovskyy, O., Nestler, T., Gaedke, M., Daniel, F., Fernández-Villamor, J.I., Chepegin, V., Fornas, J.A., Wilson, S., Kögler, C., Chang, H.: End-user-oriented telco mashups: the omelette approach. In: Proceedings of the 21st International Conference on World Wide Web. WWW 2012 Companion, pp. 235–238. ACM, New York (2012)
8. Chudnovskyy, O., Pietschmann, S., Niederhausen, M., Chepegin, V., Griffiths, D., Gaedke, M.: Awareness and control for inter-widget communication: challenges and solutions. In: Daniel, F., Dolog, P., Li, Q. (eds.) ICWE 2013. LNCS, vol. 7977, pp. 114–122. Springer, Heidelberg (2013). doi:10.1007/978-3-642-39200-9_11
9. Kröll, M., Körner, C., Strohmaier, M.: itag: automatically annotating textual resources with human intentions. J. Emerg. Technol. Web Intell. **2**(4), 333–342 (2010)
10. Matera, M., Picozzi, M., Pini, M., Tonazzo, M.: PEUDOM: a mashup platform for the end user development of common information spaces. In: Daniel, F., Dolog, P., Li, Q. (eds.) ICWE 2013. LNCS, vol. 7977, pp. 494–497. Springer, Heidelberg (2013). doi:10.1007/978-3-642-39200-9_43
11. Pietschmann, S., Radeck, C., Meißner, K.: Semantics-based discovery, selection and mediation for presentation-oriented mashups. In: Proceedings of the 5th International Workshop on Web APIs and Service Mashups - Mashups 2011. p. 1. ACM, New York (2011)
12. Radeck, C., Blichmann, G., Meißner, K.: CapView – functionality-aware visual mashup development for non-programmers. In: Daniel, F., Dolog, P., Li, Q. (eds.) ICWE 2013. LNCS, vol. 7977, pp. 140–155. Springer, Heidelberg (2013). doi:10.1007/978-3-642-39200-9_14
13. Radeck, C., Blichmann, G., Meißner, K.: Estimating the functionality of mashup applications for assisted, capability-centered end user development. In: Proceedings of the 12th International Conference on Web Information Systems and Technologies (WEBIST 2016), pp. 109–120 (2016)

14. Radeck, C., Blichmann, G., Mroß, O., Meißner, K.: Semantic mediation techniques for composite web applications. In: Casteleyn, S., Rossi, G., Winckler, M. (eds.) ICWE 2014. LNCS, vol. 8541, pp. 450–459. Springer, Cham (2014). doi:10.1007/978-3-319-08245-5_30

15. Radeck, C., Lorz, A., Blichmann, G., Meißner, K.: Hybrid recommendation of composition knowledge for end user development of mashups. In: The Seventh International Conference on Internet and Web Applications and Services. ICIW 2012, pp. 30–33 (2012)

16. Strohmaier, M.: Purpose tagging: capturing user intent to assist goal-oriented social search. In: Proceedings of the 2008 ACM Workshop on Search in Social Media. SSM 2008, pp. 35–42. ACM (2008)

17. Tietz, V., Mroß, O., Rümpel, A., Radeck, C., Meißner, K.: A requirements model for composite and distributed web mashups. In: Proceedings of the 8th International Conference on Internet and Web Applications and Services (ICIW 2013). XPS (2013)

18. Tietz, V., Pietschmann, S., Blichmann, G., Meißner, K., Casall, A., Grams, B.: Towards task-based development of enterprise mashups. In: Proceedings of the 13th International Conference on Information Integration and Web-based Applications and Services (iiWAS 2011), pp. 325–328 (2011)

Subtopic Ranking Based on Block-Level Document Analysis

Tomohiro Manabe[1,2(✉)] and Keishi Tajima[2]

[1] Yahoo Japan Corporation, Chiyoda, Tokyo 102-0094, Japan
[2] Graduate School of Informatics, Kyoto University, Sakyo, Kyoto 606-8501, Japan
manabe@dl.kuis.kyoto-u.ac.jp, tajima@i.kyoto-u.ac.jp

Abstract. We propose methods for ranking subtopics of a keyword query. Subtopics are also keyword queries which specialize and/or disambiguate search intent behind their original query. Information on subtopics are useful for search systems to generate diversified search results. Search result diversification is important when there are multiple ways to interpret the submitted query. In search result diversification, it is important to rank subtopics by their intent probabilities that users need information on the subtopics. Our subtopic ranking methods use hierarchical structure in documents in the corpus. Hierarchical structure in documents consists of nested logical blocks with headings. A heading describes the topic of a part of a document, and a block is such a part of a document. All our methods are based on two assumptions related to the structure. First, hierarchical headings in a document represent hierarchical topics discussed in the document. Second, authors write more contents about subtopics with higher intent probabilities. Based on these assumptions, our methods score each subtopic based on the total size of the blocks whose hierarchical headings represent the subtopic. We develop our methods in the following way. We first propose four methods to score a subtopic on a document, four methods to integrate subtopic scores on multiple documents, and two methods to sort subtopics based on their scores. We then combined these methods, which results in 32 subtopic ranking methods in total. We evaluated these methods on the data set for the subtopic mining subtask of the NTCIR-10 INTENT-2 task. The results indicated that our methods generated rankings statistically significantly better than the query completion snapshots by major commercial search engines.

Keywords: Web search · Search result diversification · Search intent · Subtopic mining · Hierarchical heading structure

1 Introduction

The Web is now one of the most important information resource, and the most standard way to obtain information from the Web is to submit a query consisting

© Springer International Publishing AG 2017
V. Monfort et al. (Eds.): WEBIST 2016, LNBIP 292, pp. 83–104, 2017.
DOI: 10.1007/978-3-319-66468-2_5

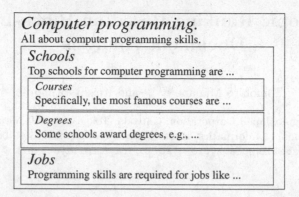

Fig. 1. Example web page with hierarchical heading structure. Each rectangle encloses block and each emphasized text is heading. Long texts are replaced by dots.

of keywords to Web search engines. Such keyword queries are sometimes ambiguous and/or referring to broad topics. For such queries, search result diversification techniques have been developed [7,9,24]. These techniques generate a page ranking including various topics so that it satisfies all information needs behind the given query. Subtopic mining is one of the most promising approaches to search result diversification [7]. Diversification methods based on subtopic mining first extract subtopic candidates of queries, then score and rank the subtopic candidates by their importance and distinctness, and finally returns a few pages each for the highly-ranked subtopic candidates. Because of the importance of subtopic mining, competitions for subtopic mining methods have been held as the subtopic mining subtasks of the NTCIR INTENT/IMine tasks [14,23,25,36]. In this paper, we focus on important structure in documents which we consider is highly related to the problem of subtopic mining: *hierarchical heading structure.* Most documents contain hierarchical heading structure reflecting their topic structure. Hierarchical heading structure consists of nested logical blocks and each block includes its own heading. A heading represents the topic of its associated block and the hierarchical descendant blocks of the block. Because of this feature of heading, hierarchical headings in a document reflect topic structure in the document. For example, Fig. 1 shows an example web page about "computer programming" (one of the NTCIR queries) containing hierarchical heading structure. In this figure, each rectangle encloses a block and each emphasized text is a heading. The hierarchical headings in this page reflect its topic structure. For example, its first level topic is computer programming, second level topics are computer programming schools and computer programming jobs, and the third level topics are courses and degrees of computer programming schools. Hierarchical heading structure of web pages are not obvious in general, but we have recently developed a method for extracting it [16].

In this paper, we propose methods to score hierarchical blocks in documents then rank subtopic candidates based on the block scores. To the best of our knowledge, this is the first paper which discusses the use of detailed hierarchical heading structure in web pages for subtopic mining. Our basic ideas are that hierarchical headings in documents reflect hierarchical topic structure in the documents, and that more contents about a topic suggests more importance of the topic. Our methods score blocks based on the quantity of their contents, then approximate the importance of a subtopic candidate by the summation of its matching blocks' scores in a corpus. A subtopic candidate matches a block if the hierarchical headings of the block represent the candidate. To diversify resulting rankings, our methods adopt a subtopic with the best score one-by-one, and every time a subtopic is adopted, our methods re-score all remaining blocks after removing blocks matching subtopics which have been already adopted. By this approach, if some remaining subtopic candidates are already referred to by the blocks matching the already-adopted subtopics, or in other words, if some remaining subtopic candidates seems to be sub-subtopics of the already-adopted subtopics, the candidates lose their scores and resulting subtopic rankings get diversified.

The remainder of this paper is organized as follows. In the next section, we clarify our research targets. After that, we concisely survey related work. We then explain our methods in Sect. 4. In Sect. 5, we evaluate our methods on a publicly available NTCIR data set and compare the evaluation results with the baselines generated by major commercial web search engines. Lastly, Sect. 6 concludes this paper.

2 Definitions

In this section, we clarify the definitions of our research targets. They are namely subtopics of keyword queries and hierarchical heading structure in documents.

2.1 Definition of Subtopics

We focus on subtopics explicitly represented by subtopic strings defined in the NTCIR-10 INTENT-2 task [23] as quoted below.

> A subtopic string of a given query is a query that *specializes and/or disambiguates* the search intent of the original query. If a string returned in response to the query does neither, it is considered incorrect.

As defined above, each subtopic is associated to the original topic behind an original query. In INTENT-2 and in this paper, a *query* means a keyword query, which is an array of one or more words.

The overview paper of INTENT-2 lists some example subtopic strings [23]. If the original query is "harry potter", "harry potter philosophers stone movie" is a true subtopic string which specializes the original query. On the other hand, "harry potter hp" is not a subtopic string because hp is just the acronym of harry potter and the string neither specializes nor disambiguates the original query. If the original query is "office", "office workplace" is a subtopic string that disambiguates the original query considering the existence of office software, but "office office" is not a subtopic string. Note that true subtopic strings may not include their original query. For example, "aliens vs predators" is a true subtopic string of the original query "avp" because avp can be an acronym of multiple terms.

2.2   Definition of Heading Structure

For ranking of subtopics, we use hierarchical heading structure in documents. We use our previous definition of the structure and its components given in [16], which is summarized below.

Heading. A *heading* is a visually prominent segment of a document describing the topic of another segment.

Block. A *block* is a coherent segment of a document which has its own heading describing its topic. As explained above, there is one-to-one correspondence between a heading and a block. We consider neither a block that consists only of its heading nor a block without its heading. This is because our research interest in this paper is the relationship between headings representing subtopics and blocks of various lengths. An entire document is also a block because it is a clearly specified segment and we can regard its title or URL as its heading.

Hierarchical Heading Structure. A block may contain another block entirely, but two blocks never partially overlap. Therefore, all blocks in a document form a hierarchical structure whose root is the *root block* representing the entire document. We call the structure *hierarchical heading structure*.

3   Related Work

Generally, a term *topic* has two meanings in informatics [10]. One is an implicit topic represented by a (fuzzy) set of terms [11,12], and the other is an explicit topic represented by a short text like a keyword query. Our research target is explicit topics. In particular, we focus on subtopics of topics which are behind keyword queries input by users. For mining such subtopics, we need four component technologies. They are namely subtopic candidate extraction, feature extraction from subtopic candidates, and subtopic ranking and diversification based on the features. We survey related work on these technologies in this order.

3.1   Subtopic Candidate Extraction

This step is not the topic of this paper. However, we briefly survey related work on this step for reference.

Query completion/suggestion by search engines generates many related queries of the original queries. This is a very popular resource of subtopic candidate strings [15,27,28,30,33,34,37], and the snapshots of them for INTENT-2 [23] is publicly available. We also use them as baseline subtopic rankings for evaluation later. Google Insights and Google keywords generator are similar services [34]. Raw query logs of search engines [2,15,28,30,33] must also be useful.

Disambiguation pages in Wikipedia contain multiple subtopics of many ambiguous article titles of Wikipedia, and are very well-organized by hand. Therefore, they are also a very popular resource of subtopic candidate strings [15,30,33,34,37]. Redirect pages and tables of contents in Wikipedia must also be useful [33].

Of course, search result documents themselves can be a resource of subtopic candidate strings. Methods based on words frequently occurring [20,29,30,35,39, 40], words frequently co-occurring with query keywords [32], pseudo-relevance feedback [2], syntactic patterns [13], search result summaries [34] have been proposed.

Titles [20,35], anchor texts of in-links [10,34], and explicitly tagged top-level headings (H1 nodes) of HTML documents [34] all describe the topics of the entire documents. Therefore, they may be important as subtopic candidate strings. Their idea is similar to ours, but they do not use detailed hierarchical heading structure, i.e., low-level headings and their associated blocks. In addition, we use it for ranking candidate subtopic strings in this paper, not for extracting the candidates.

The QDMiner system extracts *query dimensions* each of which refers to one important aspect of the original query [8]. The system is based on list extraction from web pages. Their idea of query dimension is highly relevant to the idea of subtopic, and therefore some existing methods extract them as components of subtopic candidate strings [1,28]. Some methods use lexical databases as well [2,30].

3.2 Subtopic Feature Extraction

Similarly to most existing document ranking methods, many existing methods of subtopic feature extraction are based on term frequency (TF) and/or document frequency (DF) of subtopic strings or their component terms [5,13,32,35,39]. TF of a string means the number of its occurrences in a document, and DF of a string means the number of documents which contain it. The occurrences in some types of document metadata, e.g., document titles, anchor text of in-links, and top-level headings, are more important than other occurrences [34,35].

Similarity between subtopic candidate strings and their search result documents, or between subtopic candidate strings and their original queries, is a popular feature [5,15,19,39]. Document coverage of a subtopic candidate string is the weighted summation of the scores of documents that both the string and its original query retrieved [13].

Distinctness entropy of subtopic candidate strings measures the distinctness among the document sets that the strings retrieved [13,38]. The SEM group at

INTENT-2 used the co-occurrence of subtopic candidate strings in query logs and the edit distance between the strings and their original queries [28].

Query-independent features like readability of subtopic candidate strings are also useful [28, 32].

3.3 Subtopic Ranking

Subtopic ranking is essential for filtering out noises and for ranking subtopic strings by their importance. The simplest way is to sort subtopic candidate strings in order of linear combination of features. As in the area of document ranking, however, more sophisticated functions like TFIDF (TF over DF) and BM25 [22] are also used [13, 28, 30, 32].

Many methods assign different weights for different sources of subtopic candidate strings [15, 34]. For example, the THUIR group at the IMine task of NTCIR-11 assigned the weights of 0.75 for Google keywords generator, 0.15 for Google insights, and 0.05 for query completion/suggestion by commercial search engines [34].

Ullah and Aono proposed a method that represents each subtopic candidate string by its feature vector then score them by their cosine similarity with the mean vector [27].

It is notable that the THUSAM group at INTENT-2 adopted a variant of learning-to-rank methods that are state-of-the-arts methods for document ranking [15].

3.4 Subtopic Diversification

One important application of subtopic mining is search result diversification. Therefore, diversity of ranked subtopics is also important.

Subtopic diversification step is sometimes embedded into other steps. One promising way is clustering of subtopic candidate strings and extraction of the representative string of each cluster [13, 18, 29–31, 33–35, 37]. The cluster-level entropy maximization [13], affinity propagation [31, 33, 37], a variant of K-medoids [34], and K-means [35] algorithms are used.

The THCIB group at NTCIR-10 clustered implicit topics by the affinity propagation algorithm, then assigned explicit topics to each cluster by Latent Dirichlet Allocation [31].

The Hierarchical InfoSimba-based Global K-means (HISGK-means) algorithm clusters search result snippets then labels each cluster [6, 18]. The InfoSimba is a similarity measure between snippets based on term co-occurrence, and HISGK-means recursively clusters snippets based on the measure and Global K-means. Each label is obtained as the centroid of a cluster.

Recently, some methods adopted word embedding models [15, 19]. In word embedding models, we can *subtract* subtopic candidate strings from their original query. Based on this idea, the HULTECH group at IMine recursively subtracted subtopic candidate strings from their original query then compared the difference and the remaining subtopic candidate strings every time they adopt the subtopic candidate string with the best score [19]. Their idea is similar to ours, except we recursively subtract blocks, not vectors representing words, from a web corpus.

The maximal marginal relevance (MMR) framework also concatenate items into rankings one-by-one [3]. In each iteration, the framework selects the item with the best balance of the score and dissimilarity to the already ranked items. Of course, the framework is useful for diversifying subtopic rankings [27].

As explained above, no existing method scores or diversifies subtopic candidate strings based on detailed logical hierarchical structure in documents, e.g. hierarchical heading structure, which our methods use.

4 Subtopic Ranking Based on Hierarchical Heading Structure

In this section, we propose scoring and ranking methods for subtopic candidate strings. Our proposed methods are based on matching between the strings and hierarchical heading structure in documents in a corpus. We regard that a subtopic candidate string *matches* a block if and only if all the words in the string appear either in the heading of the block or in the headings of its ancestor blocks (after basic pre-processing, i.e., tokenization, stop word filtering, and stemming). For example, a subtopic string "computer programming degrees" matches the "degrees" block in Fig. 1 because the top-level heading of the block contains "computer" and "programming" and the own heading of the block contains the remaining word "degrees". If a subtopic string matches a block, the block must refer to the subtopic according to the definition of hierarchical heading structure. Because of this definition of matching, if a subtopic string matches a block, the string must also match the hierarchical descendant blocks of the block. However, we do not consider such matching of hierarchical descendants of already matched blocks. Instead, we score each block considering its hierarchical descendant blocks.

Formally, the score of a pair of a subtopic string s and a document d is:

$$docScore(s, d) = \sum_{b \text{ in } d} match(s, b) blockScore(b) \tag{1}$$

where b is each block in d, $match(s, b)$ is 1 if and only if s matches b and does not match any ancestor block of b and is 0 otherwise. $blockScore(b)$ is the score of b.

Hereafter in this section, we first discuss the definition of $blockScore(b)$, then discuss integration of subtopic scores on multiple documents, and finally discuss ranking of multiple subtopics into a diversified ranking.

4.1 Block Scoring

First, we propose four definitions of $blockScore(b)$.

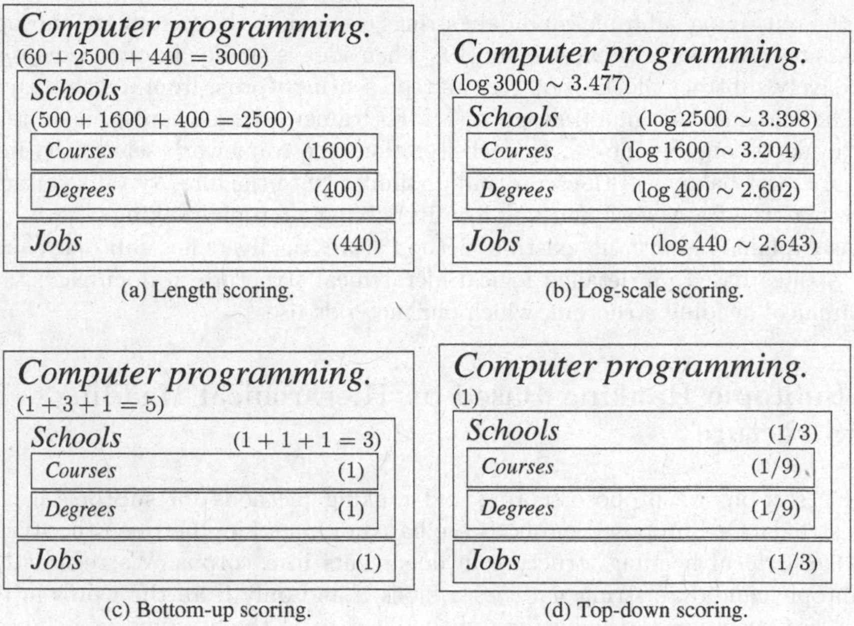

Computer programming.
(60 + 2500 + 440 = 3000)

Schools
(500 + 1600 + 400 = 2500)

Courses   (1600)

Degrees   (400)

Jobs   (440)

(a) Length scoring.

Computer programming.
(log 3000 ∼ 3.477)

Schools   (log 2500 ∼ 3.398)

Courses   (log 1600 ∼ 3.204)

Degrees   (log 400 ∼ 2.602)

Jobs   (log 440 ∼ 2.643)

(b) Log-scale scoring.

Computer programming.
(1 + 3 + 1 = 5)

Schools   (1 + 1 + 1 = 3)

Courses   (1)

Degrees   (1)

Jobs   (1)

(c) Bottom-up scoring.

Computer programming.
(1)

Schools   (1/3)

Courses   (1/9)

Degrees   (1/9)

Jobs   (1/3)

(d) Top-down scoring.

Fig. 2. Comparison of scoring results by four scoring methods of page in Fig. 1. Scores of blocks are in parentheses. Non-heading components of blocks are omitted.

Scoring by Content Length. Basically, the more description about a subtopic a document contains, the more important the subtopic is for the document author. Furthermore, the importance of the subtopic for readers, and for search engine users, is also reflected by the length of the content because generally speaking authors write documents for readers. Based on this idea, we can score blocks by the lengths of their contents. The score of a block b is:

$$\text{blockScore}(b) = \text{length}(b) \qquad (2)$$

where length(b) is the length of b. We call this *length* scoring. For example, if we score the blocks in Fig. 1 by this, we obtain the result shown in Fig. 2a. In Fig. 2, the scores of the blocks are in parentheses and non-heading components of the blocks are omitted.

Scoring by Log-Scaled Content Length. As the relevance between a document and a query keyword is assumed to be not direct proportional to the number of the query keyword occurrences in the document [22], the importance of a topic may also be not direct proportional to the content length of the block referring to the topic. Based on this idea, we propose another scoring function with logarithmic scaling:

$$\text{blockScore}(b) = \log(\text{length}(b) + 1). \qquad (3)$$

We call this *log-scale* scoring. An example result of log-scale scoring is shown in Fig. 2b.

Bottom-Up Scoring. In practice, the importance of some topics are not reflected by the content length of their matching blocks. For example, telephone number may be an important subtopic of a place, but blocks under the heading "telephone number" should contain relatively less contents, i.e., only the exact telephone number of the place, than blocks under other headings. Logarithmic scaling in the previous section reduces the effect of content length, but we also consider a scoring function that completely ignores content lengths. If we assume even importance for all blocks excluding their child blocks, the score of a block b is formulated as below:

$$blockScore(b) = 1 + \sum_{c \in b} blockScore(c) \tag{4}$$

where c is each child block of b. We call this *bottom-up* scoring. An example result of bottom-up scoring is shown in Fig. 2c.

Top-Down Scoring. On the other hand, we can assume even importance for all child blocks of a block. This assumption means that child blocks of a block are used to segment its topic into multiple subtopics of even importance. Because an original block may include meaningful contents besides its child blocks, we also assign the same importance to the contents. Formally, the score of a block b is:

$$blockScore(b) = \begin{cases} \dfrac{blockScore(p)}{1 + |p|} & \text{if } b \text{ has its parent block } p \\ 1 & \text{otherwise} \end{cases} \tag{5}$$

where $|p|$ is the number of the child blocks of p. We call this *top-down* scoring. An example result of top-down scoring is shown in Fig. 2d.

4.2   Score Integration for Multiple Pages

Next, we explain four ways to integrate the scores of a subtopic candidate string s on each document d, $docScore(s, d)$, into $score(s, D)$, which is the score of the string on an entire document collection, or a corpus, D.

Integration by Simple Summation. The simplest way to integrate the scores on multiple documents is to sum them up. Such simple summation means that the importance of a subtopic string is reflected by the length of contents (if we adopt length scoring), the number of blocks (if we adopt bottom-up scoring), and so on that refer to the subtopic in the corpus. Formally, the score of a subtopic string s on a corpus D is:

$$\text{score}(s, D) = \sum_{d \in D} \text{docScore}(s, d). \tag{6}$$

We call this method *summation* integration.

Page-Based Integration. In summation integration, documents of more length (if we adopt length or log-scale scoring) or including more blocks (if we adopt bottom-up scoring) have more chance to contribute to score(s, D). However, if we assume that each document is equally important, the scaling of docScore(s, d) defined below may be useful:

$$\text{score}(s, D) = \sum_{d \in D} \frac{\text{docScore}(s, d)}{\text{blockScore}(\text{root}(d))} \tag{7}$$

where root(d) is the root block of d, i.e., the block representing the entire document d. We call this method *page-based* integration.

Because we score each block considering its hierarchical descendant blocks, blockScore(root(d)) takes its maximum value among all the blocks in d. This division by blockScore(root(d)) scales docScore(s, d) to $[0, 1]$ if we adopt length, top-down, or bottom-up scoring methods. Note that docScore(s, d) may exceed 1 if we adopt log-scale scoring and multiple blocks in d matches s.

Note that there is no difference between summation integration and page-based integration if we adopt top-down scoring because blockScore(b) in top-down scoring is already scaled to $[0, 1]$.

Domain-Based Integration. Authors may split the contents about a topic into multiple documents in a *domain*, e.g., a set of web pages whose URLs include the same domain name, instead of splitting it into multiple blocks in a single document.

Considering such cases, domain-based scaling may be more effective than page-based scaling. To formulate such scaling, we introduce Δ, a set of domains which appear in the corpus. Each domain $\delta \in \Delta$ is a subset of the corpus D, and $\bigcup_{\delta \in \Delta} \delta = D$. A new integration function is:

$$\text{score}(s, D) = \sum_{\delta \in \Delta} \frac{\sum_{d \in \delta} \text{docScore}(s, d)}{\sum_{d \in \delta} \text{blockScore}(\text{root}(d))}. \tag{8}$$

We call this method *domain-based* integration.

Combination Integration. If we apply both page-based and domain-based scalings, the new integration function is:

$$\text{score}(s, D) = \sum_{\delta \in \Delta} \frac{1}{|\delta|} \sum_{d \in \delta} \frac{\text{docScore}(s, d)}{\text{blockScore}(\text{root}(d))}. \tag{9}$$

We call this *combination* integration.

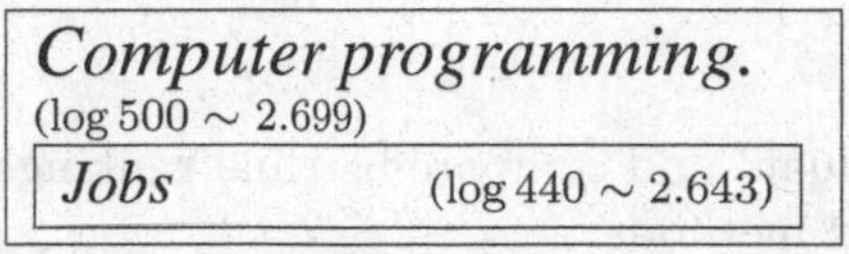

> ## Computer programming.
> (log 500 ~ 2.699)
>
> | *Jobs* | (log 440 ~ 2.643) |
> | --- | --- |

Fig. 3. Example re-scoring result of page in Fig. 1 by log-scale scoring after we rank first subtopic string "computer programming schools".

4.3 Diversifying Subtopic Ranking

Next, we explain two ways to rank multiple subtopics of a query with varied score(s, D) into a ranking for the query.

Uniform Ranking. To rank multiple subtopic strings into a ranking, we can score each of them once, then simply sort the strings by descending order of their scores. We call this *uniform* ranking method.

Diversified Ranking. However, because search result diversification is one of the most important applications of subtopic ranking, diversity of subtopic ranking is also important. Therefore, we also propose a diversification method for subtopic ranking. Our idea for the diversification is that if a block matches a subtopic candidate string which is already ranked into the ranking, the topic of the block is already referred to by the ranked subtopic string, and therefore, even if the block matches some other remaining subtopic candidate strings, the block should not contribute to the score of the candidate strings.

Based on this idea, we propose a *diversified* ranking method for subtopic strings based on hierarchical heading structure. In this method, first we score each subtopic candidate string on a corpus then put only the string with the best score into the resulting ranking. Second, we remove all the blocks matching the string from the corpus. Third, we again score the remaining subtopic candidate strings on the remaining blocks then put the string with the best score into the resulting ranking. The second and third steps are repeated until all the subtopic candidate strings are ranked or enough number of subtopics are ranked.

For example, suppose we have three subtopic strings, "computer programming school", "computer programming course", and "computer programming jobs". If we rank the strings by uniform ranking method and the log-scale scores of the blocks on the document in Fig. 2b, the ranks of the strings are in the above order because the strings respectively match the "Schools" (score: 3.398), "Courses" (score: 3.204), and "Jobs" (score: 2.643) blocks. On the other hand, if we rank the strings by diversified ranking method, "computer programming jobs" occupies the second rank. This is because after "computer programming school" is ranked first, its matching block "School" including its descendant blocks is removed from the re-calculation of the scores (Fig. 3). Then the score of "computer programming course" in this page becomes 0 because the "Courses" block referring to the subtopic candidate has already removed from this page.

5   Evaluation

In this section, we evaluate and compare baseline rankings and rankings generated with our proposed methods.

We proposed four block scoring methods, four score integration methods, and two subtopic ranking methods. We can arbitrary combine these methods. However, there is no difference between summation and page-based integration and also between domain-based and combination integration when we use top-down scoring as discussed in Sect. 4.2. Therefore, we compare 28 proposed methods in total.

5.1   Evaluation Methodology

Because we do not discuss extraction of subtopic candidate strings, we evaluate our proposed methods by re-ranking baseline subtopic rankings.

We use the official data set, including the baselines, and the evaluation measures of the subtopic mining subtask of the NTCIR-10 INTENT-2 task [23]. This is because the dataset of the latest NTCIR-12 IMine-2 task [36] is not available yet, and because first-level and second-level subtopics are distinguished in the second-latest NTCIR-11 IMine task [14] while our proposed methods do not distinguish them. All components of the NTCIR-10 data set is publicly available and most of them are on the web site of NII[1].

In the subtopic mining subtask, participants are required to return ranked list of top-10 subtopic strings for each query. Subtopic strings are expected to be sorted in descending order of their *intent probability*, i.e. the probability that search engine users submitting the given query need information on the subtopics. Multiple subtopic strings may refer to the same subtopic, but a string refers to one subtopic at most.

Official evaluation measures of the subtask are intent recall (I-rec), D-nDCG, and D♯-nDCG.

The definition of the I-rec measure is:

$$\text{Irec@10} = \frac{|I'|}{|I|} \tag{10}$$

where I is a set of known subtopics of the original query, and I' is a set of subtopics represented by any of the maximum 10 strings in a ranking to be evaluated. This measure reflects recall and diversity of subtopics in rankings.

The definition of the D-nDCG measure is:

$$\text{DnDCG@10} = \frac{\text{DDCG@10}}{\text{ideal DDCG@10}} \tag{11}$$

$$\text{where DDCG@10} = \sum_{r=1}^{10} \frac{\sum_i Pr(i|q)g_i(r)}{\log(r+1)} \tag{12}$$

---

[1] http://www.nii.ac.jp/dsc/idr/en/ntcir/ntcir.html.

where r is a rank, $Pr(i|q)$ is the intent probability of a known subtopic i behind the original query q, and $g_i(r)$ is 1 iff the string at the rank r refers to the subtopic i, and 0 otherwise. The D-nDCG measure reflects the precision and accuracy of subtopics in rankings.

The integrated measure D♯-nDCG is the weighted summation of I-rec and D-nDCG.

$$D♯nDCG@10 = \gamma Irec@10 + (1 - \gamma)DnDCG@10 \qquad (13)$$

where γ is the weight of I-rec which is fixed to 0.5 in this paper and the subtask. In other words, D♯-nDCG is arithmetic mean of I-rec and D-nDCG in this paper and the subtask.

An official evaluation tool is available online[2].

5.2   Data Set

The details of the data set is as follows.

Queries. We used 50 keyword queries in the NTCIR data set which are also used in the web track of the well-known Text Retrieval Conference (TREC) 2012 [4].

Document Sets. We used the documents on baseline document rankings generated by default scoring of Indri search engine (including query expansion based on pseudo-relevance feedback) [26] and Waterloo spam filter. The baseline rankings are prepared for the TREC 2014 web track and contains rankings for the queries prepared for the TREC 2012–2014 web tracks. Each ranking consists of 131–837 web pages for a query extracted from the ClueWeb09B document collection, and we use them as the corpus for re-ranking the baseline subtopics of the query.

The baseline rankings are available online[3].

The ClueWeb09B document collection is one of the most well-known snapshots of the web, contains 50 million web pages, and is crawled by the Lemur Project in 2009.

The document collection is also available at distribution cost[4].

Baseline Subtopic Rankings. The NTCIR data set includes snapshots of query completion/suggestion results by major commercial search engines. We used the query completion results by Google and Yahoo because they respectively achieved the best I-rec and D-nDCG scores among the baselines [23]. Because the both results contain only 10 strings at most for each query, re-ranking of them do

---

[2] http://research.nii.ac.jp/ntcir/tools/ntcireval-en.html.

[3] https://github.com/trec-web/trec-web-2014.

[4] http://www.lemurproject.org/clueweb09/.

not affect I-rec scores. Therefore, we also used *our merged baseline result* which is generated by merging all of the four baseline query completion/suggestion results and sorting them in "dictionary sort" [23]. Because the meaning of dictionary sort is ambiguous, we could not reproduce their evaluation result. We merged the results, decapitalized the strings, removed duplicated strings, and sorted the remaining strings in byte order in UTF-8 to generate our merged baseline result.

Known Intents and Intent Probabilities. The actual known subtopics, subtopic strings referring to them, and their intent probabilities are manually prepared for the subtask [23]. Note that all the actual subtopic strings in the baseline subtopic rankings must be in this data according to their annotation process [23].

5.3 Implementation Details

In this section, we explain the details of our implementation required to evaluate our methods.

Heading Structure Extraction. To extract hierarchical heading structure in web pages, we use our previously proposed heading-based page segmentation (HEPS) method [16]. It extracts each heading and block in pages as an array of adjoining sibling DOM nodes. For evaluation, we used the reference implementation 1.0.0 of HEPS[5].

Text Contents of Headings and Blocks. We used the URL and the title as the heading of each web page. As the text contents of the other headings, blocks, and entire pages, we use their corresponding *raw strings* that we previously defined [16]. Intuitively, the raw string of a component is the string of the DOM text nodes in the component. Before generating raw strings, each DOM IMG (image) nodes are replaced by its alternate text and URL, i.e., alt and src HTML attribute values, to treat the IMG nodes as text nodes.

Content Length. For length and log-scaled scoring, we used the number of UTF-8 characters in their raw strings as their length. Note that the documents in the ClueWeb09 collection are encoded in UTF-8.

Domain. For domain-based and combination integration, we distinguished the domains of web pages by the domain names in their URLs.

---

[5] https://github.com/tmanabe/HEPS.

Matching Between Subtopic Strings and Headings. Before matching subtopic candidate strings and hierarchical headings, we applied basic pre-processing for text retrieval, e.g., tokenization, stop word filtering, and stemming, to both types of strings. All URLs were tokenized by splitting by any non-word characters, and the other strings were tokenized by Stanford CoreNLP toolkit [17]. All tokens were decapitalized, filtered out if they are 33 default stop words of the Lucene library[6], and then stemmed by the Porter stemmer [21].

Subtopic Candidate Strings. After preprocessing, duplicated subtopic candidate strings and subtopic candidate strings same as their original queries were removed.

Tie Breaking. If we have multiple subtopic candidates of the same score in our unified ranking method or in any iteration of our diversified ranking method, we sorted them in the same order as the baseline subtopic ranking.

5.4 Evaluation Results

Tables 1, 2, and 3 show evaluation results. Table 1 shows the D-nDCG scores achieved by each method when they re-rank the query completion result by Google, and Table 2 shows the D-nDCG scores achieved by each method when they re-rank the query completion result by Yahoo. In Tables 1 and 2, all our methods are listed in descending order of their D-nDCG scores. Table 3 shows the scores achieved by each method when they re-rank our merged baseline result. In Table 3, all our methods are listed in descending order of their D♯-nDCG scores.

5.5 Discussion

In all the comparisons, all our proposed methods consistently achieved scores better than the baseline scores on all the measures. This fact strongly supports the effectiveness of considering hierarchical headings and lengths of blocks for subtopic ranking. This consistency is due to a considerable number of subtopic candidate strings which were assigned score 0, and this effectiveness is due to such strings which are actually not subtopics or not important subtopics. For example, let us focus on the log-scale/page-based/diversified method which achieved the best D♯-nDCG score $((0.3815 + 0.4617)/2 = \mathbf{0.4216})$ throughout this paper by re-ranking the query completion result by Yahoo. With this combination, 178 among 448 (39.7%) subtopic candidate strings were assigned score 0. In other words, no block in our corpus matched with these strings. Regardless of the choice of block scoring and score integration methods, these strings should be assigned score 0. Note that this fact does not indicate a flaw of our methods because they achieved the scores better than the baselines, and that larger corpus must support our methods to rank the zero-scored strings correctly.

---

[6] http://lucene.apache.org/.

Table 1. Comparison with query completion result by Google. Our methods are listed in descending order of their D-nDCG scores. Best score is in bold font. For all methods and baseline, I-rec score is .3841

Scoring	Integration	Ranking	D-nDCG
Log-Scale	Domain-Based	Uniformed	**.4502**
Log-Scale	Combination	Uniformed	.4501
Log-Scale	Domain-Based	Diversified	.4487
Log-Scale	Combination	Diversified	.4485
Bottom-Up	Page-Based	Diversified	.4479
Bottom-Up	Page-Based	Uniformed	.4474
Length	Combination	Uniformed	.4474
Log-Scale	Page-Based	Uniformed	.4474
Log-Scale	Summation	Diversified	.4470
Log-Scale	Page-Based	Diversified	.4470
Top-Down	Domain-Based	Uniformed	.4468
Top-Down	Combination	Uniformed	.4468
Log-Scale	Summation	Uniformed	.4467
Bottom-Up	Domain-Based	Uniformed	.4466
Top-Down	Summation	Diversified	.4460
Top-Down	Page-Based	Diversified	.4460
Length	Combination	Diversified	.4458
Length	Domain-Based	Uniformed	.4457
Bottom-Up	Combination	Uniformed	.4454
Length	Page-Based	Diversified	.4453
Top-Down	Page-Based	Uniformed	.4451
Top-Down	Summation	Uniformed	.4451
Top-Down	Domain-Based	Diversified	.4446
Top-Down	Combination	Diversified	.4446
Bottom-Up	Domain-Based	Diversified	.4446
Bottom-Up	Combination	Diversified	.4444
Length	Page-Based	Uniformed	.4442
Length	Domain-Based	Diversified	.4432
Length	Summation	Diversified	.4418
Length	Summation	Uniformed	.4416
Bottom-Up	Summation	Diversified	.4409
Bottom-Up	Summation	Uniformed	.4397
Query completion result of Google			.3735

Table 2. Comparison with query completion result by Yahoo. Our methods are listed in descending order of their D-nDCG scores. Best score is in bold font. For all methods and baseline, I-rec score is .3815

Scoring	Integration	Ranking	D-nDCG
Log-Scale	Page-Based	Diversified	**.4617**
Bottom-Up	Domain-Based	Diversified	.4609
Log-Scale	Page-Based	Uniformed	.4608
Log-Scale	Summation	Diversified	.4601
Length	Domain-Based	Diversified	.4587
Bottom-Up	Domain-Based	Uniformed	.4585
Log-Scale	Summation	Uniformed	.4584
Top-Down	Domain-Based	Diversified	.4584
Top-Down	Combination	Diversified	.4584
Length	Combination	Diversified	.4583
Bottom-Up	Combination	Diversified	.4577
Top-Down	Domain-Based	Uniformed	.4569
Top-Down	Combination	Uniformed	.4569
Bottom-Up	Summation	Diversified	.4568
Length	Combination	Uniformed	.4566
Bottom-Up	Page-Based	Diversified	.4565
Bottom-Up	Combination	Uniformed	.4564
Top-Down	Summation	Diversified	.4562
Top-Down	Page-Based	Diversified	.4562
Length	Domain-Based	Uniformed	.4560
Log-Scale	Domain-Based	Diversified	.4557
Bottom-Up	Page-Based	Uniformed	.4557
Log-Scale	Combination	Diversified	.4551
Length	Summation	Diversified	.4549
Length	Page-Based	Diversified	.4549
Top-Down	Page-Based	Uniformed	.4548
Top-Down	Summation	Uniformed	.4548
Bottom-Up	Summation	Uniformed	.4541
Log-Scale	Domain-Based	Uniformed	.4537
Log-Scale	Combination	Uniformed	.4536
Length	Page-Based	Uniformed	.4528
Length	Summation	Uniformed	.4521
Query completion result of Yahoo			.3829

Table 3. Comparison with our merged baseline result. Our methods are listed in descending order of their D♯-nDCG scores. Best scores are in bold font.

Scoring	Integration	Ranking	I-rec	D-nDCG	D♯-nDCG
Log-Scale	Summation	Uniformed	**.4009**	**.3997**	**.4003**
Log-Scale	Page-Based	Uniformed	.3986	.3981	.3984
Length	Summation	Uniformed	.3974	.3945	.3959
Log-Scale	Combination	Uniformed	.3956	.3921	.3939
Log-Scale	Domain-Based	Uniformed	.3956	.3913	.3934
Length	Page-Based	Uniformed	.3974	.3882	.3928
Bottom-Up	Page-Based	Uniformed	.3918	.3930	.3924
Length	Combination	Uniformed	.3900	.3948	.3924
Top-Down	Combination	Uniformed	.3895	.3947	.3921
Top-Down	Domain-Based	Uniformed	.3895	.3947	.3921
Bottom-Up	Combination	Uniformed	.3880	.3944	.3912
Length	Domain-Based	Uniformed	.3855	.3930	.3893
Top-Down	Summation	Uniformed	.3872	.3906	.3889
Top-Down	Page-Based	Uniformed	.3872	.3906	.3889
Bottom-Up	Domain-Based	Uniformed	.3827	.3937	.3882
Top-Down	Combination	Diversified	.3869	.3710	.3790
Top-Down	Domain-Based	Diversified	.3869	.3710	.3790
Bottom-Up	Summation	Uniformed	.3726	.3824	.3775
Length	Summation	Diversified	.3855	.3682	.3768
Log-Scale	Page-Based	Diversified	.3840	.3695	.3768
Top-Down	Summation	Diversified	.3847	.3686	.3767
Top-Down	Page-Based	Diversified	.3847	.3686	.3767
Length	Combination	Diversified	.3836	.3693	.3764
Bottom-Up	Page-Based	Diversified	.3830	.3694	.3762
Bottom-Up	Combination	Diversified	.3813	.3707	.3760
Log-Scale	Summation	Diversified	.3812	.3694	.3753
Length	Page-Based	Diversified	.3852	.3639	.3746
Length	Domain-Based	Diversified	.3812	.3663	.3737
Log-Scale	Domain-Based	Diversified	.3813	.3659	.3736
Bottom-Up	Domain-Based	Diversified	.3780	.3681	.3731
Log-Scale	Combination	Diversified	.3813	.3640	.3727
Bottom-Up	Summation	Diversified	.3757	.3652	.3704
Our merged baseline result			.3310	.3066	.3188

Next, let us continue focusing on the log-scale/page-based/diversified method. The method also achieved its D-nDCG score (0.4470) better than the score of the query completion result by Google (0.3735) and its I-rec, D-nDCG, and D♯-nDCG scores (0.3840, 0.3695, and 0.3768, respectively) better than the scores of our merged result (0.3310, 0.3066, and 0.3188, respectively). Moreover, according to Student's paired t-test (where each pair consists of the scores of the baseline and our proposed method for a query), all the D-nDCG and D♯-nDCG scores were statistically significantly different from the baseline scores ($p < 0.05$). This fact supports the effectiveness of this combination of our proposed methods. Only the I-rec score was not statistically significant ($p = 0.0656$). Hereafter in this paper, we discuss statistical significance based on the same test procedure.

Comparison of Block Scoring Methods. Log-scale scoring achieved the best scores in all the three comparisons. This fact may suggest that the importance of a topic is reflected by the content length of the block referring to the topic, but the importance is not direct proportional to the length. Moreover, 11 among the 15 best results shown in Tables 1, 2, 3 are using log-scale scoring. This fact may suggest the robustness of log-scale scoring. However, the advantage of log-scale scoring over the others was small. For example, the D-nDCG score of the re-ranked Yahoo result by the *log-scale*/page-based/diversified method was not statistically significantly different from the scores of the *bottom-up*/page-based/diversified ($p = 0.1481$), *top-down*/page-based/diversified ($p = 0.1204$), and *length*/page-based/diversified ($p = 0.0972$) methods. To prove the advantage of log-scale scoring, we need more experiments on larger corpora.

Comparison of Score Integration Methods. Score integration methods had only small impact. In the comparison with the Google result (Table 1), the log-scale/*domain-based*/uniform method achieved the best D-nDCG score, but its difference from the second-best score by log-scale/*combination*/uniform method was quite small (0.0001). In the comparison with the Yahoo result (Table 2), the log-scale/*page-based*/diversified method achieved the best D-nDCG score, but its difference from the score by the log-scale/*summation*/diversified method was also small (0.0016). In the comparison with our merged result (Table 3), the differences between the best log-scale/*summation*/ uniform method and the second-best log-scale/*page-based*/uniform method were also small (I-rec@10: 0.0023, D-nDCG@10: 0.0016, D♯-nDCG: 0.0019). All these five differences were not statistically significant.

In this experiment, there was no substantial difference between our score integration methods.

Effect of Diversified Ranking Method. Because I-rec can measure diversity of rankings, we focus on the I-rec score comparison with our merged result (Table 3). Unfortunately, no diversified method achieved its I-rec score better than 0.3869 while multiple uniformed methods achieved their I-rec scores better than 0.39.

In detail, the top-down/combination/*diversified* method achieved the best I-rec score (0.3869) among the methods with diversified ranking while the log-scale/summation/*uniformed* method achieved the best I-rec score (0.4009) among all the methods. However, the I-rec score difference between the methods was not statistically significant ($p = 0.2759$).

The I-rec score difference between the best log-scale/summation/*uniformed* method and the log-scale/summation/*diversified* method was also not statistically significant ($p = 0.1028$).

The facts show that our proposed ranking diversification method did neither improve nor worsen resulting rankings.

6   Conclusion and Future Work

We proposed subtopic ranking methods based on the ideas that hierarchical headings in a document reflect the topic structure in the document and that the length of contents referring to a topic reflects the importance of the topic. Based on these ideas, all our methods score subtopic candidate strings based on the lengths of the blocks whose hierarchical headings match the strings. Our methods consist of three steps: block scoring, integration of block scores, and ranking of subtopic candidate strings based on the integrated score of their matching blocks. We proposed four methods to score blocks, four methods to integrate block scores, and two methods to rank strings.

We evaluated our total 32 methods by using the publicly available NTCIR data set. The results indicated (1) our methods statistically significantly improved the baseline rankings by commercial search engines, (2) our corpus was not large enough for our methods to score less important subtopic strings correctly, (3) log-scale scoring seems effective and robust, (4) there is no substantial difference among score integration methods, and (5) our ranking diversification method was not effective.

Using a larger corpus for scoring subtopic candidate strings is one interesting future direction of this study. This is because it may allow us to measure the detailed difference of our proposed methods, to measure the effectiveness of our methods to rank less important subtopic strings, and to measure the effect of corpus size to our methods.

Another interesting future direction is to improve our diversified ranking method. In this paper, we completely removed blocks matching with already ranked strings. However, instead of such complete removal, we can reduce the scores of the blocks. This approach may be effective to score subtopics which ordinarily appear as sub-subtopics of other subtopics.

In this paper, we considered only re-ranking of already extracted subtopic candidate strings. However, of course, extraction of subtopic candidate strings is also an important step of subtopic mining. Therefore, extraction of hierarchical headings as subtopic candidate strings is also an important future direction of this study. However, to evaluate subtopic extraction methods, we need to expand the set of known subtopics because the NTCIR data set contains only a limited number of actual subtopics, which requires either some automatic method or a considerable amount of effort by human assesers.

Acknowledgment. This work was supported by JSPS KAKENHI Grant Number 13J06384 and 26540163.

References

1. Bah, A., Carterette, B., Chandar, P.: Udel @ NTCIR-11 IMine track. In: NTCIR (2014)
2. Bouchoucha, A., Nie, J., Liu, X.: Université de montréal at the NTCIR-11 IMine task. In: NTCIR (2014)
3. Carbonell, J., Goldstein, J.: The use of MMR, diversity-based reranking for reordering documents and producing summaries. In: SIGIR, pp. 335–336 (1998)
4. Clarke, C.L.A., Craswell, N., Voorhees, E.M.: Overview of the TREC 2012 web track. In: TREC (2012)
5. Das, S., Mitra, P., Giles, C.L.: Phrase pair classification for identifying subtopics. In: Baeza-Yates, R., Vries, A.P., Zaragoza, H., Cambazoglu, B.B., Murdock, V., Lempel, R., Silvestri, F. (eds.) ECIR 2012. LNCS, vol. 7224, pp. 489–493. Springer, Heidelberg (2012). doi:10.1007/978-3-642-28997-2_48
6. Dias, G., Cleuziou, G., Machado, D.: Informative polythetic hierarchical ephemeral clustering. In: WI, pp. 104–111 (2011)
7. Dou, Z., Hu, S., Chen, K., Song, R., Wen, J.R.: Multi-dimensional search result diversification. In: WSDM, pp. 475–484 (2011)
8. Dou, Z., Hu, S., Luo, Y., Song, R., Wen, J.R.: Finding dimensions for queries. In: CIKM, pp. 1311–1320 (2011)
9. Drosou, M., Pitoura, E.: Search result diversification. SIGMOD Rec. **39**(1), 41–47 (2010)
10. He, J., Hollink, V., de Vries, A.: Combining implicit and explicit topic representations for result diversification. In: SIGIR, pp. 851–860 (2012)
11. Hu, Y., Qian, Y., Li, H., Jiang, D., Pei, J., Zheng, Q.: Mining query subtopics from search log data. In: SIGIR. pp. 305–314 (2012)
12. Jiang, D., Ng, W.: Mining web search topics with diverse spatiotemporal patterns. In: SIGIR, pp. 881–884 (2013)
13. Kim, S.J., Lee, J.H.: Subtopic mining using simple patterns and hierarchical structure of subtopic candidates from web documents. Inf. Process. Manage. **51**(6), 773–785 (2015)
14. Liu, Y., Song, R., Zhang, M., Dou, Z., Yamamoto, T., Kato, M.P., Ohshima, H., Zhou, K.: Overview of the NTCIR-11 IMine task. In: NTCIR (2014)
15. Luo, C., Li, X., Khodzhaev, A., Chen, F., Xu, K., Cao, Y., Liu, Y., Zhang, M., Ma, S.: THUSAM at NTCIR-11 IMine task. In: NTCIR (2014)
16. Manabe, T., Tajima, K.: Extracting logical hierarchical structure of HTML documents based on headings. PVLDB **8**(12), 1606–1617 (2015)
17. Manning, C.D., Surdeanu, M., Bauer, J., Finkel, J., Bethard, S.J., McClosky, D.: The Stanford CoreNLP natural language processing toolkit. In: ACL, pp. 55–60 (2014)
18. Moreno, J.G., Dias, G.: HULTECH at the NTCIR-10 INTENT-2 task: discovering user intents through search results clustering. In: NTCIR (2013)
19. Moreno, J.G., Dias, G.: HULTECH at the NTCIR-11 IMine task: mining intents with continuous vector space models. In: NTCIR (2014)
20. Oyama, S., Tanaka, K.: Query modification by discovering topics from web page structures. In: Yu, J.X., Lin, X., Lu, H., Zhang, Y. (eds.) APWeb 2004. LNCS, vol. 3007, pp. 553–564. Springer, Heidelberg (2004). doi:10.1007/978-3-540-24655-8_60

21. Porter, M.F.: An algorithm for suffix stripping. Readings in Information Retrieval, pp. 313–316. Morgan Kaufmann Publishers Inc., San Francisco (1997)
22. Robertson, S.E., Walker, S.: Some simple effective approximations to the 2-poisson model for probabilistic weighted retrieval. In: SIGIR, pp. 232–241 (1994)
23. Sakai, T., Dou, Z., Yamamoto, T., Liu, Y., Zhang, M., Song, R.: Overview of the NTCIR-10 INTENT-2 task. In: NTCIR (2013)
24. Santos, R.L., Macdonald, C., Ounis, I.: Exploiting query reformulations for web search result diversification. In: WWW, pp. 881–890 (2010)
25. Song, R., Zhang, M., Sakai, T., Kato, M.P., Liu, Y., Sugimoto, M., Wang, Q., Orii, N.: Overview of the NTCIR-9 INTENT task. In: NTCIR (2011)
26. Strohman, T., Metzler, D., Turtle, H., Croft, W.: Indri: a language model-based search engine for complex queries. In: International Conference on Intelligent Analysis (2005)
27. Ullah, M.Z., Aono, M.: Query subtopic mining for search result diversification. In: ICAICTA, pp. 309–314 (2014)
28. Ullah, M.Z., Aono, M., Seddiqui, M.H.: SEM12 at the NTCIR-10 INTENT-2 English subtopic mining subtask. In: NTCIR (2013)
29. Wang, C., Danilevsky, M., Desai, N., Zhang, Y., Nguyen, P., Taula, T., Han, J.: A phrase mining framework for recursive construction of a topical hierarchy. In: KDD, pp. 437–445 (2013)
30. Wang, C.J., Lin, Y.W., Tsai, M.F., Chen, H.H.: Mining subtopics from different aspects for diversifying search results. Inf. Retr. 16(4), 452–483 (2013)
31. Wang, J., Tang, G., Xia, Y., Zhou, Q., Zheng, T.F., Hu, Q., Na, S., Huang, Y.: Understanding the query: THCIB and THUIS at NTCIR-10 intent task. In: NTCIR (2013)
32. Wang, Q., Qian, Y., Song, R., Dou, Z., Zhang, F., Sakai, T., Zheng, Q.: Mining subtopics from text fragments for a web query. Inf. Retr. 16(4), 484–503 (2013)
33. Xia, Y., Zhong, X., Tang, G., Wang, J., Zhou, Q., Zheng, T.F., Hu, Q., Na, S., Huang, Y.: Ranking search intents underlying a query. In: Métais, E., Meziane, F., Saraee, M., Sugumaran, V., Vadera, S. (eds.) NLDB 2013. LNCS, vol. 7934, pp. 266–271. Springer, Heidelberg (2013). doi:10.1007/978-3-642-38824-8_23
34. Xue, Y., Chen, F., Damien, A., Luo, C., Li, X., Huo, S., Zhang, M., Liu, Y., Ma, S.: THUIR at NTCIR-10 INTENT-2 task. In: NTCIR (2013)
35. Yamamoto, T., Kato, M.P., Ohshima, H., Tanaka, K.: KUIDL at the NTCIR-11 IMine task. In: NTCIR (2014)
36. Yamamoto, T., Liu, Y., Zhang, M., Dou, Z., Zhou, K., Markov, I., Kato, M.P., Ohshima, H., Fujita, S.: Overview of the NTCIR-12 IMine-2 task. In: NTCIR (2015)
37. Yu, H., Ren, F.: TUTA1 at the NTCIR-11 IMine task. In: NTCIR (2014)
38. Zeng, H.J., He, Q.C., Chen, Z., Ma, W.Y., Ma, J.: Learning to cluster web search results. In: SIGIR, pp. 210–217 (2004)
39. Zheng, W., Fang, H., Cheng, H., Wang, X.: Diversifying search results through pattern-based subtopic modeling. Int. J. Semant. Web Inf. Syst. 8(4), 37–56 (2012)
40. Zheng, W., Wang, X., Fang, H., Cheng, H.: An exploration of pattern-based subtopic modeling for search result diversification. In: JCDL. pp. 387–388 (2011)

Improving Serendipity and Accuracy
in Cross-Domain Recommender Systems

Denis Kotkov[1]([✉]), Shuaiqiang Wang[2], and Jari Veijalainen[1]

[1] Faculty of Information Technology, University of Jyvaskyla, P.O.Box 35, FI-40014
Jyvaskyla, Finland
deigkotk@student.jyu.fi,jari.veijalainen@jyu.fi
[2] Manchester Business School, The University of Manchester, Manchester, UK
shuaiqiang.wang@manchester.ac.uk

Abstract. Cross-domain recommender systems use information from
source domains to improve recommendations in a target domain, where
the term *domain* refers to a set of items that share attributes and/or
user ratings. Most works on this topic focus on accuracy but disregard
other properties of recommender systems. In this paper, we attempt to
improve serendipity and accuracy in the target domain with datasets
from source domains. Due to the lack of publicly available datasets,
we collect datasets from two domains related to music, involving user
ratings and item attributes. We then conduct experiments using collaborative filtering and content-based filtering approaches for the purpose
of validation. According to our results, the source domain can improve
serendipity in the target domain for both approaches. The source domain
decreases accuracy for content-based filtering and increases accuracy for
collaborative filtering. The improvement of accuracy decreases with the
growth of non-overlapping items in different domains.

Keywords: Recommender systems · Serendipity · Cross-domain
recommendations · Collaborative filtering · Content-based filtering ·
Data collection

1 Introduction

Recommender systems use past user behavior to suggest items interesting to
users [17]. An item is "a piece of information that refers to a tangible or digital
object, such as a good, a service or a process that a recommender system suggests
to the user in an interaction through the Web, email or text message" [12].
Recommender systems use algorithms to generate recommendations.

Traditional recommendation algorithms mainly aim to improve accuracy,
which indicates how good an algorithm is at suggesting items a user usually
consumes. In this paper, they are referred to as *accuracy-oriented algorithms*.

Shuaiqiang Wang—The research was conducted while the author was working for
the University of Jyvaskyla, Finland.

© Springer International Publishing AG 2017
V. Monfort et al. (Eds.): WEBIST 2016, LNBIP 292, pp. 105–119, 2017.
DOI: 10.1007/978-3-319-66468-2_6

Generally speaking, accuracy-oriented algorithms often suggest popular items, as these items are widely consumed by individuals. To improve accuracy, recommendation algorithms also tend to suggest items similar to a user profile (a set of items rated by the user [12]), as these items match previous user tastes. As a result, a user is recommended (1) items that are popular and therefore familiar to the user [6] and (2) items that the user can easily find him/herself, which is referred to as the *overspecialization problem* [21]. In particular, as two main categories of recommendation algorithms, collaborative filtering algorithms often suggest popular items due to the popularity bias in most datasets, while content-based filtering algorithms often suffer from the overspecialization problem due to insufficient information regarding attributes of items.

Typically, the main reason why a user joins a recommender system is to find novel and interesting items the user would not find him/herself [21]. To improve user satisfaction, a recommender system should suggest serendipitous items [12]. In this paper, we follow the definitions of [2,10,12], which indicate that serendipitous items must be relevant, novel and unexpected to a user.

The mentioned problems can be tackled by cross-domain recommender systems, which could predict serendipitous items by enriching the training data from the target domain with additional datasets from other domains. Here the term *domain* refers to "a set of items that share certain characteristics that are exploited by a particular recommender system" [9]. These characteristics are item attributes and user ratings. Recommender systems that take advantage of multiple domains are called *cross-domain recommender systems* [4,9,13].

In this paper, we explore the *cross-domain recommendation task* [4,13], that requires one *target domain* and at least one *source domain*. The former refers to the domain from which suggested items are picked from, and similarly the latter refers to the domain that contains auxiliary information.

In this work, we seek to address the following research question: Can the source domain improve serendipity in the target domain? Due to the lack of publicly available datasets for cross-domain recommender systems [3,11,13], we collected data from Vkontakte[1] (VK) – Russian online social network (OSN) and Last.fm[2] (FM) – music recommender service. We then matched VK and FM audio recordings and developed the cross-domain recommender system that suggests VK recordings to VK users based on data from both domains. Each audio recording is represented by its metadata excluding the actual audio file. VK recordings thus represent the target domain, while the source domain consists of FM recordings. VK and FM recordings share titles and artists, but have different user ratings and other attributes.

We regard items that share certain attributes and belong to different domains as *overlapping*, while those that do not as *non-overlapping*. In our case, VK and FM recordings that have the same titles and artists are overlapping items.

To address the research question and illustrate the potential of additional data, we chose simple but popular recommendation algorithms to conduct exper-

---

[1] http://vk.com/.
[2] http://last.fm/.

iments for validation: collaborative filtering based on user ratings and content-based filtering based on the descriptions of the items.

Our results indicate that the source domain can improve serendipity in the target domain for both collaborative filtering and content-based filtering algorithms:

– The traditional collaborative filtering algorithms tend to suggest popular items, as most datasets contain rich information regarding these items in terms of user ratings. Combing datasets of different domains decreases the popularity bias.
– Content-based filtering algorithms often suffer from the overspecialization problem due to poor data regarding item attributes. Enriching item attributes alleviates the problem and increases serendipity.

According to our results, the source domain has a negative impact on accuracy for content-based filtering, and a positive impact on accuracy of collaborative filtering. Furthermore, with the growth of non-overlapping items in different domains, the improvement of accuracy for collaborative filtering decreases. This paper has the following contributions:

– We initially investigate the cross-domain recommendation problem in terms of serendipity.
– We collect a novel dataset to conduct the experiments for addressing the research question.

The rest of the paper is organized as follows. Section 2 overviews related works. Section 3 describes the datasets used to conduct experiments. Section 4 is dedicated to recommendation approaches, while Sect. 5 describes conducted experiments. Finally, Sect. 6 draws final conclusions.

2   Related Works

In this section, we survey state-of-the-art efforts regarding serendipity and cross-domain recommendations.

2.1   Serendipity in Recommender Systems

According to the dictionary[3], serendipity is "the faculty of making fortunate discoveries by accident". The term was coined by Horace Walpole, who referenced the fairy tale, "The Three Princes of Serendip", to describe his unexpected discovery [16].

Currently, there is no agreement on definition of serendipity in recommender systems. Researchers employ different definitions in their studies. In this paper, we employ the most common definition, which indicates that serendipitous items are relevant, novel and unexpected [2,10,12].

---

[3] http://www.thefreedictionary.com/serendipity.

Given the importance of serendipity, researchers have proposed different serendipity-oriented recommendation algorithms. For example, Lu et al. presented a serendipitous personalized ranking algorithm [15]. The algorithm is based on matrix factorization with the objective function that incorporates relevance and popularity of items. Another matrix factorization based algorithm is proposed by Zheng, Chan and Ip [24]. The authors proposed the unexpectedness-augmented utility model, which takes into account relevance, popularity and similarity of items to a user profile. In contrast, Zhang et al. provided the recommendation algorithm *Full Auralist* [23]. It consists of three algorithms, each being responsible for relevance, diversity and unexpectedness. To the best of our knowledge, studies that focus on improving serendipity using source domains are of restricted availability.

2.2 Cross-Domain Recommendations

Cross-domain recommender systems use multiple domains to generate recommendations, which can be categorized based on domain levels [4,5]:

- Attribute level. Items have the same type and attributes. Two items are assigned to different domains if they have different values of a particular attribute. A pop song and jazz song might belong to different domains.
- Type level. Items have similar types and share some common attributes. Two items are assigned to different domains if they have different subsets of attributes. A photograph and animated picture might belong to different domains. Even though both items have common attributes, such as a title, publisher and tags, other attributes might be different (duration attribute for animated pictures).
- Item level. Items have different types and all or almost all attributes. Two items are assigned to different domains if they have different types. A song and book might belong to different domains, as almost all attributes of the items are different.
- System level. Two items are assigned to different domains if they belong to different systems. For example, movies from IMDb[4] and MovieLens[5] might belong to different domains.

Depending on whether overlapping occurs in the set of users or items [7], there are four situations that enable cross-domain recommendations: (a) no overlap between items and users, (b) user sets of different domains overlap while item sets do not overlap, (c) item sets overlap while user sets do not overlap, and (d) item and user sets overlap.

Most efforts on cross-domain recommendations focus on the situation when users or both users and items overlap [13]. For example, Sang demonstrated the feasibility of utilizing the source domain. The study was conducted on a

---

[4] http://www.imdb.com/.
[5] https://movielens.org/.

dataset collected from Twitter[6] and YouTube[7]. The author established relationships between items from different domains using topics [19]. Similarly to Sang, Shapira, Rokach and Freilikhman also linked items from different domains, where 95 participants rated movies and allowed the researches to collect data from their Facebook pages [20]. The results suggested that source domains improve the recommendation performance [20]. Another study with positive results was conducted by Abel et al. The dataset contained information related to the same users from 7 different OSNs [1]. Sahebi and Brusilovsky demonstrated the usefulness of recommendations based on source domains to overcome cold start problem [18].

Most works on cross-domain recommendations focus on accuracy. To the best of our knowledge, the efforts on the impact of source domains on the target domain in terms of serendipity involving a real cross-domain dataset are very limited. In this paper, we investigate whether source domains can improve serendipity in the target domain when only items overlap on system level.

3 Datasets

Due to the lack of publicly available datasets for cross-domain recommender systems with overlapping items [3,11] we collected data from VK and FM. The construction of the dataset included three phases (Fig. 1): (1) VK recordings collection, (2) duplicates matching, and (3) FM recordings collection.

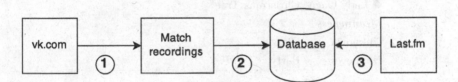

Fig. 1. Data collection chart.

3.1 VK Recordings Collection

The VK interface provides the functionality to add favored recordings to users' pages. By generating random user IDs we collected accessible VK users' favored audio recordings using VK API. Each audio recording is represented by its metadata excluding the actual audio file. Our VK dataset consists of $97,737$ ($76,177$ unique) audio recordings added by 864 users.

Each VK user is allowed to share any audio or video recording. The interface of the OSN provides the functionality to add favored recordings to the users page. VK users are allowed not only to add favored audio recordings to their

---

[6] https://twitter.com/.

[7] https://www.youtube.com/.

pages, but also to rename them. The dataset thus contains a noticeable number of duplicates with different names. To assess this number we randomly selected 100 VK recordings and manually split them into three categories:

– Correct names - the name of the recording is correctly written without any grammatical mistakes or redundant symbols.
– Misspelled names - the name is guessable, even if the name of the recording is replaced with the combination of artist and recording name or lyrics.
– Meaningless names - the name does not contain any information about the recording. For example, "unknown" artist and "the song" recording.

Out of 100 randomly selected recordings we detected 14 misspelled and 2 meaningless names. The example can be seen from Table 1.

Table 1. Examples of recordings.

Artist name	Recording name
Correct names	
Beyonce	Halo
Madonna	Frozen
Misspelled	
Alice DJ	Alice DJ - Better of Alone.mp3
Reamonn	Oh, tonight you kill me with your smile
● Lady Gaga	Christmas Tree
Meaningless	
Unknown	Classic
Unknown	Party

3.2 Duplicates Matching

To match misspelled recordings, we developed a duplicate matching algorithm that detects duplicates based on recordings' names, mp3 links and durations. The algorithm compares recordings' names based on the Levenshtein distance and the number of common words excluding stop words.

We then removed some popular meaningless recordings such as "Unknown", "1" or "01", because they represent different recordings and do not indicate user preferences. Furthermore, some users assign wrong popular artists' names to the recordings. To restrict the growth of these kinds of mistakes, the matching algorithm considers artists of the duplicate recordings to be different. By using the presented matching approach, the number of unique recordings decreased from 76, 177 to 68, 699.

3.3   FM Recordings Collection

To utilize the source domain we collected FM recordings that correspond to 48,917 selected VK recordings that were added by at least two users or users that have testing data. Each FM recording contains descriptions such as FM tags added by FM users. FM tags indicate additional information such as genre, language or mood. Overall, we collected 10,962 overlapping FM recordings and 20,214 (2,783 unique) FM tags.

It is also possible to obtain FM users who like a certain recording (top fans). For each FM recording, we collected FM users who like at least one more FM recording from our dataset according to the distribution of VK users among those recordings. In fact, some unpopular FM recordings are missing top fans. We thus collected 17,062 FM users, where 7,083 of them like at least two recordings from our database. FM users liked 4,609 FM recordings among those collected.

3.4   The Statistics of the Datasets

In this work, we constructed three datasets. Each of them includes the collected FM data and different parts of the VK data (percentage indicates the fraction of overlapping items):

- 100% - the dataset contains only overlapping recordings picked by VK and FM users;
- 50% - the dataset contains equal number of overlapping and non-overlapping recordings;
- 7% - the dataset contains all collected VK and FM recordings. The fraction of overlapping recordings is 6.7%.

The 7% dataset contains all the collected and processed data. We presented results for 50% and 100% datasets to demonstrate how serendipity and accuracy change when a dataset contains different fraction of overlapping items.

Table 2. The statistics of the datasets.

	100%		50%		7%	
	VK	FM	VK	FM	VK	FM
Users	665	7,083	795	7,083	864	7,083
Ratings	14,526	40,782	33,680	40,782	96,737	40,782
Items	4,609	4,609	9,218	4,609	68,699	4,609
Artists	1,986	1,986	4,595	1,986	31,861	1,986
Tags	-	20,167	-	20,167	-	20,167

The statistics of the datasets are presented in Table 2. The number of VK users varies in different datasets, due to the lack of ratings after removing non-overlapping VK recordings.

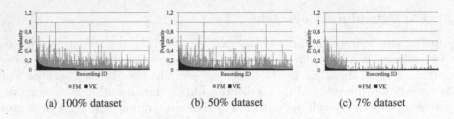

(a) 100% dataset   (b) 50% dataset   (c) 7% dataset

Fig. 2. Popularity distributions of VK and FM datasets.

According to Fig. 2, each recording has different popularity among VK and FM users. The FM dataset contains rich information in terms of user ratings regarding recordings unpopular in the VK dataset. In the figure, popularity is based on the number of users who picked a particular item:

$$Popularity_i = \frac{Freq(i)}{Freq_{max}},\tag{1}$$

where $Freq(i)$ is the number of users who picked recording i, while $Freq_{max}$ corresponds to the maximum number of users picked the same recording in a dataset.

4   Recommendation Approaches

In this section, we implement and observe simple but popular collaborative filtering and content-based filtering algorithms to demonstrate the impact of the data from source domains.

4.1   Item-Based Collaborative Filtering

We chose item-based collaborative filtering as the first experimental algorithm. It is a representative recommendation algorithm that has been widely used in industry due to its scalability [8]. In item-based collaborative filtering, each audio recording (item) is represented as a vector in a multidimensional feature space, where each feature is a user's choice (rating). VK recording is represented as follows: $i^{vk} = (u_{1,i}^{vk}, u_{2,i}^{vk}, ..., u_{n,i}^{vk})$, and each element $u_{k,i}^{vk} \in \{0, 1\}$ for $k = 1, ..., \|U\|$, where U is a set of users, while $u_{k,i}^{vk}$ equals to 1 if VK user k picks VK recording i^{vk} and 0 otherwise. To integrate the source domain (FM) with our target domain (VK), we included FM users as follows: $i^{vkfm} = (u_{1,i}^{vk}, u_{2,i}^{vk}, ..., u_{n,i}^{vk}, u_{1,i}^{fm}, u_{2,i}^{fm}, ..., u_{n,i}^{fm})$.

To generate recommendations, item-based collaborative filtering first detects recordings that are most similar to recordings picked by the target user. The algorithm then ranks recordings based on the obtained similarities.

To measure similarity, we used conditional probability, which is a common similarity measure for situations in which users only indicate items they like

without specifying how much they like these items (unary data) [8]. Conditional
probability is calculated as follows:

$$p(i,j) = \frac{Freq(i \wedge j)}{Freq(i) \cdot Freq(j)^\alpha}, \tag{2}$$

where $Freq(i)$ is the number of users that picked item i, while $Freq(i \wedge j)$ is the
number of users that picked both items i and j. The parameter α is a damping
factor to decrease the similarity for popular items. In our experiments $\alpha = 1$.

Item vectors based on FM users contain remarkably more dimensions than
vectors based on VK users. To alleviate the problem, we compared recordings
using the following rule:

$$sim(i,j) = \begin{cases} p(i^{vk}, j^{vk}), & \exists i^{vk} \wedge \exists j^{vk} \wedge \\ & (\nexists i^{fm} \vee \nexists j^{fm}) \\ p(i^{fm}, j^{fm}), & \exists i^{fm} \wedge \exists j^{fm} \wedge \\ & (\nexists i^{vk} \vee \nexists j^{vk}) \\ p(i^{vkfm}, j^{vkfm}), & \exists i^{vk} \wedge \exists j^{vk} \wedge \\ & \exists i^{fm} \wedge \exists j^{fm} \end{cases} \tag{3}$$

We compared items in each pair using domains that contain user ratings for
both items. To rank items in the suggested list, we used sum of similarities of
recordings [8]:

$$score(u,i) = \sum\nolimits_{j \in I_u} sim(i,j), \tag{4}$$

where I_u is the set of items picked by user u (user profile).

4.2   Content-Based Filtering

We chose content-based filtering algorithm, as this algorithm uses item attributes
instead of user ratings to generate recommendations. In our case, these attributes
are VK - FM artists and FM tags. Each FM artist corresponds to a particular
VK artist.

To represent items, we used a common weighting scheme, term frequency-
inverse document frequency (TF-IDF). TF-IDF weight consists of two parts:

$$tfidf_{attr,i} = tf_{attr,i} \cdot idf_{attr}, \tag{5}$$

where $tf_{attr,i}$ corresponds to the frequency of attribute $attr$ for item i (term
frequency), while idf_{attr} corresponds to the inverse frequency of attribute $attr$
(inverse document frequency). The term frequency is based on the number of
times an attribute appears among attributes of an item with respect to the
number of item attributes:

$$tf_{attr,i} = \frac{n_{attr,i}}{n_i}, \tag{6}$$

where n_i is the number of attributes of item i, while $n_{attr,i}$ is the number of times
attribute $attr$ appears among attributes of item i. In our case, $n_{attr,i} = 1$ for each

item, while n_i varies depending on the item. The term frequency increases with the decrease of the number of item attributes. The inverse document frequency is based on the number of items with an attribute in the dataset:

$$idf_{attr} = ln\frac{||I||}{||I_{attr}||},\tag{7}$$

where I is a set of all the items, while I_{attr} is a set of items that have attribute $attr$. The inverse document frequency is high for rare attributes and low for popular ones. TF-IDF weighting scheme assigns high weights to rare attributes that appear in items with low number of attributes.

An audio recording is represented as follows: $i^a = (a_{1,i}, a_{2,i}, ..., a_{d,i})$, where $a_{k,i}$ corresponds to the TF-IDF weight of artist a_k [14]. The user is represented as follows: $u^a = (a_{1,u}, a_{2,u}, ..., a_{d,u})$, where $a_{k,u}$ corresponds to the number of recordings picked by user u performed by artist a_k.

To integrate FM data, we considered FM tags as follows: $i^{at} = (a_{1,i}, a_{2,i}, ..., a_{d,i}, t_{1,i}, t_{2,i}, ..., t_{q,i})$, where $t_{k,i}$ corresponds to the TF-IDF weight of tag t_k [14]. The user vector then is denoted as follows: $u^{at} = (a_{1,u}, a_{2,u}, ..., a_{d,u}, t_{1,u}, t_{2,u}, ..., t_{q,u})$, where $t_{k,u}$ is the number of recordings picked by user u having tag t_k.

The recommender system compares audio recordings' vectors and a user vector using cosine similarity [8]:

$$cos(u, i) = \frac{u \cdot i}{||u||||i||},\tag{8}$$

where u and i are user and item vectors. To suggest recordings, content-based filtering ranks recordings according to $cos(u, i)$. In our experiments, we used $cos(u^a, i^a)$ for VK data and $cos(u^{at}, i^{at})$ for VK and FM data.

5   Experiments

In this section, we detail experiments conducted to demonstrate whether the source domain improves serendipity and accuracy in the target domain when only items overlap.

5.1   Evaluation Metrics

To assess the performance of algorithms we used two metrics: (1) $Precision@K$ to measure accuracy and (2) a traditional serendipity metric $Ser@K$.

$Precision@K$ is a commonly used metric to assess quality of recommended lists with binary relevance. In our datasets, recordings added by a user to his/her page are relevant, while the rest of the recordings are irrelevant to the user. $Precision@K$ reflects the fraction of relevant recordings retrieved by a recommender system in the first K results. The metric is calculated as follows:

$$Precision@K = \frac{1}{||U||}\sum_{u \in U}\frac{||RS_u(K) \cap REL_u||}{K},\tag{9}$$

where U is a set of users, while $RS_u(K)$ is a set of top-K suggestions for user u. Recordings from the test set (ground truth) for user u are represented by REL_u.

The traditional serendipity metric is based on (1) a primitive recommender system, which suggests items known and expected by a user, and (2) a set of items similar to a user profile. Evaluated recommendation algorithms are penalized for suggesting items that are irrelevant, generated by a primitive recommender system or included in the set of items similar to a user profile. Similarly to [2], we used a slight modification of the serendipity metric:

$$Ser@K = \frac{1}{||U||} \sum_{u \in U} \frac{||(RS_u(K) \setminus PM \setminus E_u) \cap REL_u||}{K}, \tag{10}$$

where PM is a set of suggestions generated by the primitive recommender system, while E_u is a set of recordings similar to recordings picked by user u. We selected the 10 most popular recordings for PM following one of the most common strategies [15,24]. Set of items similar to a user profile E_u represents all the recordings that have common artists with recordings user u picked. User u can easily find recordings from set E_u by artist name, we therefore regard these recordings as obvious.

5.2   Results

Following the datasets sampling strategy in [8], we split each of our datasets into training and test datasets and applied 3-fold cross-validation. We selected 40% of the users who picked the most VK recordings, and chose 30% of their ratings as the testing dataset. We then regarded the rest of the ratings as the training dataset.

To compare the results of various baselines, we used offline evaluation. The recommender system suggested 30 popular VK recordings to each testing VK user excluding recordings that the user has already added in the training set. In each approach the recommendation list consists of the same items. We chose popular items for evaluation, as the users are likely to be familiar with those items.

In this study, we demonstrate serendipity and accuracy improvements resulting from the source domain with three simple but popular algorithms: (1) POP, (2) Collaborative Filtering (CF), and (3) Content-Based Filtering (CBF). It is important to note that POP is a non-personalized recommendation algorithm, which orders items in the suggested list according to their popularity in the VK dataset. For the CF and the CBF algorithms, we obtained two performance results based on (1) data collected from VK and (2) data collected from both VK and FM.

- **POP** - ordering items according to their popularity using the VK dataset.
- **CF(VK)** - item-based collaborative filtering using the VK dataset.
- **CF(VKFM)** - item-based collaborative filtering using VK and FM datasets.
- **CBF(VK)** - content-based filtering using the VK dataset.

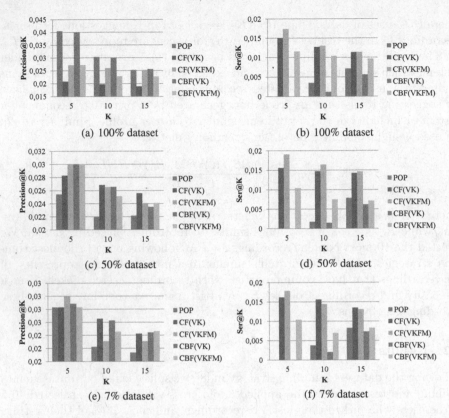

Fig. 3. *Precision@K* and *Ser@K* for experiments conducted using datasets with different fractions of non-overlapping items.

– **CBF(VKFM)** - content-based filtering using VK and FM datasets.

Figure 3 demonstrates the experimental results based on three datasets presented in Sect. 3. From the figure we can observe that:

1. The source domain can improve serendipity in the target domain. On all datasets, CBF based on VK and FM data outperforms CBF based on only VK data in terms of serendipity. For collaborative filtering the situation is very similar, except the decrease of serendipity for recommendation lists of length 10 and 15 on the 7% dataset. For the 50% dataset, the CF algorithm achieves 0.0156, 0.0147 and 0.0142 in terms of *Ser@5*, *Ser@10* and *Ser@15* based on VK data, while these numbers are 0.0190, 0.0164 and 0.0146 based on VK and FM data, making the improvement of 22.2%, 11.7% and 2.7%, respectively.

2. For collaborative filtering, the source domain can improve accuracy in the target domain when only items overlap. For the 100% dataset, the CF algorithm achieves 0.0208, 0.0196 and 0.0189 in terms of *Precision@5*, *Precision@10* and *Precision@15* based on VK data, while these numbers are 0.0271, 0.0260

and 0.0252 based on VK and FM data, making the improvement of 30.6%, 32.4% and 33.7%, respectively.

3. The improvement of accuracy declines with the growth of non-overlapping items for collaborative filtering. The improvement of CF in terms of *Precision*@5 decreases as follows: 30.6%, 6.1% and 6.0% using 100%, 50% and 7% datasets, respectively.

4. The source domain decreases accuracy of content-based filtering. For the 100% dataset, CBF based on VK and FM data decreases *Precision*@5, *Precision*@10 and *Precision*@15 by 31.9%, 24.0% and 11.2%, respectively.

5. Despite being accurate, popularity baseline has a very low serendipity. POP outperforms other algorithms in terms of accuracy on the 100% dataset. Meanwhile, the algorithm fails to suggest any serendipitous items in top-5 recommendations on each dataset.

According to observations 1 and 2, CF(VKFM) outperforms CF(VK) in terms of both serendipity and accuracy. The improvement of accuracy illustrates the global correlation of user preferences in different domains [9,22]. Although, the data belongs to different domains, user ratings from the source domain indicate similarities between items that improve the recommendation performance in the target domain. The improvement of serendipity is caused by the growth of accuracy and by different popularity distributions in VK and FM datasets.

Observation 3 supports the claim [9], that the improvement caused by the source domain rises with the growth of the overlap between target and source domains. The decrease of accuracy for the CF algorithm with the FM data is caused by the different lengths of item vectors in source and target domains, where vectors of FM items contain significantly more dimensions than vectors of VK items.

Observations 1 and 4 indicate that the FM data positively contributes to serendipity and negatively affects accuracy of the content-based filtering algorithm. As users tend to add recording of the same artist, CBF(VK) significantly outperforms CBF(VKFM). However, most recordings suggested by CBF(VK) are obvious to a user, as the user can find these recordings him/herself. As a result, the serendipity of CBF(VK) is very low. FM tags help recommend similar recordings of artists novel to the user. Recordings that share the same FM tags do not necessarily share the same artists, which results in the decrease of accuracy and increase of serendipity.

Observation 5 indicates that POP has very low serendipity, despite being accurate. Popular recommendations are likely to be accurate, as users tend to add familiar recordings. However, popular recordings are widely recognized by users and therefore regarded as obvious.

6   Conclusion

In this paper, we first initially investigated the cross-domain recommendation problem in terms of serendipity. We collected data from VK and FM and built three datasets that contain different fractions of non-overlapping items from source and target domains. We then conducted extensive experiments with collaborative filtering and content-based filtering algorithms to demonstrate the impact of source domains on performance gains of the target domain.

According to our results, the source domain can improve serendipity in the target domain when only items overlap on system level for both collaborative filtering and content-based filtering algorithms. The integration of the source domain resulted in the decrease of accuracy for content-based filtering and the increase of accuracy for collaborative filtering. Similarly to [9] our results indicated that the more items overlap in source and target domains with respect to the whole dataset the higher the improvement of accuracy for collaborative filtering.

Acknowledgement. The research at the University of Jyväskylä was performed in the MineSocMed project, partially supported by the Academy of Finland, grant #268078. The communication of this research was supported by Daria Wadsworth.

References

1. Abel, F., Herder, E., Houben, G.J., Henze, N., Krause, D.: Cross-system user modeling and personalization on the social web. User Model. User-Adap. Inter. **23**, 169–209 (2013)
2. Adamopoulos, P., Tuzhilin, A.: On unexpectedness in recommender systems: or how to better expect the unexpected. ACM Trans. Intell. Syst. Technol. **5**, 1–32 (2014)
3. Berkovsky, S., Kuflik, T., Ricci, F.: Mediation of user models for enhanced personalization in recommender systems. User Model. User-Adap. Inter. **18**, 245–286 (2008)
4. Cantador, I., Cremonesi, P.: Tutorial on cross-domain recommender systems. In: Proceedings of the 8th ACM Conference on Recommender Systems, New York, NY, USA, pp. 401–402 (2014)
5. Cantador, I., Fernández-Tobías, I., Berkovsky, S., Cremonesi, P.: Cross-domain recommender systems. In: Ricci, F., Rokach, L., Shapira, B. (eds.) Recommender Systems Handbook, pp. 919–959. Springer, Boston (2015). doi:10.1007/978-1-4899-7637-6_27
6. Celma Herrada, Ò.: Music recommendation and discovery in the long tail. Ph.D. thesis, Universitat Pompeu Fabra (2009)
7. Cremonesi, P., Tripodi, A., Turrin, R.: Cross-domain recommender systems. In: 11th IEEE International Conference on Data Mining Workshops, pp. 496–503 (2011)
8. Ekstrand, M.D., Riedl, J.T., Konstan, J.A.: Collaborative filtering recommender systems. Found. Trends Hum. Comput. Interact. **4**, 81–173 (2011)
9. Fernández-Tobías, I., Cantador, I., Kaminskas, M., Ricci, F.: Cross-domain recommender systems: a survey of the state of the art. In: Proceedings of the 2nd Spanish Conference on Information Retrieval, pp. 187–198 (2012)
10. Iaquinta, L., Semeraro, G., de Gemmis, M., Lops, P., Molino, P.: Can a recommender system induce serendipitous encounters? IN-TECH (2010)
11. Kille, B., Hopfgartner, F., Brodt, T., Heintz, T.: The plista dataset. In: Proceedings of the 2013 International News Recommender Systems Workshop and Challenge, pp. 16–23. ACM, New York (2013)

12. Kotkov, D., Veijalainen, J., Wang, S.: Challenges of serendipity in recommender systems. In: Proceedings of the 12th International Conference on Web Information Systems and Technologies. SCITEPRESS (2016)
13. Kotkov, D., Wang, S., Veijalainen, J.: Cross-domain recommendations with overlapping items. In: Proceedings of the 12th International Conference on Web Information Systems and Technologies, vol. 2, pp. 131–138. SCITEPRESS (2016)
14. Lops, P., de Gemmis, M., Semeraro, G.: Content-based recommender systems: state of the art and trends. In: Ricci, F., Rokach, L., Shapira, B., Kantor, P. (eds.) Recommender Systems Handbook, pp. 73–105. Springer, Boston (2011). doi:10.1007/978-0-387-85820-3_3
15. Lu, Q., Chen, T., Zhang, W., Yang, D., Yu, Y.: Serendipitous personalized ranking for top-n recommendation. In: Proceedings of the IEEE/WIC/ACM International Joint Conferences on Web Intelligence and Intelligent Agent Technology, pp. 258–265. IEEE Computer Society, Washington, DC (2012)
16. Remer, T.G.: Serendipity and the Three Princes: From the Peregrinaggio of 1557. University of Oklahoma Press, Norman (1965)
17. Ricci, F., Rokach, L., Shapira, B.: Introduction to recommender systems handbook. In: Ricci, F., Rokach, L., Shapira, B., Kantor, P. (eds.) Recommender Systems Handbook, pp. 1–35. Springer, Boston (2011). doi:10.1007/978-0-387-85820-3_1
18. Sahebi, S., Brusilovsky, P.: Cross-domain collaborative recommendation in a cold-start context: the impact of user profile size on the quality of recommendation. In: Carberry, S., Weibelzahl, S., Micarelli, A., Semeraro, G. (eds.) UMAP 2013. LNCS, vol. 7899, pp. 289–295. Springer, Heidelberg (2013). doi:10.1007/978-3-642-38844-6_25
19. Sang, J.: Cross-network social multimedia computing. User-centric Social Multimedia Computing. ST, pp. 81–99. Springer, Heidelberg (2014). doi:10.1007/978-3-662-44671-3_5
20. Shapira, B., Rokach, L., Freilikhman, S.: Facebook single and cross domain data for recommendation systems. User Model. User-Adap. Inter. 23, 211–247 (2013)
21. Tacchini, E.: Serendipitous mentorship in music recommender systems. Ph.D. thesis, Università degli Studi di Milano (2012)
22. Winoto, P., Tang, T.: If you like the devil wears prada the book, will you also enjoy the devil wears prada the movie? A study of cross-domain recommendations. New Gener. Comput. 26, 209–225 (2008)
23. Zhang, Y.C., Séaghdha, D.O., Quercia, D., Jambor, T.: Auralist: introducing serendipity into music recommendation. In: Proceedings of the 5th ACM International Conference on Web Search and Data Mining, pp. 13–22. ACM, New York (2012)
24. Zheng, Q., Chan, C.-K., Ip, H.H.S.: An unexpectedness-augmented utility model for making serendipitous recommendation. In: Perner, P. (ed.) ICDM 2015. LNCS, vol. 9165, pp. 216–230. Springer, Cham (2015). doi:10.1007/978-3-319-20910-4_16

A Layered Architecture for Sentiment Classification of Products Reviews in Italian Language

Franco Chiavetta[1,2], Giosuè Lo Bosco[2,3(✉)], and Giovanni Pilato[4]

[1] Istituto Tecnico Settore Tecnologico Vittorio Emanuele III,
Via Duca della Verdura 48, 90143 Palermo, Italy
franco.chiavetta@istruzione.it
[2] Dipartimento di Matematica e Informatica,
Università degli studi di Palermo, Via Archirafi 34, 90123 Palermo, Italy
giosue.lobosco@unipa.it
[3] Dipartimento di Scienze per l'Innovazione tecnologica,
Istituto Euro-Mediterraneo di Scienza e Tecnologia,
Via Michele Miraglia 20, 90139 Palermo, Italy
[4] ICAR-CNR, Viale Delle Scienze - Edificio 11, 90128 Palermo, Italy
giovanni.pilato@cnr.it

Abstract. The paper illustrates a system for the automatic classification of the sentiment orientation expressed into reviews written in Italian language. A proper stratification of linguistic resources is adopted in order to solve the lacking of an opinion lexicon specifically suited for the Italian language. Experiments show that the proposed system can be applied to a wide range of domains.

1 Introduction

Sentiment analysis has the goal of extracting from the web the current opinion toward someone or something through the classification of texts generated by users [1]. The development of automatic tools for Sentiment Analysis is required by the massive and growing amount of user generated opinions currently available on the Web. The research activity in this field is now 15 years old and it is mostly focused on English language texts.

In this work we propose a method for Sentiment Analysis applied to texts written in Italian language. In particular, we have developed and evaluated a linguistic algorithm aimed at classifying Amazon products reviews by using a lexicon-based approach. As a matter of fact in literature the vast majority of approaches in sentiment analysis is suited for the English language, while there is a lack of resources for the Italian language.

Sentiment analysis can be applied to several types of user generated textual contents. This paper is focused on the analysis of Amazon products reviews, a type of user generated content on which research particularly focuses its attention. This is because buyers who are looking online for a certain product without having already decided on a brand or a specific model, trust the opinions

© Springer International Publishing AG 2017
V. Monfort et al. (Eds.): WEBIST 2016, LNBIP 292, pp. 120–141, 2017.
DOI: 10.1007/978-3-319-66468-2_7

expressed by those who have already purchased and the average score of reviews may result in the choice of one product over another one.

We have developed and tuned our classification system making first experiments on reviews of books. Then we have carried out its testing on the following additional products categories: "Electronics" (mainly smartphones, but also products for networking), "Mobile Apps", "Music" (CD and vinyl), "Movies" (DVD and Blue-ray). We considered reviews from different categories because, in general, the linguistic level of a review, e.g. the syntactical and grammatical correctness and the richness of used vocabulary, the presence of domain specific terms, changes with the kind of reviewed product.

From the size point of view, a review is usually shorter than a full article of a blog and longer than a microblogging post (e.g. a "tweet"). While the reduced number of available characters to post a tweet does not allow defining complicated and articulated sentences, forcing the writer to employ common opinion-bearing words which easily reveal his sentiment, a review usually replaces the more common opinion-bearing adjectives with more complicated sentences transferring the user sentiment, including irony: a feature that cannot be easily identified. In the design of a sentiment classification algorithm all these factors must be taken into consideration in order to choose the appropriate strategy.

The proposed system splits a text into sentences, and sentences into clauses and then, using NLP techniques, it analyses the context of each evaluable word in order to search neighbor elements that can change/emphasize its polarity, like "valence shifters" [2] and similar combinations. Furthermore, the "out of context" sentiment polarity of a given word is obtained considering what we called "cloud" of the word obtained by deeply searching semantically related terms in a properly combined set of annotated linguistic resources. Polarity scores associated to all the word senses in the cloud are hence combined to assign an overall polarity to the word.

Experiments confirm, in terms of classification accuracy, that the method we propose for Sentiment Analysis of texts written in Italian language reaches similar performances to those reported in literature for the English language.

2   Sentiment Classification Approaches

A "sentiment classifier" is a computational model to predict the "sentiment polarity" of a text, i.e. a positive or a negative opinion toward the target product. A sentiment classifier can be developed by making use of machine learning models or opinion-lexicon based approaches. An extended survey on the sentiment classification approaches is given in the work by Hassan et al. [3].

Based mostly on supervised learning, machine learning approaches are able to predict the polarity class of a document after a proper learning phase of positive and negative examples. Lexicon based approaches [4] make use of lexical resources named *opinion lexicon* [5], that give an association of words to the corresponding sentiment orientation usually represented by positive and negative "scores". The effectiveness of the approach is highly dependent both on the correctness of the preprocessing steps (e.g. the right "part-of-speech" detection) and on the consistency and quality of the opinion lexicon and the coverage, i.e. the number of contained terms.

In the simplest form an opinion lexicon is a text file [6]. Words can be tagged with strings (e.g. {"Positive", "Negative"}), binary values (e.g. $\{-1, +1\}$) or continuous numerical scores in a given range (e.g. $[-1.0, +1.0]$) whose values represent their sentiment polarity strength. The annotation can be done either manually or by automatic semi-supervised processes that, using linguistic resources like corpora [7], a thesaurus, or a more sophisticated one like Wordnet [8,9], generate the lexicon. According to the chosen linguistic resources and to the annotating process, the resulting opinion lexicon can contain polarities with different meanings. Prior polarities do not need deep semantic analysis or word sense disambiguation [10] to assign a sentiment score to a word. An example of opinion lexicon based on prior polarities is MPQA [11].

In contrast with the prior polarity of a word, there exist the so called *posterior polarities* i.e. the polarities associated to each *word sense*. In such a case, the association *words* ↔ *polarities* is therefore one-to-many.

The most popular opinion lexicon containing posterior polarities associated to English words is SentiWordNet [12].

For what concerns sentiment detection at document level, many approaches try to learn discriminative features from data by using neural networks, which consider only text information [13,14]. Other approaches, like the one presented in [15], take into account also the user and product together with the analyzed document in order to develop an unified neural framework. Empirical studies on the use of Support Vector Machines and Artificial Neural Networks at document-level sentiment analysis has been reported in [16]. According to this study, ANN gives better or at least comparable results to SVMs. In particular, for what concerns the benchmark dataset of Movies reviews, ANN outperformed SVM. However the same study confirmed some potential limitations of both models.

More recently Dong et al. in [17] proposed an Adaptive Recursive Neural Network (AdaRNN) for target-dependent Twitter sentiment classification. The methodology exploits the ability of deep learning models. In particular, their model propagates the sentiments of words towards the target relying on both context and syntactic structure. In [18] Bagging, Boosting, and Random Subspace ensemble have been evaluated over ten public sentiment analysis datasets, showing that using ensemble methods can lead to obtain better results than base learners. In particular, the Random Subspace [19] has obtained the better comparative results.

At present sentiment analysis research is moving from the bag of words to the bag of sentences approach [20].

In [21] the differential effects of the features of various speech acts on sentiment strength have been analyzed. In particular they collected review data from three online customer review sites (Amazon.com, Bn.com, tripadvisor.com) by considering text-based comments with their associated star ratings across two different contexts: books and hotels. The stars have been used by considering that one or two stars are usually associated with negative evaluations, while four or five stars are often related to positive evaluations.

The approach uses dictionaries extracted by the LIWC software, enriched by adding words having strong positive and negative meaning; besides the approach takes into account the presence of attenuation words, positive or negative boosting, and negations, deriving four main sentiment strength variables and their negated forms.

Unfortunately, most of the research activities on Sentiment Analysis is focused on English language. Worse, most of the available resources needed by lexicon based approaches to sentiment classification, such as opinion lexicons, manually labeled corpora and NLP tools, are only available for the English language. The lack of linguistic resources is really a critical issue in all the research works regarding Sentiment Analysis in languages different from English. Several works on sentiment analysis methods applied to non English languages have been proposed, such as German language [22] Japanese Language [23,24], Arabic language [25] and Italian language [26].

Moreover, several solutions to automatically generate resources for a new language, by starting from lexical resources already available for the English language, have been investigated. To work around the lack of resources and tools for a generic language, another common approach is to translate the text in a preprocessing phase by "state of the art" automatic translators, and subsequently applying all traditional steps of the sentiment analysis framework on the obtained English text [27]. Such solution, however, presents several problems including translation precision and disambiguation of words.

3   The Proposed Approach

The overall architecture of the developed system is shown in Fig. 1.

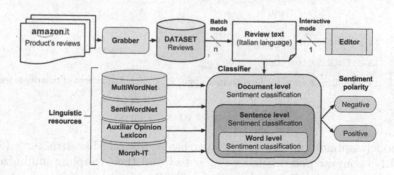

Fig. 1. The system architecture.

The core element is a classifier tuned to perform a sentiment classification task on product reviews written in Italian language. The approach classifies a document on the basis of the average sentiment strengths of its sentences.

The sentiment expressed in the sentences is obtained through the use of tools suited for the Italian language, in all the steps preceding a "scoring phase", i.e. the part of the process that attributes scores to each word in any given sentence of the text. In Sect. 3.1, we describe the approach to obtain scores for Italian words. To this purpose, we will make use of a "concept-based" scoring technique by using Wordnet related lexical resources. In Sect. 3.2 we illustrate the classification algorithm. Experiments and result are illustrated in the Sect. 4.

3.1 Resources for Concept-Based Scoring

To compute the sentiment polarity of a text by the average sentiment strengths of its sentences we need polarity scores for the largest number of terms as possible. Human beings associate sentiment to "concepts" and not to words (i.e. language-dependent strings), often by mediating between different meaning. To simulate this behavior we have to assign scores to a word considering the *cloud of concepts* it evokes (i.e. the set of terms semantically related to it by relationships like *synonymy* or the *IS-A* relationship or similar): we call this approach *concept-based scoring*. Concept-based scoring can be based on Wordnet-like (annotated) resources because they contain two parallel components:

- a *lexical* component, collecting words understood as character strings organized into syntactic categories (nouns, verbs, adjectives, adverbs).
- a *semantic* component, where words are clustered into *synsets* (i.e. lists of synonyms each expressing the same concept) and semantic relationships between concepts (hyperonymy, hyponymy, antinomy, meronymy, etc.) are also represented. Unfortunately, at the best of our knowledge, there are not freely available and well tested high coverage opinion lexicons containing posterior polarities of Italian words. Therefore, to support concept-based storing of Italian words, we modeled a "layered" opinion lexicon made of existing resources organized in a stack as shown in Fig. 2.

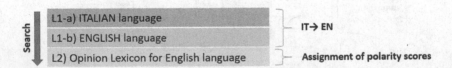

Fig. 2. Linguistic resource layers.

This model assumes that: (1) each layer has a Wordnet-like structure; (2) L1-a and L1-b contain well aligned *word senses* and their coupling minimizes the *lexical gap* between Italian and English; (3) L2 is (as much as possible) a copy of L1-b with annotation of posterior polarities; (4) the size of layers in number of terms can assure an high coverage.

To realize the L1-a and L1-b layers we investigated the use of a "multilingual Wordnet". Since there exist few structural differences between English and Italian languages (see [28]), i.e. there are relatively few cases when a synset of one

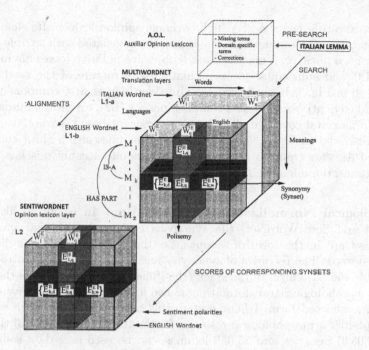

Fig. 3. The stack of lexical resources used as opinion lexicon.

language has no correspondence in the other language (*lexical gap*) we have chosen "MultiWordNet"[1], a multilingual wordnet represented by a set of relational databases built by the "expansion model"[2]. MultiWorNet contains a large Italian Wordnet strongly "aligned" to the English Princeton WordNet (PWN) [8], with a percentage of lexical gap between Italian and English synsets around 1% only. Here the term "alignment" indicates that the corresponding terms have the same index keys in the respective relational DB tables. The alignment between Italian and English languages is represented into the three dimensional "lexical matrix" of MultiWordNet as illustrated in the middle of Fig. 3: in the matrix words in a language are indicated by W_j; meanings are indicated by M_i; languages are indicated by L_k. Moreover, the main lexical and semantic relations are also shown. The E_{ij}^l represents intersections. Concerning the second component of the stack (L2), we have compared several opinion lexicons [29–32]. We have chosen SentiWordnet [12] as the best to couple with MultiWordnet because it has been obtained from the annotation of all 117659 synsets of the English

---

[1]MultiWordNet is included into the Open Multilingual Wordnet project (http://compling.hss.ntu.edu.sg/omw/).

[2]In this model the Wordnet for a foreign language is built by adding synsets in correspondence with the PWN synsets, whenever possible, and importing semantic relations from PWN by assuming that, if there are two synsets in PWN and a relation holding between them, the same relation holds between the corresponding synsets in the foreign language.

PWN, representing hence a very high coverage opinion lexicon. Its elements are named *senti_synsets* because each one is a synset associated with a triple (P,N,O) of scores, i.e. a positive, a negative and a objective polarity scores having values in [0.0, 1.0] and sum equal to one. Finally, the structure of the used stack is represented in Fig. 3: being based on MultiWordnet as first component (L1-a, L1-b), and on SentiWordNet as second component (L2), we get a minimal lexical gap and a maximal coverage allowing to use concept-based scoring.

As illustrated in Figs. 1 and 3 our system includes also a third component we named *Auxiliar Opinion Lexicon*, used to take into account misclassification, missing terms, domain specific terms.

Morphological Normalization/Lemmatization: In resources like Multi-WordNet and SentiWordNet, the synonyms contained within a synset or a senti_synset are in the form of *lemmas*, i.e. the canonical form (or dictionary form) of a word. The retrieval of synonyms and meanings associated to an Italian word in the L1-a layer of the stack (the Italian Wordnet) requires therefore a previous morphological transformation named *lemmatization* that, given a word, returns its inflected form. In our system this task is currently done by means of "Morph-it!", a morphological resource for the Italian language [33] that, containing 505,074 entries and 35,056 lemmas, can be used as a data source for a lemmatizer, morphological analyser, morphological generator.

3.2 Sentiment Classification

The sentiment classification of a document (a review) is executed by the main function $DocumentLevelSC(D, \tau)$ described in the Algorithm 1 figure. Its parameters are the document D and a threshold $\tau \in \mathbb{R}$ used to decide the positive or negative overall polarity of D. In the preprocessing step the $TextCleaner(D)$ function returns a text with fewer ambiguities and errors: it converts all the letters to lower-case, unescapes "html entities", deletes some escape sequences as "\n", "\r", "\t", reduces letters repeated more then three times, recodes accented vowels, corrects "chat style" terms to the corresponding Italian words and other "cleaning" operations. In the tokenization step the $GetSentences(D)$ function splits D into a list of sentences[3] $s_1, s_2, ..., s_k$ detecting sentences boundaries on the basis of punctuation marks ('.', '!', '?'). The overall polarity of the review D is hence obtained comparing the average of the polarity strengths of its sentences (*APS* for short) with the positivity threshold τ. The classifier returns the label 'POS' if APS is above or equal τ, else the label 'NEG' is returned. The most important sub-task here is the $SentenceLevelSC(s)$ function, which assigns a polarity strength score, s_score_i to a sentence $s_i \in D$.

---

[3] A sentence is a linguistic unit consisting of one or more words that are grammatically linked.

Algorithm 1. Sentiment Classification of a document.

---

procedure DOCUMENTLEVELSC(D, τ)

    $D \leftarrow TextCleaner(D)$ ▷ Preprocessing

    $\{s_1, s_2, ..., s_k\} \leftarrow GetSentences(D)$ ▷ Tokenization

    for $i \leftarrow 1, k$ **do**   ▷ Classification of all sentences

        $s\_score_i \leftarrow SentenceLevelSC(s_i)$ ▷ (Algorithm 2)

    end for

    $APS \leftarrow (\sum_{i=1}^{k} s\_score_i)/k$ ▷ Average polarity

    if $APS \geq \tau$ **then**

        $res \leftarrow POS$ ▷ Positive label

    else

        $res \leftarrow NEG$ ▷ Negative label

    end if

    return res ▷ Document polarity class

end procedure

Sentiment Classification of Sentences: A sentence is considered composed by one or more clauses separated by conjunctions ("ma" = "but", "e' '= "and"...), punctuation (',' ";", ":"), or both. We assume that each clause is a portion of text that can express a sentiment independently from other clauses in the same sentence. This assumption obliges us to search clauses separators during the sentence analysis. The first step in $SentenceLevelSC(s)$ function is a part of speech tagging of s with a tool specifically designed for the Italian language: the $POS\_Tagger(s)$ function returns a list TS of r pairs (p, t) where each p is a word of the sentence s and t a *tag* indicating the part of speech p represents. The second step is a parsing of the sequence of pairs (p_i, t_i), $i = 1, 2, ...r$. The overall sentence score is given summing positive and negative scores, named pt_scores_i, associated to the pairs (p_i, t_i), with $i = 1, 2, ...r$. Each pt_scores_i is the product of three factors:

1. the result of the $Weight(p_i, t_i)$ function based on a lookup table (see Table 3) to give different enhancements according to the part of speech tag t_i or to give a proper amplification to a negation term in p_i;
2. the result of the $Sign(F, sp)$ function that, during the parsing, at each step $i = 1, 2, ...r$, keeps or inverts the sign of the polarity based on the *local context* extracted from s and TS.
3. the result of the $WordLevelSC(p_i, t_i)$ function that calculates a positive or negative score for each word in the sentence independently by its local context (Algorithm 3).

Local Context Window: At each step $i = 1, 2, ...r$ of the parsing in the Algorithm 2, the function $GetLocalContext(i, s, TS)$ maintains a local window F of elements from TS and from s preceding the currently analyzed term p_i. So F contains the unigram $((p_i, t_i))$, the bigram $((p_{i-1}, t_{i-1}), (p_i, t_i))$, the trigram $((p_{i-2}, t_{i-2}), (p_{i-1}, t_{i-1}), (p_i, t_i))$ if $i = 1, i = 2, i \geq 3$ respectively. The function also adds to F clause separators as punctuation marks in s, if any, preceding the word p_i.

Algorithm 2. Sentiment Classification of a sentence.

procedure SENTENCELEVELSC(s)
  $\{(p_1, t_1), (p_2, t_2), ..., (p_r, t_r)\} \leftarrow POS\_Tagger(s)$
  $TS \leftarrow \{(p_1, t_1), (p_2, t_2), ..., (p_r, t_r)\}$ ▷ tagged sentences
  $s\_score \leftarrow 0$ ▷ initialization
  $sp \leftarrow +1$ ▷ initial polarity sign (positive)
  for $i \leftarrow 1, r$ **do**   ▷ sequence parsing
    $a \leftarrow Weight(p_i, t_i)$ ▷ amplifications
    $F \leftarrow GetLocalContext(i, s, TS)$ ▷ current window
    $ns \leftarrow Sign(F, sp)$ ▷ calculate new sign
    $w\_score \leftarrow WordLevelSC(p_i, t_i)$ ▷ (Algorithm 3)
    $pt\_score_i \leftarrow a \times ns \times w\_score$ ▷ score for(p_i, t_i)
    $s\_score \leftarrow s\_score + pt\_score_i$ ▷ accumulation
    $sp \leftarrow ns$ ▷ polarity sign update
  end for
  return s_score ▷ sentence polarity strenght
end procedure

The Function Sign (F, Sp): The window F is extracted because the polarity of a term can be flipped if its local context contains some particular combination of items called *valence shifter* [2]. According to the Italian grammar, there are several lexical items combinations acting as valence shifters. Common examples are (a) negation at different levels of syntactic constituency, (b) lexicalized negation in the verb or in adverbs, (c) conditional counterfactual subordinators, (d) double negations with copulative verbs, (e) modals and other modality operators. Since polarities are represented as signed scores, the parser starts initializing with +1 to the sp variable; then at each step i the sign is updated in the ns variable calling the $Sign(F, sp)$ The function uses its parameters F, sp and a set of lists of Italian words to detects items combinations representing valence shifters by using a sequence of *IF-THEN/IF-THEN-ELSE* rules. If the presence of a valence shifter is detected in the current position, the sign to be given to the pt_score_i is flipped, otherwise it is maintained. The sign is also reset each time the function find either conjunctions or punctuation marks in the local context, as colon and semicolon, individuating the start of a new independent clause into the analysed sentence.

Sentiment Classification of Words by Concept-Based Scoring: The function $WordLevelSC(p, t)$ in Algorithm 2 assigns a positive or negative prior polarity score[4] to a single Italian word p, regardless of its local context, on the basis of Algorithm 3. Since we do not perform word sense disambiguation, we have to consider that many words are *polysemous*, e.g. they have multiple meanings and, moreover, the meanings of a word can convey sentiments with opposite

---

[4]We remember that in the used resources both positive and negative polarity scores are unsigned values in the range [0.0, 1.0].

Algorithm 3. Sentiment Classification of a word.

```
 1: procedure WORDLEVELSC(p, t)
 2:     w_score ← 0.0
 3:     lemma ← Normalize(p, t)
 4:     (poss, negs) ← SearchAOL(lemma, t)
 5:     if min(poss, negs) ≥ 0.0 then
 6:         if max(poss, negs) = poss then
 7:             w_score ← poss
 8:         else
 9:             w_score ← −negs
10:         end if
11:         return w_score
12:     end if
13:     senti_synsets_list ← SearchLemmas(lemma, t)
14:     if senti_synsets_list = ∅ then
15:         senti_synsets_list ← SearchCloud(lemma, t)
16:     end if
17:     if senti_synsets_list = ∅ then
18:         senti_synsets_list ← SearchTranslations(p, t)
19:     end if
20:     if ocnti_synsets_list ≠ ∅ then
21:         poss ← 0.0,    negs ← 0.0
22:         ws ← 0.0                                      ▷ weights sum initialization
23:         for all ss ∈ senti_synsets_list do
24:             ps ← ss.pos_score()
25:             ns ← ss.neg_score()
26:             sn ← ss.sense_number()
27:             tt ← ss.tag()
28:             if tt = t then
29:                 ppt ← 1.0
30:             else
31:                 ppt ← 0.75                           ▷ tag mismatch penalty
32:             end if
33:             w ← (1 / 2^{sn−1}) × ppt
34:             ws ← ws+w
35:             poss ← poss + w × ps
36:             negs ← negs + w × ns
37:         end for
38:         poss ← poss/ws
39:         negs ← negs/ws
40:         if min(poss, negs) ≥ 0.0 then
41:             if max(poss, negs) = poss then
42:                 w_score ← poss
43:             else
44:                 w_score ← −negs
45:             end if
46:             return w_score
47:         end if
48:     end if
49:     return w_score
50: end procedure
```

polarities. Instead of using the most frequent meanings our approach uses all the meanings of each given word.

At the beginning the word p is "normalized" into a *lemma* (step 3) by means of Morph-IT (see Subsect. 3.1) and some heuristics to allow retrieval in the stack of lexical resources.

Then the Algorithm 3 tries to search the input pair (p, t) first into the Auxiliar Opinion Lexicon (AOL), in which corrections and terms missing in the lexical resources are stored. The AOL database can also contain domain specific terms: in our application it stores terms typically used in literary criticism and books reviews[5]. If the search in AOL is successful the function returns the polarity score with a proper sign (steps 4–12). Otherwise, the *SearchLemmas*() function searches in the Italian Wordnet lemmas which are synonyms of p, with and without using also its POS-tag t (step 13).

If this attempt fails, the *SearchCloud*() function in Algorithm 3 searches "meanings" in the "cloud" of p i.e. terms semantically close as linked by relationships of type *Is-a*, the set of hyperonyms (and secondarily hyponyms) of p (step 15).

Finally, if also this search fails, the *SearchTranslations*() function algorithm attempts to find other senses, if any, starting from alternative translations of p (step 18).

Each of last three functions uses an Italian lemma to search synsets in the Italian Wordnet, then extracts the corresponding aligned synsets in the English WordNet and finally returns a list of senti-synsets (or an empty list) from SentiWordNet exploiting the alignment again. The final part of the algorithm extracts information from each one of the n senti-synsets s_i in particular positive ($pos(s_i)$) and negative ($neg(s_i)$) posterior polarity scores (steps 24 and 25), sense_number (step 26), tag t (step 27).

Finally, two weighted means are then calculated:

$$poss = \frac{\sum_{i=1}^{n} w(s_i) \times pos(s_i)}{\sum_{i=1}^{n} w(s_i)} \qquad negs = \frac{\sum_{i=1}^{n} w(s_i) \times neg(s_i)}{\sum_{i=1}^{n} w(s_i)}$$

with

$$w(s_i) = \frac{1}{2^{sense\_number-1}} \times ppt$$

where the first factor gives lower weight to less frequent meanings and vice versa, while the second factor is equal to 1.0 for senti-synsets having tag equal to t, or act as a penalty for senti-synsets having POS-tag different from t (we used $ppt = 0.75$ in case of tags mismatch). The Algorithm 3 finally returns the greater of the two weighted means, providing it with a proper sign. This value is the polarity given to the word p with tag t.

---

[5] During the development of the proposed methodology, we have found that some terms in SentiWordNet have opposite polarity signs with respect to the corresponding Italian terms. Moreover, some errors are due to the POS tagger which in some cases applies wrong tags labelling some adjectives as verbs and some verbs as nouns.

4   Development and Refinement of the Classifier, Creation of the AOL, Test

In order to test the proposed method we have developed a framework including: (*a*) a *grabber* to capture products reviews from amazon.it web pages, (*b*) a relational database storing the *dataset*, (*c*) the *classifier*, (*d*) two *wrapper procedures* allowing to run the classifier in two possible modes: a *batch mode*, and an interactive *editor mode*. This framework allowed us to properly parametrize and refine the classifier and to realize a prototype of the AOL performing a first set of experiments on manually written texts and on a preliminary dataset based on books reviews. We have chosen this category of products as first attempt because we expected a better linguistic level respect to the other ones, and this aspect was particularly important to better validate and correct the set of IF-THEN-ELSE rules, as well as the set of weights and parameters of the classifier.

In a second phase, we have collected a much larger dataset containing reviews from several categories in order to evaluate the performances of the classifier.

As known, each Amazon review is written by a single Amazon user and reviews are accompanied by a rating (the number of stars) and a "title". Since Amazon users often write in the title their overall impression about the bought product, our system adds the title as first sentence to the text of each review.

4.1   The Development Dataset

The first dataset was created grabbing from Amazon.it 8255 reviews related to 85 books of various authors and topics. Table 1 shows the number of reviews for each rating level. In this dataset the average lenght of a review is 384 characters, with a standard deviation around 538. The longest review has 19263 characters. We consider positive the reviews having rating above or equal to 4 stars, while those having a rating less or equal to 2 stars are negative. The distribution of reviews per class is given in Table 2 showing that the development dataset, while containing some thousands of reviews, is not perfectly balanced according to the rating. As you see the POS class has a majority (over two thirds) of highly positive reviews, while NEG class is well balanced with almost the same percentage of reviews of two stars and one star. The disproportion between the number of reviews at 4 or 5 stars (POS class) and those with 1 or 2 (NEG class) is "physiological" in the sense that on Amazon.it abundantly prevail, as is normal, the positive reviews. For classification purposes, this disproportion clearly puts the POS class in a "better position" than the NEG one because selecting randomly from the first there is a higher probability of highly positive sentiment strength.

4.2   Creation of the Auxiliar Opinion Lexicon During Early Experiments

The Auxiliary Opinion Lexicon (AOL) has been built to take into account

Table 1. The development dataset.

Rating (stars)	5	4	2	1
# reviews	4342	1963	508	494
Occurrences per review (Avg.)				
adjectives	6.6	7.1	7.5	6.8
nouns	13.5	13.9	15.9	14.3
verbs	8.5	8.6	11.0	10.6
adverbs	0.8	0.7	0.9	0.9

Table 2. Subdivision of the reviews in classes.

Polarity class	Rating	#	%
POS rating ≥ 4	5 stars	4342	68.87%
	4 stars	1963	31.13%
	Total	6305	100.0%
NEG rating ≤ 2	2 stars	508	50.70%
	1 star	494	49.30%
	Total	1002	100.0%

- Missing terms (some Italian terms are missing in Multiwordnet/Sentiwordnet or represents lexical gaps)
- Misclassification (some terms in SentiWordNet have opposite polarity signs with respect to the corresponding Italian terms. e.g. raccomandato (negative) corresponds to recommended (positive))
- Domain specific terms

The absence of this component in the first experiments determined in fact a remarkable percentage of errors in the word level sentiment classification and an overall accuracy not higher than about 60%. The preliminary version of the AOL has been manually created by the following procedure.

First, we applied an Italian Part-Of-Speech tagging to each review in the development dataset; then, all the terms tagged as adjectives, nouns, adverbs and verbs have been lemmatized and searched in the Multiwordnet/Sentiwordnet resource, saving all missing terms in a file. Finally, we have given a priori polarity to each missing term in the file by a manual annotation.

Misclassification errors have been corrected by applying again an Italian Part-Of-Speech tagging to each review in the development dataset and saving in a second file each distinct noun, adjective, adverb and verb together with the polarity assigned it by the word-level classification; then we manually checked if their scores were consistent with corresponding sentiment polarity normally understood in the Italian language. All the misclassified terms have been added to the first file. Regarding domain specific terms for book reviews, we have obtained, from a set of specialized websites and blogs, a list of Italian words (most of which are adjectives and adverbs) typically used in literary criticism; the list has been also expanded using specific terms found in a collection of Italian books reviews on the web. After this set of steps the size of the first release of the AOL was around 800 terms. In the AOL all variations of form of a word representing its declension are compacted into a single stemmed prefix in order to reduce the file size and to facilitate the search.

4.3   Early Experiments on the Development Dataset

The set of weights and the positivity threshold τ on which our classifier depends have been experimentally determined by using two wrapper procedures of the classifier. The first wrapper allows the interactive use of the classifier by means of a GUI whose visual components realize a text Editor. On the edited text we can run the classifier to obtain a detailed trace of the text analysis. This inter-activity allowed us to study misclassification errors and to correct them acting on parameters, e.g. the weights used in parsing of sentences (Algorithm 2) and the positivity threshold τ used in the Algorithm 1. This experimental modality has allowed us to refine also the set of IF-THEN-ELSE rules used in the parsing process (Algorithm 2). Experiments showed that too high weights values tend to give document level average scores with too large standard deviations, not allowing to find a good separation threshold between positive and negative classes. It was also noted that one of the most influential weights for a more correct classification are those given to adjective and adverbs, and to the negatives (the term 'no' and the first successive terms) that are more frequently present in negative sentences. The set of weights found, reported in Table 3 showed a good behaviour of the Sentence Level SC.

Table 3. Look up table of the Weight() function.

Part of speech	Weight
'JJ'	1.1
'RB'	1.1
'VB'	1.06
'VBN'	1.06
'VBG'	1.03
'NN'	1.06
Negation	1.1

Once the classifier has been preliminarily tuned, we estimated the average document polarity for each rating level by using the second wrapper that allows to apply the classification task on subsets of the development dataset in batch mode. To take into account the different review rating distribution as described in Table 2, we extracted a subset of 200 reviews composed of 50 randomly selected reviews for each one of 1,2,4 and 5 stars rating levels. Then we have run the classification in batch mode obtaining the average document polarity scores shown in Table 4.

Table 4. Batch mode experiments results on samples of given rating.

Polarity class	Rating (stars)	Average document polarity
POS	5	+0.098
	4	+0.035
NEG	2	−0.03
	1	−0.07

Using these results and on the basis of the distribution of the rating in the POS and NEG class, we have calculated the expected Document polarity strength for the POS an NEG class as the weighted mean:

$$\mu_{POS} = (0.098 \times 68,87 + 0.035 \times 31.13)/100 = 0.079$$

$$\mu_{NEG} = (-0.03 \times 50,7 - 0.07 \times 49.3)/100 = -0.045$$

where weights are rating percentages.

Finally, the τ parameter has been determined as the arithmetic mean of the above values:

$$\tau = (\mu_{POS} + \mu_{NEG})/2 = (0.079 - 0.045)/2 = 0.017$$

a threshold value slightly positive that adjusts imbalance between the POS and NEG classes.

The last set of early experiments we performed has been finalized to have an estimate of the accuracy reached with the classifier refinement. For this purpose, we have applied the classifier in batch mode on six lots of 200 randomly selected reviews each and 3 of these lots having rating greater than or equal to 4, while the other three having rating less than or equal to 2. The results of these experiments led to the following values of True Positive (TP), False Negative (FN), True Negative (TN) and False Positive (FP): TP = 513, FN = 87, TN = 482, and FP = 118, giving an accuracy of 82.91%, while in terms of precision we have values ranging from 81.29% to 84.71% and in terms of recall we have values ranging from 82.0% to 85.5% obtained from the classifications.

4.4 Baseline Test

In order to have a term of comparison we have realized a baseline test using a reduced lexicon of Italian words that we refer as *OLIT*. It is available to download from Github[6]. This lexicon contains 1382 positive and 3052 negative

---

[6]https://github.com/steelcode/sentiment-lang-italian.

Italian words. We have randomly selected from the dataset one thousand positive (i.e. having rating ≥ 4) and one thousand negative reviews (i.e. having rating ≤ 2). Each review has been preprocessed with the same preprocessor used in the classifier (first step of Algorithm 1). Then for each review it was done the count of positive and negative words of OLIT found in the text and it has been classified positive if the count of positive words exceeds that of the negative, classified negative vice versa, classified neutral if the two counts were equal. This classification paradigm has shown a true positive rate of 78.10% (vs. 85.5% of the proposed classifier) and a true negative rate of 49.63% (vs. 84.71% of the proposed classifier).

4.5 The Complete Dataset and the Final Test

After the completion of the preliminary tests aimed at tuning the classifier and at the creation AOL's, it was made a massive gathering of products reviews in the following categories:

- Books (novels, fiction, essays, fantasy, etc.)
- Electronics (mobile phones, smartphones, networking products, etc.)
- Mobile Apps (games, social apps, utilities, etc.)
- Movies (DVD and BlueRays on various kind of film genres)
- Music (CD and vinyl containing albums of various musical genres)

In total, we collected more than 103, 000 reviews distributed on various categories and ratings as shown in the Table 5. Table 6 shows statistics (mean and standard deviation) about the length of the text in the reviews depending on product category and level of rating.

Reviews with 3 stars rating were not used, we considered as positive reviews the ones showing ratings of 5 and 4 stars, and as negative reviews the others with rating 1 and 2 stars. Reviews with ratings 2 are generally the most rare, especially for "Mobile Apps" and "Music" categories, as if a user plans to publish a negative judgement, he usually uses the minimum rating (1 star).

Table 5. The complete dataset.

Category	Products	Reviews	5 stars	4 stars	3 stars	2 stars	1 star
Books	205	12733	5222	3276	1970	1086	1179
Electronics	288	31299	19412	7330	1926	1063	1568
MobileApps	337	12215	6507	2735	1122	607	1244
Music	484	17544	12989	2509	919	462	665
Movies	432	29681	19945	5536	2028	1002	1170
Total	**1746**	**103472**	**64075**	**21386**	**7965**	**4220**	**5826**

Table 6. Statistic on review text lenght per rating level.

Category	5 stars		4 stars		2 stars		1 star	
	Avg	StdDev	Avg	StdDev	Avg	StdDev	Avg	StdDev
Books	311	391	323	485	360	414	443	544
Electronics	373	586	429	672	461	481	411	436
MobileApps	204	164	201	142	216	142	206	139
Music	247	331	290	376	361	397	355	379
Movies	263	362	333	443	399	381	405	408

4.6   Final Experiments on the Complete Dataset

The performances of the classifier have been finally measured through a series of experiments on the complete dataset. For each one of the five categories (books, electronics, movies, music, apps) we randomly selected a sample of 1200 reviews from the dataset, equally distributed per rating level (300 for each rating class, excluding 3 stars rating). The classifier has been used as it was tuned in the early experiments based on a restricted set of books reviews. The performances of the classifier has been measured in terms of accuracy, precision and recall for each product category. In Table 7 the values of Accuracy (A), Precision on positives (π_{pos}), Recall on positives (ρ_{pos}), Precision on negatives (π_{neg}), Recall on negatives (ρ_{neg}) are shown.

The estimated average accuracy of the classifier computed on the chosen categories is 82.18%. The best performances have been obtained on Electronics products reviews (estimated accuracy of 86%), while the worst ones have been observed for the Movies reviews (79.17%).

Table 7. Performance of the classification method by product category.

Category	TP	FN	TN	FP	A	π_{POS}	ρ_{POS}	π_{NEG}	ρ_{NEG}
Books	491	109	517	83	84,00%	85,54%	81,83%	82,59%	86,17%
Electronics	524	76	508	92	86,00%	85,06%	87,33%	86,99%	84,67%
MobileApps	508	92	481	119	82,42%	81,02%	84,67%	83,94%	80,17%
Music	508	92	444	156	79,33%	76,51%	84,67%	82,84%	74,00%
Movies	505	95	445	155	79,17%	76,52%	84,17%	82,41%	74,17%

4.7   Considerations on Some Kinds of Misclassification

Several misclassification errors have been analyzed by tracing the classification process in interactive modality. We observed that some errors were due to imperfections in the components of the system or to the lack in the framework of some functionalities as a "spelling correction" module. We noticed in fact a certain sensibility to "typing errors" like missing spaces between words, or missing or wrong letters in them that our preprocessing step cannot resolve. Other sources of errors are given by the POS tagger that in some cases assigns erroneous tags.

Anyway, the majority of misclassification were related to the nature of the analyzed documents. Many reviews contain sarcasm. Very often, users insert into negatively rated reviews positive sentences regarding Amazon's delivery service and vice versa. Sometimes the review is on the book format rather than on its contents.

Regarding the category "books", several Amazon users introduce in their reviews comparisons with previous works of the book author, and hence we can have a mix of positive and negative sentences on different objects. Moreover, in reviewing a book the user of Amazon often has a tendency to show his skills as a "literary critic", and hence periods are sometimes very long and articulated and generally complexes.

Similar observations have been done regarding reviews on "electronics" products, that are on average quite long and articulated, full of technical terms on products description.

Conversely, reviews on MobileApps tend to be short, with clearly expressed opinions, some technical terms. In these reviews there are not traces of opinions on delivery service because MobileApps are directly purchased in online stores. It is also not expected the presence of any package and hence reviews regard almost exclusively to products quality, their proper functionality and compatibility with users' systems.

Among the other considered categories, the ones where the classifier performed at worst were "Movies" and "Music" categories, due mostly to the low values of the "recall" index ρ_{NEG} on negative reviews (see Table 7). In most cases, unlike other products such as books or electronics, a user buys a CD or DVD when he already knows the music album or movie. Bad reviews on these two categories of products are more concentrated on delayed delivery, damaged packaging, presence of defects on the media, wrong item, rather than on the product itself.

4.8   On Three Stars Reviews and Neutral Class

In this work we have not considered three stars reviews because Amazon users normally use this level of rating to manifest neither satisfaction nor displeasure with a particular product. As consequence, they tend to write texts without a clear positive or negative sentiment strength that can be considered neutral in a document-level classification. In lexicon-based approaches the overall neutrality of a text can derive either by the absence of polarized words, or by the presence of an almost equal number of positive and negative terms, resulting in a near-zero sentiment strength. In several sentiment analysis tasks neutral texts can be ignored when it can be assumed that they not convey significant information with regard to the opinion the users have about products or given targets. Moreover, depending on the nature of the data and of the application, it may be useful or necessary to assume that the examined text can also be neutral (NEU). In these cases neutral class should not be considered as a boundary between positive and negative classes but as a class of its own, representing either the lack of sentiment, or a balanced mix of positive and negative sentiments in the same text. Our binary classifier, comparing a single overall measure to a unique threshold to decide on positiveness or negativeness of a given text (see Algorithm 1), has good performances on clearly opinionated reviews, but cannot recognize neutral ones. In order to classify also neutral (three stars) reviews, and hence to expand the range of its possible applications, we are developing a new version of the system including an updated release of the lexicon-based classifier. This new system is giving encouraging results and a better overall accuracy in the early experiments, according to what is stated in [34].

4.9   Automatic Construction/Expansion of the AOL and Domain-Orientation

Even if manual construction of the AOL can provide high quality and accuracy, it is a really an heavy task. Automatic approaches have to been investigated in order to add missing terms in the main lexical resources (SentiWordnet/Multiwordnet), in order to correct the polarities given by differences between Italian and English languages and to introduce domain specific terms. While corrections and missing terms are mostly related to ordinary language words, and thus their polarity can be easily deduced/assigned from their common senses, domain specific terms are critical because their number can be very large and, moreover, they may differ in each domain. A possible simple strategy to construct a domain-related lexicon consists in the adoption of annotated domain-related reviews corpus in the way that the assignment or update of the polarity of a word is subjected to the statistic of its occurrence in labeled reviews (e.g. Tf-Idf scores or some of their variants) strongly suggest a given polarity class. In [35] authors use Bayesian decision theory to handle sentiment scores as stocastic variable and using this view to apply polarity adjustments in order to improve the performances in a specific domain. In [36] authors combine domain-specific word embeddings with a label propagation procedure to generate accurate domain-specific sentiment lexicons starting from a small sets of seed words, reaching state-of-the-art performances comparable with approaches that rely on hand-curated resources. As a future work we consider to investigate the construction of the domain specific part of the AOL following the approach given in [37].

5   Conclusions and Future Works

In this work it has been illustrated the evolution of a previously proposed approach [38] suited for the Italian language, showing that concept-based scoring of words allows us both to abstract from the used language and to classify the sentiment of single words. Differently from other schemes that use SentiWordnet simply like a dictionary to score documents, our approach uses the lexical resources to find terms semantically close to the one to be scored, finding the so called "cloud of concepts" of the considered word. Moreover, errors and missing terms, as well as dominion specific terms can be corrected by using an Auxiliary Opinion Lexicon integrating the main resources. At sentence level SC, concept-based scoring together with NLP techniques using language specific grammars rules of the underlying language (IT), can be used to properly combine scores given to words. Even if manual construction of the AOL can provide high quality and accuracy, it is a really an heavy task. Future works will include the adaptive activation of domain specific AOL, the refinement of the set of rules used in the sign function, the improvement of other components of the system and introduction of an opinion summarization stage. Furthermore, we will focus our efforts on recognizing irony and sarcasm in particular for the Italian language, by considering an hybrid machine learning and rule based approach.

References

1. Liu, B.: Sentiment Analysis and Opinion Mining. Morgan & Claypool Publishers, San Rafael (2012)
2. Polanyi, L., Zaenen, A.: Contextual valence shifters. In: Croft, W.B., Shanahan, J., Qu, Y., Wiebe, J. (eds.) Computing Attitude and Affect in Text: Theory and Applications. The Information Retrieval Series, vol. 20, pp. 1–10. Springer, Netherlands (2006)
3. Hassan, A., Korashy, H., Medhat, W.: Sentiment analysis algorithms and applications - a survey. Ain Shams Eng. J. 5, 1093–1113 (2014)
4. Taboada, M., Brooke, J., Tofiloski, M., Voll, K., Stede, M.: Lexicon-based methods for sentiment analysis. Comput. Linguist. 37, 267–307 (2011)
5. Hu, M., Liu, B.: Mining and summarizing customer reviews. In: Proceedings of the ACM International Conference on Knowledge Discovery & Data Mining (SIGKDD), pp. 168–177 (2004)
6. http://www.cs.uic.edu/~liub/FBS/opinion-lexicon-English.rar
7. Littman, P., Turney, M.: Unsupervised learning of semantic orientation from a hundred-billion-word corpus. Technical report, National Research Council Canada, Institute for Information Technology (2002)
8. Fellbaum, C.: WordNet: An Electronic Lexical Database. MIT Press, Cambridge (1998)
9. Dragut, E.C., Yu, C., Sistla, P., Meng, W.: Construction of a sentimental word dictionary. In: ACM International Conference on Information and Knowledge Management (CIKM 2010), pp. 1761–1764 (2010)
10. Navigli, R.: Word sense disambiguation: a survey. ACM Comput. Surv. 41, 10:1–10:69 (2009)
11. Wilson, T., Wiebe, J., Hoffmann, P.: Recognizing contextual polarity in phrase-level sentiment analysis. In: Proceedings of the Conference on Human Language Technology and Empirical Methods in Natural Language Processing (HLT/EMNLP 2005), pp. 347–354 (2005)
12. Esuli, A., Sebastiani, F., Baccianella, S.: Sentiwordnet 3.0: an enhanced lexical resource for sentiment analysis and opinion mining. In: Proceedings of the 7th Conference on International Language Resources and Evaluation (LREC 2010), pp. 2200–2204 (2010)

13. Socher, R., Perelygin, A., Wu, J., Chuang, J., Manning, C.D., Ng, A., Potts, C.: Recursive deep models for semantic compositionality over a sentiment treebank. In: EMNLP, pp. 1631–1642 (2013)

14. Kalchbrenner, N., Grefenstette, E., Blunsom, P.: A convolutional neural network for modelling sentences. In: ACL, pp. 655–665 (2014)

15. Tang, D., Qin, B., Liu, T.: Learning semantic representations of users and products for document level sentiment classification. In: ACL (1), Jul 2015, pp. 1014–1023 (2015)

16. Moraes, R., Valiati, J., Neto, W.: Document-level sentiment classification: an empirical comparison between SVM and ANN. Expert Syst. Appl. **40**(2), 621–33 (2013)

17. Dong, L., Wei, F., Tan, C., Tang, D., Zhou, M., Xu, K.: Adaptive recursive neural network for target-dependent twitter sentiment classification. In: ACL (2), 22 June 2014, pp. 49–54 (2014)

18. Wang, G., Sun, J., Ma, J., Xu, K., Gu, J.: Sentiment classification: the contribution of ensemble learning. Decis. Support Syst. **57**, 77–93 (2014)

19. Ho, T.: The random subspace method for constructing decision forests. IEEE Trans. Pattern Anal. Mach. Intell. **20**(8), 832–844 (1998)

20. Buschken, J., Allenby, G.M.: Sentence-based text analysis for customer reviews. Mark. Sci. **35**(6), 953–75 (2016)

21. Ordenes, F.V., Ludwig, S., Ruyter, K.D., Grewal, D., Wetzels, M.: Unveiling what is written in the stars: analyzing explicit, implicit, and discourse patterns of sentiment in social media. J. Consum. Res. **43**(6), 875–894 (2017)

22. Kim, S.M., Hovy, E.: Identifying and analyzing judgment opinions. In: Proceedings of the Joint Human Language Technology/North American Chapter of the ACL Conference (HLT-NAACL-06), pp. 200–207 (2006)

23. Kanayama, H., Nasukawa, T.: Fully automatic lexicon expansion for domain-oriented sentiment analysis. In: Proceedings of the Conference on Empirical Methods in Natural Language Processing (EMNLP 2006), pp. 355–363 (2006)

24. Takamura, H., Inui, T., Okumura, M.: Latent variable models for semantic orientations of phrases. In: Proceedings of the 11th Conference of the European Chapter of the Association for Computational Linguistics (EACL 2006), pp. 201–208 (2006)

25. Abbasi, A., Hsinchun, C., Arab, S.: Sentiment analysis in multiple languages: feature selection for opinion classification in web forums. ACM Trans. Inf. Syst. **26**, 1–34 (2008)

26. Casoto, P., Dattolo, A., Tasso, C.: Sentiment classification for the italian language: a case study on movie reviews. J. Internet Technol. **9**, 365–373 (2008)

27. Bautin, M., Vijayarenu, L., Skiena, S.: International sentiment analysis for news and blogs. In: Proceedings of the International Conference on Weblogs and Social Media (ICWSM 2008), pp. 19–26 (2008)

28. Bentivogli, L., Girardi, C., Pianta, E.: Multiwordnet, developing an aligned multilingual database. In: Proceedings of the First International Conference on Global WordNet, pp. 293–302 (2002)

29. Agerri, R., Garcia-Serrano, A.: Q-wordnet: extracting polarity from wordnet senses. In: Proceedings of the Seventh International Conference on Language Resources and Evaluation (LREC 2010) (2010)

30. Cambria, E., Olsher, D., Rajagopal, D.: Senticnet 3: a common and common-sense knowledge base for cognition-driven sentiment analysis. In: Twentyeight AAAI Conference on Artificial Intelligence (AAAI-14), pp. 1515–1521 (2014)

31. Strapparava, C., Valitutti, A.: Wordnet-affect: an affective extension of wordnet. In: Proceedings of the 4th International Conference on Language Resources and Evaluation (LREC 2004), pp. 1083–1086 (2004)
32. Compagnoni, S., Demontis, V., Formentelli, A., Gandini, M., Cerini, G.: Micro-WNOp: a gold standard for the evaluation of automatically compiled lexical resources for opinion mining. In: Language Resources and Linguistic Theory: Typology, Second Language Acquisition, English linguistics. Franco Angeli Editore (2007)
33. Zanchetta, E., Baroni, M.: Morph-it! a free corpus-based morphological resource for the Italian language. In: Proceedings of Corpus Linguistics 2005 (2005)
34. Koppel, M., Schler, J.: The importance of neutral examples for learning sentiment. Comput. Intell. **22**(2), 100–109 (2006)
35. Hammer, H., Yazidi, A., Bai, A., Engelstad, P.: Building domain specific sentiment lexicons combining information from many sentiment lexicons and a domain specific corpus. In: Amine, A., Bellatreche, L., Elberrichi, Z., Neuhold, J.E., Wrembel, R. (eds.) Computer Science and Its Applications: 5th IFIP TC 5 International Conference, CIIA 2015. Saida, Algeria (2015)
36. Hamilton, W.L., Clark, K., Leskovec, J., Jurafsky, D.: Inducing domain-specific sentiment lexicons from unlabeled corpora (2016). http://nlp.stanford.edu/projects/socialsent
37. Agathangelou, P., Katakis, I., Kokkoras, F., Ntonas, K.: Mining domain-specific dictionaries of opinion words. In: 15th International Conference on Web Information System Engineering (WISE 2014), pp. 47–62 (2014)
38. Chiavetta, F., Lo Bosco, G., Giovanni, P.: A lexicon-based approach for sentiment classification of Amazon books reviews in Italian language. In: 12th International Conference on Web Information Systems and Technologies (WEBIST), pp. 159–170 (2016)

Mobile and Context-Aware Event Recommender Systems

Daniel Herzog[✉] and Wolfgang Wörndl

Department of Informatics, Technical University of Munich,
Boltzmannstr. 3, Garching b. München 85748, Germany
{herzogd,woerndl}@in.tum.de

Abstract. Personalized event recommendations are a challenging task. Unlike other items such as movies or restaurants, events often come with an expiration date. User ratings are usually not available before the event date and become dispensable after the event has taken place. In this work, we present the benefits and challenges of mobile and context-aware event recommender systems (RSs). We summarize basics and related work covering the most important requirements for developing event RSs. We developed a hybrid algorithm for context-aware event recommendations and integrated it into an Android prototype. Results of a two-week user study show that our RS provides useful recommendations. Based on our findings, we outline future challenges in the field of event recommendations: Improving the context-awareness, recommendations for different user and event types and an integration of event recommendations into city trip planners.

Keywords: Recommender system · Event recommendations · Content-boosted Collaborative Filtering · Context-awareness · Mobile application

1 Introduction

Recommender systems (RSs) are information filtering and decision support tools providing personalized recommendations by identifying information or products which best satisfy the user's needs. RSs are increasingly used in a mobile context due to the widespread use of smartphones and tablets. These devices allow more accurate recommendations because they can identify the context of the recommendation in a more detailed manner [25]. Example of context factors are the current time, the user's location and if she or he is accompanied by someone. Mobile devices are able to collect this type of information as they are often equipped with sensors which allow them to identify context data like the user's current position or speed of travel.

Event recommendations pose a new challenge in the field of RSs. Minkov et al. [20] explain that events, as opposed to movies or restaurants, usually take place only one-time under the same conditions, thus they come with an expiration date. User ratings, which can be considered for recommendations, are

V. Monfort et al. (Eds.): WEBIST 2016, LNBIP 292, pp. 142–163, 2017.
DOI: 10.1007/978-3-319-66468-2_8

usually not available before the event takes place and no longer of importance when the event is over or expired. This lack of ratings makes it impossible to recommend, for example, future events other users with similar preferences have liked. Hence, additional data has to be collected and processed by more sophisticated techniques in order to generate recommendations for events. Event recommendations are moreover a good example showing the importance of context in RSs. For instance, in case of a bad weather forecast, recommendations for outdoor events could be inappropriate.

Different techniques are available for recommending items such as events. Hybrid recommenders use the combination of two or more techniques in order to overcome weaknesses of single techniques and to improve the quality of recommendation. Melville et al. [19] present Content-boosted Collaborative Filtering (CBCF), a hybrid recommendation technique which generates better recommendations than a pure content-based (CB) or a pure collaborative filtering (CF) approach by combining these two techniques.

In this work, we present the idea of mobile event RSs and highlight their benefits as well as challenges for developers. In our previous work in [13], we developed and evaluated an event RS which is presented in Sect. 3. In addition, this work is extended by an extensive overview of event recommendation basics and additional related work which is summarized in Sect. 2. Furthermore, we introduce new challenges in the research of event RSs in Sect. 4.

2 Background and Related Work

This section provides an overview over the most important recommendation techniques which we combined to a hybrid algorithm. We present the requirements of mobile RSs and explain the idea of context-aware recommendations. Finally, we show the characteristics and challenges of event recommendations. Important related work substantiates the theoretical basics.

2.1 Recommendation Techniques

Different techniques and algorithms can be implemented in RSs in order to generate personalized recommendations. These techniques differ in the information they collect and how they rate items. Two popular techniques are CB predictions and CF.

CB systems try to recommend items which are similar to those the user has liked in the past [3]. A profound knowledge of the item representation is mandatory because CB RSs analyze item descriptions and attributes to identify similar items. Pazzani and Billsus [22] differentiate between structured and unstructured data to represent items: items represented by structured data comprise a set of attributes and there is a known set of values that each of these attributes may have. Unstructured data have no well-defined values, e.g., a text field allowing entry into every possible text. In most cases, semi-structured data, a combination of attributes with a known set of values and free-text fields, is chosen.

One advantage of CB recommending is that no critical mass of users is necessary to provide recommendations. Nevertheless, CB recommending comes with some limitations. As the *New User Problem* explains, a new user has to rate a significant number of items before the system can offer accurate recommendations for her or him. Furthermore, CB systems aim to recommend items which tightly fit a user's profile, thus a lack of diversity can be an issue [1].

Case-based recommendations are a special case of CB recommenders. According to Smyth [31], cases are solutions to a given recommendation problem. The simplest scenario is the recommendation of the top k most similar cases matching a user query. Case-based recommendations can be used for recommending items with a structured item representation as they allow the use of sophisticated approaches to judge how cases respond to the user query. Formula 1 [31] is one exemplary approach how to calculate the similarity between a case and the query:

$$Similarity(q, c) = \frac{\sum_{i=1}^{n} w_i \cdot sim_i(q_i, c_i)}{\sum_{i=1}^{n} w_i}. \tag{1}$$

In this formula, n is the number of attributes of the item. sim_i is the similarity between an attribute i of a query q and a case c. The attribute similarity can be calculated with formula 2 [31] and is weighted by w:

$$sim_i(q_i, c_i) = 1 - \frac{|q_i - c_i|}{max(q_i, c_i)}. \tag{2}$$

The presented formulas depend on the selected similarity metric. Smyth differentiates between symmetric and asymmetric similarity metrics. A symmetric similarity metric reduces the similarity by the same value if the case attribute value is lower or higher than the query attribute value. An asymmetric metric prefers either higher or lower values.

In contrast, CF recommends items other users with similar preferences have liked [3]. In the majority of cases, nearest neighbor algorithms are implemented in CF recommenders. Schafer et al. [27] differentiate between *User-Based Nearest Neighbor* and *Item-Based Nearest Neighbor* algorithms. While *User-Based Nearest Neighbor* algorithms call users who rate objects similar neighbors, *Item-Based Nearest Neighbor* algorithms rate items based on similarities between items [26]. Like CB systems, CF has some limitations. In addition to the *New User Problem*, the *New Item Problem* is an issue because items not rated by a substantial number of users cannot be recommended [1]. These problems define the *Cold-Start Problem* - a serious problem for event recommendations. Because users cannot rate unique future events before actually attending them, most of the items in the system remain unrated [11]. The limitation of such a sparsely filled user-item rating matrix is called sparsity [19]. Sparsity causes a low probability of finding a set of users with significantly similar ratings, thus leading to fewer or no recommendations.

The presented limitations of CB and CF recommenders can be illustrated using a simple example. Table 1 shows a user-item rating matrix with two users A and B and five events. Four events are assigned to the genre comedy, thus they are assumed to be similar. The other event is a musical. User A already provided a good rating to two comedy events, indicated by the + symbol. User B gave positive ratings to the two other comedy events and to the musical. A CB RS is able to recommend to each user the comedy events not previously rated as these events are similar. As CB recommendation is not taking other users into account, no further recommendations for User A are possible. A CF approach, however, is not able to recommend any event to any user. User A and B had not initially rated any common events, thus they cannot be identified as neighbors.

Table 1. Exemplary user-item rating matrix for events.

	User A	User B
Comedy 1	+	
Comedy 2	+	
Comedy 3		+
Comedy 4		+
Musical 1		+

Hybrid RSs combine two or more techniques in order to overcome such limitations. One example of a hybrid recommending method is CBCF. CBCF is a feature augmentation hybrid which uses the output from a CB prediction to generate recommendations in the subsequent CF phase [6]. The initial CB prediction is executed on the user-item rating matrix containing all ratings given by the users. The predicted ratings are then stored in the user-item rating matrix, now called pseudo user-item rating matrix, which is characterized by a lower sparsity. Finally, the CF algorithm is executed on the pseudo matrix [19]. In the presented example (Table 1), the CB approach extends the user-item rating matrix by CB predictions, in this case, two comedy events for each user. Based on the new pseudo matrix, CF is able to identify User A and B as neighbors. This allows the recommendation of the musical to User A since it was highly rated by a user with similar preferences.

2.2   Context-Aware Recommender Systems

Traditional RSs are 2-dimensional as they consider two entities when recommending items: the user and the item. Context-aware RSs add context as a third entity to the recommendation process [2]. This means that a predicted rating of an item does not only depend on the user and the item itself. The contextual situation in which the item will be consumed has an influence on the probability of a recommendation as well [4]. For example, the weather or the distance should be considered before recommending a location to the user.

Context is a broad term and various definitions exist. Dey et al. [10] describe context as "any information that can be used to characterize the situation of entities (i.e., whether a person, place, or object) that are considered relevant to the interaction between a user and an application, including the user and the application themselves". Woerndl et al. [35] differentiate between user context, temporal context, geographic context and social context.

Even though context-aware RSs promise a significant increase of the recommendations' quality, incorporating contextual information into the recommendations is challenging task [4]. Firstly, the relevance of the different context factors has to be estimated. Then, past ratings for items under the different contextual conditions have to be collected to predict ratings for other items under these conditions. If the context factors are too narrow, not enough ratings for each context are available to recommend items. In this case, the context should be generalized to reduce this sparsity effect [2]. For example, when recommending a movie on Saturday, it may be helpful to look for past user ratings for movies on weekends.

Adomavicius and Tuzhilin [2] present three different paradigms for incorporating context in RSs: *contextual pre-filtering*, *contextual post-filtering* and *contextual modeling*. In the *contextual pre-filtering* paradigm, context is used to select or construct the data set which a 2-dimensional RS uses as input to predict ratings. In *contextual post-filtering*, however, ratings are predicted on the entire data set using a 2-dimensional RS. Context filters the output of this RS before recommending it to the user. When applying a *contextual modeling*, the context is incorporated into the rating prediction technique instead of using a traditional 2-dimensional RS.

Context-aware RSs promise better recommendations than 2-dimensional RSs and lead to a higher user satisfaction [21]. Nevertheless, the users should always have the feeling that they can decide for themselves, instead of having systems thinking and deciding for them [29]. This is why the user should be provided with mechanisms to adjust the influence of context factors on the recommendation process. In a *contextual pre-filtering* paradigm, the adjustment could be done by defining thresholds such as the maximum distance to a location when selecting the data set for the RS.

2.3 Mobile Recommender Systems

Due to the widespread use of devices like smartphones and tablets, RSs are increasingly accessed through these mobile devices. Mobile devices allow to receive important information or interesting recommendations anywhere and anytime but they come with some limitations [25]. Compared to notebooks or desktop computers, displays of smartphones and tablets are smaller. Physical keyboards are often replaced by touch-screens and poor wireless networks can limit the access to information providers.

These limitations underline the importance of RSs in mobile scenarios. Users cannot easily browse through large lists of items searching for a specific result. On the other hand, even typing search queries or entering preferences can be a hassle for mobile users. This is why RSs should proactively recommend items when the current situation seems appropriate. Woerndl et al. [35] present a model for proactive recommendations composed of two phases. At first, they evaluate if the current situation is appropriate for a recommendation by observing different context factors such as the current time, the user's location or social context, e.g., if the user is alone or accompanied by others. If a recommendation is appropriate, the second phase determines which items should be recommended. As the system pushes recommendations to the user only when they are appropriate, the user effort can be reduced.

2.4   Event Recommendations

Compared to movie recommendations, research has paid little attention to RSs for events. First results show that hybrid methods deliver the most promising event recommendations. Minkov et al. [20] present an approach which considers the individuals' preferences for past events and combines these preferences with other peoples' likes and dislikes. Dooms et al. [11] conducted a user-centric evaluation of different event recommender algorithms. Their results stress that a hybrid of content-based and collaborative filtering performs better than other algorithms in most quality factors like accuracy, satisfaction and usefulness. The hybrid approach of Khrouf and Troncy [14] combines content-based and collaborative filtering and is enriched by Linked Data to overcome data sparsity. Cornelis et al. [7] model user and item similarities as fuzzy relations in their hybrid approach.

A big challenge when developing event RSs is to consider the characteristics of different event types which can be suggested to users. Some work has recently been done to recommend events in event-based social networks (EBSNs). These social networks help users to create social events, invite people that might be interested in participating and to keep track of the participants. Therefore, compared to conventional social networks, EBSNs do not only contain online social interactions but also include a face-to-face social interaction when participating in an event in the offline physical world [16]. Examples of such social events are seminars, reunions or group buying auctions [32]. Meetup[1] is a well-known EBSN in which users can join groups to create or find suitable events. Macedo and Marinho [17] investigated the reasons of the *Cold-Start Problem* in EBSNs. Users give positive RSVPs[2] not at all or only close to the occurrence of the event, leading to a high sparsity of RSVP data. This means, after creating a new event, a pure CB recommender is necessary to overcome the *New Item Problem*. Close to the occurrence of the event, when more RSVP data is available, CF can be applied. Furthermore, their results show that the distance to an event plays an important role, RSs should favor events nearby. Qiao et al. [23] recommend social events using Matrix Factorization while considering social relations and implicit feedback. In an experiment, they used Meetup data of five American cities to show that their model outperforms baseline approaches. Macedo et al. [18] developed a context-aware, hybrid event RS. It takes social, geographic and temporal

---

[1] http://www.meetup.com.

[2] "Répondez s'il vous plaît", French for "Please respond". In EBSNs users can usually provide Yes, No and Maybe responses to event invitations.

context factors into account. In a study they showed that this approach outperforms a state-of-the-art context-aware event recommender based on matrix factorization by up to 79%. Quercia et al. [24] analyzed mobile phone location data to understand how the user's current location influences the acceptances of social event recommendations. They found out that recommending events that are popular among residents of an area is more beneficial than recommending nearby events. This finding can be seen as another promising solution for the *Cold-Start Problem* in event RSs. If the event is location independent, Daly and Geyer [8] suggest using the popularity as a metric for overcoming the *Cold-Start Problem*.

Some RSs recommend groups or participants for social events or predict the user attendance. Zhang et al. [36] present a group recommender which recommends EBSN groups using matrix factorization. A study using Meetup data from New York City and Los Angeles shows the effectiveness of their approach PTARMIGAN which outperforms all baselines methods. Outlife is an event recommender which groups friends in social groups [9]. It allows the creation of recommendations for specific groups of friends and can recommend friends who should be invited to an event. Boutsis et al. [5] developed PRESENT, a middleware that predicts whether a user will attend an event. The authors assume that users in social groups behave similar. This is why PRESENT uses a Mixed Markov Model to extract the behavioral patterns of the users in social groups. An experiment using a large Meetup data set shows that their approach achieves an average prediction for the user attendance of over 73%.

Cultural events, on the other side, constitute a highly taste-dependent domain and group activity [15]. The decision if a group of people visits an cultural event is dependent on the taste of the group members and the relation between them. Examples of cultural events are concerts, sporting events or exhibitions. Often, visitors have to buy tickets in advance or at the door to join a cultural event. The different genres can have a great influence on which factors are relevant for a recommendation. For example, an opera or musical enthusiast expects an event location that meets certain requirements such as an elegant atmosphere or an excellent acoustic. On the other side, the location could be less important for exhibitions where the artist is more relevant. Another differentiating feature is the uniqueness of an event. While some events such as exhibitions or plays can be part of a series that is repeated regularly, a concert of a band on a world tour can take place only one time under the same conditions as the location changes after each concert.

Trust is an important factor for personalized event recommendations. Experiments show that people prefer recommendations from trusted people such as friends to recommendations provided by a RS [30]. Cultural events are an example for a strong group activity. It is likely that a person joins an event only because her or his friends do but still likes the event [15,32]. This is true for business events such as conferences but also for cultural events such as concerts [5]. Lee [15] developed PITTCULT, a trust-based, cultural event RS which allows users to rate the trustworthiness of other users. Recommendations are then generated based on those ratings. The results of a small study show that the users like the idea of a trust-based RS.

Distributed events are collections of smaller, single but very similar events that occur at the same day [28]. Examples are festivals with different performances or conferences where participants have to choose between different talks. Schaller et al. explain that visitors of distributed leisure events are looking for interesting and diverse events that allow a tight plan. As the last goal is hard to achieve when manually browsing available events, RSs can support users in creating a personalized event schedule.

A few mobile applications offering personalized event recommendations were already released. One example is Bandsintown[3], an application available for Android and iOS devices which focuses on music events. Recommendations made for events take into consideration music selections locally stored on the user's device. Furthermore, external sources like Facebook or Twitter can be connected to the application in order to collect additional information about user preferences in regard to music. Other examples of mobile applications which offer some kinds of event recommendations are the EVENTIM DE application, offered by the German ticketing and event company CTS Eventim[4] and XING EVENTS, an application of the German based social network for professionals XING[5].

The fact that the ticketing and event industry has already started to implement personalized recommendations in their offers underlines the significance of the topic for the different players involved in this industry. Event recommendations are moreover a good example showing the importance of context in RSs. For instance, in case of a bad weather forecast, recommendations for outdoor events could be inappropriate.

3   A Mobile and Context-Aware Event Recommender System

Section 2 shows the potential of hybrid and context-aware event RSs. To the best of our knowledge, there is no work examining the use of CBCF within a context-aware RS to recommend all kinds of events. In this section, we introduce our event recommendation algorithm which we implemented in an Android application. The application and the recommendations were evaluated in a user study which we present subsequently.

3.1   Applying Context-Aware Content-Boosted Collaborative Filtering for Mobile Event Recommendations

The example presented in Table 1 illustrates the strengths of hybrid recommenders. CB recommenders identify events similar to those the user already

---

[3] http://bandsintown.com.
[4] http://www.eventim.de.
[5] https://www.xing.com.

liked. To arrive at this conclusion, past feedback has to be analyzed but no critical mass of users is necessary. CF promises an increase in the variety of the recommendations but because of the lack of ratings for future events, CF has to be combined with other techniques. This is why we use CBCF for our event recommender as it combines these two techniques and promises better recommendations than pure CB or CF recommenders [19]. Furthermore, we want to show that CBCF can be used for context-aware recommendations. We briefly introduced the idea of our algorithm and first results of a field study in [12].

Section 2.2 summarizes three different paradigms for incorporating contextual information into a recommendation process introduced by Adomavicius and Tuzhilin [2]. Our suggested context-aware CBCF approach implements *contextual pre-filtering* to diminish the amount of events available for recommendations before the actual recommendation process takes place. This approach is advantageous because events which are impossible to recommend are excluded immediately: for example, an event taking place too far away from the user's location. In future work, we plan to try the other paradigms for incorporating context as well and compare those results to the solution presented in this paper.

After the pre-filtering phase, our algorithm analyzes user feedback on past recommendations in order to predict the ratings of the remaining events in the CB recommendation phase. These predictions are entered in the pseudo rating matrix. Finally, the CF phase is executed in order to consider all predicted ratings of all users and identify additional recommendations. This step is necessary to increase the variety of our event recommendations. To sum up, the proposed recommendation algorithm comprises three phases:

1. Contextual pre-filtering
2. Content-based prediction
3. Collaborative filtering

In the following, we describe these phases in detail.

Contextual Pre-filtering. Before predicting ratings for the events available in the database, the number of possible recommendations is decreased by taking context into account. Relevant context factors in this work were identified in expert interviews with selected representatives from the German event and ticketing industry. These context factors are:

– Current position: It is likely that the user prefers selected venues but the travel distance to these venues has to be appropriate. The system should be able to identify the user's current location and the user should be able to set a radius around it. Only venues within this radius should be considered for recommendation.
– Temporary preference of selected genres: The algorithm should ignore certain genres during the recommendation process, e.g., when a genre is inappropriate for the user's companions. The user should be able to select or deselect genres in order to tell the system the appropriate genres.

- Budget: The algorithm has to respect the user's available budget. For this purpose, the user has to set an upper limit for event prices or the sum she or he can spend per week or month.
- Weekday: Recommendations have to respect the identified days the user is available for events (e.g., only on weekends). The user should be able to tell the system the weekdays for the pre-filtering of events.
- Time of day: Recommendations are only useful when the user is available at the suggested time of day (e.g., not during the morning). The user should be able to tell the system the times of day for the pre-filtering of events.
- Scheduling conflict: If the user already purchased tickets for a recommended event, no further events which take place at the same time should be recommended. The RS has to identify such conflicts automatically and exclude events if necessary.

As described, these factors are used as criteria for exclusion. If the context of a potential recommendation exceeds a defined threshold, e.g., the distance to the venue, the corresponding event will not be considered for recommendation. The developed prototype in Sect. 3.2 allows the user to set and modify these thresholds as explained above.

Content-Based Prediction. After excluding events which do not satisfy the context constraints, the classical CBCF approach can be executed. At first, the CB prediction phase of CBCF has to be adapted to the special case of event recommendations. In this section, we describe how we analyze event attributes rated by the user in the past in order to estimate ratings for events comprising these attributes. At this point, context is no longer the focus. Nevertheless, the presented context factors are reflected in the item representation during the CB prediction, e.g., when determining how much the user likes a certain venue.

As explained, items can be represented by structured data, unstructured data and semi-structured data. Based on the expert interviews we conducted, events are mainly characterized by structured data. A Munich-based event and ticketing company provided a dataset with approximately 3700 real events which were used for the survey in Sect. 3.3. The dataset includes the following, relevant event attributes:

- The event name
- The name and address of the venue
- The genre
- The exact date when the event starts
- The vendor

The dataset did not provide information about the ticket price which therefore was not considered in this work. The structured characteristic of events is the reason why we propose a case-based approach for the CB prediction of ratings.

In order to adapt CBCF to event recommendations, we propose a slightly different similarity metric than the symmetric and asymmetric similarity metrics presented in Sect. 2.1. Nominal case attributes such as the genre or the venue are treated as binary values. If an event takes place at a certain venue, its value is 1 for this venue and 0 for all other venues. The query attributes depend on the user's history. If a user liked 90% of all recommendations of a venue, the query value q_i for this venue is 0.9. The attribute similarity is calculated with Formula 2 using q_i equals 0.9 and the case value c_i equals 0 or 1 as input. Other attributes, such as the event's price, could apply an asymmetric similarity metric. If the price is lower than the average as identified by the user's history, the similarity will be less reduced than for a higher price.

The challenge is to find a way to calculate the query value q_i for each attribute. As described, user feedback for an upcoming event is usually not available up-front, hence the user's history has to be used as a basis for the calculation. For event recommendations, two scenarios are possible: the user either likes or rejects a recommendation. Additionally, if the user actually purchases tickets for a recommended event, this would be considered a more positive feedback than just liking the recommendation. In this work, we count all liked, rejected and purchased recommendations and calculate the share of the positive feedback. Thereby, liked events are increased by factor 3 and events with purchased tickets by factor 5 as we assume that users often have to reject recommendations only because of time constraint issues. If a user liked one theater recommendation, rejected another theater recommendation but purchased tickets for a third theater performance, q_i for $i = theater$ will be calculated as $\frac{8}{9} \approx 0.8889$. This value means that the user likes the attribute theater in a recommendation with a probability of 88.89%.

If q_i can be calculated for a sufficient number of attributes, i.e., past feedback is available for these attributes, a prediction is called accurate. Formula 1 can be used to calculate the similarity between the item and the query corresponding to the value of the recommended item for the user. This value is stored in the pseudo user-item rating matrix and used for the upcoming CF phase.

Collaborative Filtering. Recommendations which were not rated during the CB phase are candidates for the upcoming CF phase. Rating recommendations in the CF phase is of prime importance because focusing solely on the user history could lead to a poor diversity of recommendations. As explained, *User-Based Nearest Neighbor* and *Item-Based Nearest Neighbor* algorithms are available for CF. In this work, we implement a *User-Based Nearest Neighbor* algorithm as it is already used for the CBCF approach in [19].

Some assumptions have to be made to reach valuable predictions. Only users with a similarity of at least 50% are considered as neighbors. The CF fills the pseudo matrix with additional ratings. In the end, the events with the highest value for the user are recommended. Every recommendation has to have a value of at least 0.5 on a scale from 0 to 1. In order to achieve a high serendipity, we divide the events in three groups. Around one third of the recommendations are events which take place within 7 days, one third within one month and one third not within one month. If not enough events are available for a group, the list of recommendations is filled with the best available recommendations. We limit the maximum number of recommendations at one request to 10 to avoid overwhelming the user with events. As a result, our context-aware CBCF method is able to recommend a set of events which respect the user's context and expectations and promise a satisfying diversity.

3.2 Developed Mobile Prototype

We developed an Android application to implement our algorithm and to evaluate the RS. The application can be installed on devices running Android 4 or newer.

For our prototype, the dataset is stored in a MySQL database connected to a RESTful web service we developed. When a client demands recommendations from the web service, it transmits the user id and the current context information to the server. The web service then is able to provide personalized recommendations based on the user-item rating matrix which is stored centrally in the MySQL database. These recommendations are received by the application and displayed to the user.

In this section, we briefly present the application. The application can be used without a login. A unique, device-dependent id allows personalized recommendations without creating a user account. After starting the app, a request is sent to the server automatically and the user immediately receives a list of new recommendations (Fig. 1). Recommendations are presented as cards, a design principal made popular through applications such as Tinder and Google Now. The main advantages of this representation are the low cognitive load because of the small number of items visible and the fact that the user can navigate through the app and provide feedback with only one hand [33]. In the developed app, the cards provide the most interesting information about the recommended event such as its name, the genre, the location and the date. Furthermore, the calculated rating for the user is expressed as a percentage and presented together with a short explanation. For example, the explanation "dein Feedback" (German for "your feedback") indicates that the event is recommended because of a rating from the CB recommendation phase. The user can swipe recommendations to the right to give a positive rating to a recommendation and to the left in order to reject the recommendation and to provide a negative rating.

Clicking on a recommendation displays a detailed view of the selected event. At the selected event, the user can find additional information concerning the venue or find Facebook friends who are attending the event. A button linking to the ticket vendor is also available. For testing purposes, the prototype assumes that a user clicking this button eventually purchases a ticket.

Using the *Navigation Drawer*, the app's menu bar, the app user can call up the settings view allowing her or him to modify the thresholds for the *contextual pre-filtering* (cf. Sect. 3.1). Figure 2(a) shows a screenshot of the geographical context settings. The user can choose the radius threshold for the *contextual pre-filtering* of events by moving the slider thumb. The radius is drawn around a certain position which can be either determined by activating the device's GPS

Fig. 1. New recommendations provided by the RS.

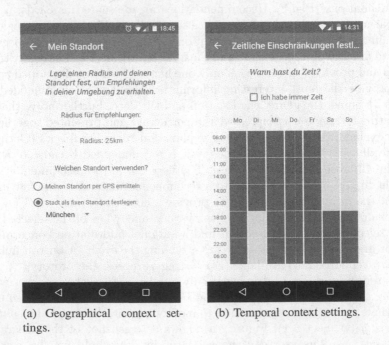

(a) Geographical context settings.

(b) Temporal context settings.

Fig. 2. Context settings.

sensor or chosen from a predefined list with cities. In this example, the current user position is set to the city center of Munich and only events within a radius of 25 km are considered for recommendation. In the second settings view, the user can determine her or his desired weekdays and times of day for the pre-filtering phase by selecting the corresponding time slots as illustrated in Fig. 2(b). For this purpose, we offer a calendar view which splits every day of the week into five times of day from morning (6 am until 11 am) until night (10 pm until 6 am). This design allows the user to select time slots for each day individually. This selection option is important for event recommendations because we believe a potential visitor cannot attend events every day at the same time. The additional check box allows users to select and deselect all slots at once. The third setting view displays a list of genres which can be selected or deselected by the user in order to determine appropriate genres for the pre-filtering phase.

3.3 Field Study

In this section, we describe the field study conducted to evaluate the developed RS. The main goal of the study was to test the recommendations in a realistic scenario. The study was intended to deliver insights into the quality of the RS. The method of influencing the context-awareness in the app settings also had to be evaluated. The study results are presented and interpreted at the end of this section.

Setting and Procedure. The field study was conducted as a two-week beta test, meaning, the users installed the application on their own smartphones. Users were advised to use the application as if they were using an application they installed voluntarily in everyday life. This means that during the test, users were allowed to use the system whenever and wherever they wanted to, in the desired intensity. Nevertheless, they were recommended to use the app at least for a certain amount of time to get a first impression of the system and the delivered recommendations.

After two weeks, the beta test terminated and a survey was sent to the participants. The main objective of the survey was to evaluate: the algorithm, the offered method to influence the context-awareness, the user interfaces and the RS as a whole. Table 2 lists all evaluation statements included in the survey. The participants had to rate these statements using a 5-point Likert scale with 1 representing no agreement at all and 5 representing complete agreement.

Further personal questions were added to the survey in order to obtain an overview of the participant's background, personal experience with events and personal experience with similar RSs.

Participants. The participants were selected to achieve a cross-sectional survey of event visitors. Different age groups were considered as were casual visitors and so-called expert visitors who attend events on a regular basis. Even though the

Table 2. Survey statements.

#	Statement
1	Overall, I like the recommender system
2	The recommendations meet my expectations
3	The recommendations are sufficiently diversified
4	My feedback leads to better recommendations
5	The system provides sufficient means to express my expectations
6	I like the way I can set local constrains
7	I like the way I can set temporal constrains
8	I like the way I can choose certain genres
9	The user interfaces are intuitive
10	I like the presentation of new recommendations

participants were obligated to own a smartphone, less technophilic participants were as important as more experienced users.

Twenty-one participants started the field study of whom 16 terminated successfully after two weeks by completing the survey. Of the 16 participants who completed the study, one was younger than 18 years old, three were between the ages of 18 and 25, nine were between 26 and 35, two were between 36 and 45 and one was older than 45 years old. The average technical affinity of the participants is 3.73 (σ: 0.88) on a 5-point Likert scale according to their own estimation. Mobile event applications were used by 62.5% of the participants once a month or less often and by 18.8% at least once a week. The participants reported different experiences with RSs such as the Amazon website. RSs were used several times per week by 25% and 43.8% used them once per month or less often. About a third of the participants, 37.5%, can be called expert visitors as they attend events requiring a ticket purchase once per month or more often whereas 62.5% purchase tickets not more often than a few times per year.

Results. The results in Fig. 3 show that the participants are satisfied with our solution ($\varnothing$: 3.75, σ: 0.83). Only 25% of the participants rated the system with a 3 or less. We also wanted to know if the received recommendations met their expectations. The responses are slightly above average ($\varnothing$: 3.38, σ: 0.60). According to the survey results, the recommendations can be called sufficiently diversified ($\varnothing$: 3.63, σ: 1.05). The participants believe that their feedback improves the personalized recommendations ($\varnothing$: 3.69, σ: 0.77). The frequency of usage differed between participants. The 16 participants would have bought a total of 16 tickets based on the recommendations which means one sold ticket per person during the two week study period. A majority of the participants, 87.5%, mentioned that they would like to continue using the system to find interesting events in the future.

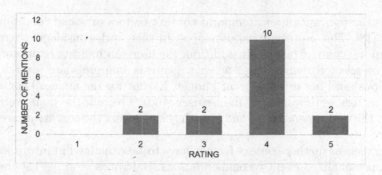

Fig. 3. Overall satisfaction with the RS.

In general, the users were satisfied with the choice of settings which allowed them to modify the context-awareness ($\varnothing$: 3.5, σ: 0.79). They particularly liked how they were able to influence the geographical context ($\varnothing$: 3.94, σ: 0.75). A higher variance of ratings can be observed when asking the participants about the calendar view ($\varnothing$: 3.56, σ: 1.17) and the list of genres ($\varnothing$: 3.44, σ: 1.12). A free text field at the end of the survey allowed the participants to add further thoughts. Some participants requested further options to modify the context-awareness, for example, the user's current budget for events.

The developed Android application is only one example of how our algorithm can be implemented in a mobile event RS. According to the participants, the apps' user interfaces are intuitive ($\varnothing$: 4.06, σ: 0.97) and they were pleased with the chosen card layout for the new recommendations ($\varnothing$: 4.07, σ: 0.77). This confirms our belief that the card layout is an appropriate way to present recommendations and to offer a quick and easy solution for providing feedback at the same time.

The results of our study show that CBCF can be used for context-aware event recommendations. The user's feedback on past recommendations is a valuable basis to fill the user-item rating matrix which can be extended by a CB prediction. The CF algorithm based on this matrix is able to provide accurate recommendations and ensures a sufficient diversity of events. Furthermore, our system is able to provide recommendations even if only one user is using the system.

4 Future Challenges of Mobile Event Recommendations

In this chapter, we summarize important future challenges in the research field of mobile event RSs.

4.1 Improving the Context-Awareness

Previous research has shown that incorporating context factors can improve the quality of recommendations. Only a few existing event RSs are context-aware and take the user's location, temporal context factors or social conditions into account [18]. The prototype we developed in this work considers geographical and temporal context factors. In addition, the user can indicate temporary preferences of selected genres (e.g., when a genre is inappropriate for the user's companions) and her or his current budget. Except for the financial context, all context factors were evaluated in our user study. Overall, the users were satisfied with the recommendations and how they can adjust the context-awareness of the RS.

Nevertheless, further context factors have to be examined in future works to improve personalized event recommendations. Baltrunas et al. [4] list the problems that have to be solved to develop context-aware RSs. First of all, context-factors have to identified and their relevance has to be determined. Examples of context factors which seem to be relevant for event recommendations and which should be examined in future works are:

- The time of recommendation: Tourist could be interested in spontaneous recommendations on the go when they are out exploring a city while others prefer long-term planning [12].
- The user's travel purpose: A tourist could be interested in different events than a local while somebody commuting to work is not interested in short-term event recommendations.
- The availability of tickets: A recommendation can become obsolete or at least less interesting if not enough tickets are available for the user and her or his companions.
- Weather, Season, Temperature: Outdoor events are higher in demand when the weather is nice.
- The user's current mood: The user's mood has an influence on the choice of an event, for example, an exhilarant or a serious event.

Baltrunas et al. developed a methodology to assess and exploit context relevance in mobile RSs. They used their approach to find out how relevant different context factors are for different points of interest (POIs) and how they influence the user's ratings. This methodology should be applied accordingly to examine context factors such as the proposed ones for event recommendations. An appropriate generalization of context factors for event recommendations has to be examined to overcome the sparsity problem [2].

Due to the complexity of the event domain and the diverse user behavior patterns, the relevance of context-factors can be different for each event or user type. For example, tourists who spend only a very short time visiting a city cannot visit events if the venue is too far away while locals are more flexible. Future event RSs should learn the user's preferences with regard to the relevance and the importance of context factors and adapt the recommendations accordingly.

Improvements are also possible in regards to other solutions of context incorporation. In our work, we used *contextual pre-filtering* only, but *contextual post-filtering*, *contextual modeling* and the combination of different paradigms should be considered as well in future works. Our *contextual pre-filtering* approach helps to immediately exclude inappropriate events but this technique can still be improved. One approach is to examine if users are willing to accept little violations of the thresholds if an event really satisfies their needs. If, for example, a user does not want to travel more than 100 km to an event, we do not consider it for recommendation. In fact, users might still be interested in an event that takes place 110 km away from her or his current position if the user likes the recommended event a lot. In this case, the recommendation's predicted rating could be reduced but the event is still considered for recommendation if no better events are available nearby.

4.2   Recommendations for Different Event and User Types

Section 2.4 lists related work for different event types. Social events are often created in EBSNs and shared with like-minded people while users often have to pay an organizer or an association to get tickets for cultural events. Other event types, such as distributed events, are similar to social events or cultural events but they come with some characteristics that complicate the event recommending problem. In our prototype, we used a case-based approach for the CB prediction of ratings where each event attribute is assigned with a weight. It seems obviously that the genre or venue of a location is more important to a visitor than the vendor. Nevertheless, this can change for different users or events. In classical concerts, the location can be more important to some visitors than the artists while a visitor of a rock concert only joins the event because of the band. An event RS containing an content-based or case-based component should use flexible attribute weights for different event types and according to the user's preferences.

Cultural events are often unique, they take place only one time under the exact same or very similar conditions. Other events, such as exhibitions or plays, can be part of a series of events, i.e., be repeated permanently. When using a generalization for the context (e.g., weekend for the event date), the conditions can be exactly the same. Such events do not come with the described limitations of event recommendations as their ratings are still valid after the event has taken place. Future event RSs should recognize if an event is unique and use past ratings to improve recommendations of future events of the same series.

Social events differ from cultural events as they are often created and shared by friends or like-minded people. A RS predicting a rating for a social event should consider different information than a cultural event RS. For example, instead of applying a CF approach comparing ratings of all users, ratings of friends or a social group should be preferred.

To sum up, an event RS should distinguish between social events, unique cultural events, series of events and other event types and use different techniques for different event types and users. However, the user must not perceive any difference in the way recommendations are presented. Events should be recommended whenever they are suitable for the user and regardless of the event type.

4.3   Integrating Event Recommendations into City Trip Applications

City trip applications combine multiple POIs to interesting and reasonable routes while respecting certain limitations such as time and the traveler's budget. Typical POIs considered for a trip are restaurants, museums or monuments. The problem of combining POIs to such routes is called the Tourist Trip Design Problem (TTDP) [34].

We believe that events are another example of items which should be combined with these POIs to city trips. Tourist visiting a city for a short time can be interested in going to a museum for an exhibition or visit an event in a famous building such as the Sydney Opera House. These events should be part of a trip containing other attractions as well as lunch breaks and transportation between the locations. To add events to a city trip, the presented context factors in Sect. 4.1 are critical to determine, for example, if the user is a tourist and which kinds of activities are appropriate.

More complicate variants of the TTDP have to applied to incorporate events in city trip applications. For example, multiple constraints should be considered as events require some time but can also be expensive. Hence, not only the duration of the whole trip but also the overall costs have to be kept below a limit.

5   Conclusion

In this work, we summarized our research in the field of mobile event recommendations. We presented the most important techniques and developed an own, hybrid and context-aware methodology to recommend events. We implemented our algorithm in an Android application and evaluated our RS in a user study. Results show that our event RS provides satisfying recommendations.

We outlined the most important challenges which should be met by future works. Our RS considers the most common context factors but additional research has to be done to better adapt the recommendations to the user's needs. As we presented the diversity of events by presenting different types of events and their characteristics, future works should develop methods that allow optimized recommendations for all event and user types. RSs that consider these characteristics can be extended to city trip applications that recommend complete routes including attractions and events.

To conclude this work, we want to emphasize the various potential applications and benefits of event RSs [20]. Integrated into a location-based service, users can find interesting events nearby or close to preferred locations which they might overlook otherwise. On the other hand, event organizers and artists can promote their events to potential visitors. In addition, they can use past preferences of the users to predict the number of future visitors for similar events. Consequently, more research should be done to overcome the difficulties of event recommendations and to exploit the maximum potential of mobile event RSs.

Acknowledgment. This work is part of the TUM Living Lab Connected Mobility (TUM LLCM) project and has been funded by the Bavarian Ministry of Economic Affairs and Media, Energy and Technology (StMWi) through the Center Digitisation. Bavaria, an initiative of the Bavarian State Government.

References

1. Adomavicius, G., Tuzhilin, A.: Toward the next generation of recommender systems: a survey of the state-of-the-art and possible extensions. IEEE Trans. Knowl. Data Eng. **17**(6), 734–749 (2005). http://dx.doi.org/10.1109/TKDE.2005.99
2. Adomavicius, G., Tuzhilin, A.: Context-aware recommender systems. In: Ricci, F., Rokach, L., Shapira, B., Kantor, P.B. (eds.) Recommender Systems Handbook, pp. 217–253. Springer, Boston (2001). doi:10.1007/978-0-387-85820-3_7
3. Balabanović, M., Shoham, Y.: Fab: content-based, collaborative recommendation. Commun. ACM **40**(3), 66–72 (1997). http://doi.acm.org/10.1145/245108.245124
4. Baltrunas, L., Ludwig, B., Peer, S., Ricci, F.: Context relevance assessment and exploitation in mobile recommender systems. Personal Ubiquitous Comput. **16**(5), 507–526 (2012). http://dx.doi.org/10.1007/s00779-011-0417-x
5. Boutsis, I., Karanikolaou, S., Kalogeraki, V.: Personalized event recommendations using social networks. In: Proceedings of the 2015 16th IEEE International Conference on Mobile Data Management (MDM 2015), vol. 01, pp. 84–93. IEEE Computer Society, Washington, DC (2015). http://dx.doi.org/10.1109/MDM.2015.62
6. Burke, R.: Hybrid recommender systems: survey and experiments. User Model. User Adapted Interact. **12**(4), 331–370 (2002). http://dx.doi.org/10.1023/A:1021240730564
7. Cornelis, C., Guo, X., Lu, J., Zhang, G.: A fuzzy relational approach to event recommendation. In: Prasad, B. (ed.) IICAI, pp. 2231–2242 (2005)
8. Daly, E.M., Geyer, W.: Effective event discovery: using location and social information for scoping event recommendations. In: Proceedings of the Fifth ACM Conference on Recommender Systems (RecSys 2011), pp. 277–280. ACM, New York (2011). http://doi.acm.org/10.1145/2043932.2043982
9. De Pessemier, T., Minnaert, J., Vanhecke, K., Dooms, S., Martens, L.: Social recommendations for events. In: 5th ACM RecSys Workshop on Recommender Systems and the Social Web (2013)
10. Dey, A.K., Abowd, G.D., Salber, D.: A conceptual framework and a toolkit for supporting the rapid prototyping of context-aware applications. Hum. Comput. Interact. **16**(2), 97–166 (2001). http://dx.doi.org/10.1207/S15327051HCI16234_02
11. Dooms, S., De Pessemier, T., Martens, L.: A user-centric evaluation of recommender algorithms for an event recommendation system. In: Proceedings of the RecSys 2011 : Workshop on Human Decision Making in Recommender Systems (Decisions@RecSys 2011) and User-Centric Evaluation of Recommender Systems and Their Interfaces - 2 (UCERSTI 2) Affiliated with the 5th ACM Conference on Recommender Systems (RecSys 2011), pp. 67–73 (2011)
12. Herzog, D., Woerndl, W.: Spontaneous event recommendations on the go. In: Proceedings of the 2nd International Workshop on Decision Making and Recommender Systems (DMRS 2015), Bolzano, 22–23 October 2015
13. Herzog, D., Wörndl, W.: Extending content-boosted collaborative filtering for context-aware, mobile event recommendations. In: Proceedings of the 12th International Conference on Web Information Systems and Technologies, vol. 2, pp. 293–303. SCITEPRESS (2016)

14. Khrouf, H., Troncy, R.: Hybrid event recommendation using linked data and user diversity. In: Proceedings of the 7th ACM Conference on Recommender Systems (RecSys 2013), pp. 185–192. ACM, New York (2013). http://doi.acm.org/10.1145/2507157.2507171

15. Lee, D.H.: Pittcult: trust-based cultural event recommender. In: Proceedings of the 2008 ACM Conference on Recommender Systems (RecSys 2008), pp. 311–314. ACM, New York (2008). http://doi.acm.org/10.1145/1454008.1454060

16. Liu, X., He, Q., Tian, Y., Lee, W.C., McPherson, J., Han, J.: Event-based social networks: linking the online and offline social worlds. In: Proceedings of the 18th ACM SIGKDD International Conference on Knowledge Discovery and Data Mining (KDD 2012), pp. 1032–1040. ACM, New York (2012). http://doi.acm.org/10.1145/2339530.2339693

17. Macedo, A.Q., Marinho, L.B.: Event recommendation in event-based social networks. In: Proceedings of International Workshop on Social Personalization (2014)

18. Macedo, A.Q., Marinho, L.B., Santos, R.L.: Context-aware event recommendation in event-based social networks. In: Proceedings of the 9th ACM Conference on Recommender Systems (RecSys 2015), pp. 123–130. ACM, New York (2015). http://doi.acm.org/10.1145/2792838.2800187

19. Melville, P., Mooney, R.J., Nagarajan, R.: Content-boosted collaborative filtering for improved recommendations. In: Eighteenth National Conference on Artificial Intelligence, pp. 187–192. American Association for Artificial Intelligence, Menlo Park (2002). http://dl.acm.org/citation.cfm?id=777092.777124

20. Minkov, E., Charrow, B., Ledlie, J., Teller, S., Jaakkola, T.: Collaborative future event recommendation. In: Proceedings of the 19th ACM International Conference on Information and Knowledge Management (CIKM 2010), pp. 819–828. ACM, New York (2010). http://doi.acm.org/10.1145/1871437.1871542

21. Oku, K., Nakajima, S., Miyazaki, J., Uemura, S.: Context-aware SVM for context-dependent information recommendation. In: Proceedings of the 7th International Conference on Mobile Data Management (MDM 2006), p. 109. IEEE Computer Society, Washington, DC (2006). http://dx.doi.org/10.1109/MDM.2006.56

22. Pazzani, M.J., Billsus, D.: Content-based recommendation systems. In: Brusilovsky, P., Kobsa, A., Nejdl, W. (eds.) The Adaptive Web. LNCS, vol. 4321, pp. 325–341. Springer, Heidelberg (2007). doi:10.1007/978-3-540-72079-9_10

23. Qiao, Z., Zhang, P., Zhou, C., Cao, Y., Guo, L., Zhang, Y.: Event recommendation in event-based social networks. In: Proceedings of the Twenty-Eighth AAAI Conference on Artificial Intelligence (AAAI 2014), pp. 3130–3131. AAAI Press (2014). http://dl.acm.org/citation.cfm?id=2892753.2893014

24. Quercia, D., Lathia, N., Calabrese, F., Di Lorenzo, G., Crowcroft, J.: Recommending social events from mobile phone location data. In: Proceedings of the 2010 IEEE International Conference on Data Mining (ICDM 2010), pp. 971–976. IEEE Computer Society, Washington, DC (2010). http://dx.doi.org/10.1109/ICDM.2010.152

25. Ricci, F.: Mobile recommender systems. Inf. Technol. Tour. **12**(3), 205–231 (2011)

26. Sarwar, B., Karypis, G., Konstan, J., Riedl, J.: Item-based collaborative filtering recommendation algorithms. In: Proceedings of the 10th International Conference on World Wide Web (WWW 2001), pp. 285–295. ACM, New York (2001). http://doi.acm.org/10.1145/371920.372071

27. Schafer, J.B., Frankowski, D., Herlocker, J., Sen, S.: Collaborative filtering recommender systems. In: Brusilovsky, P., Kobsa, A., Nejdl, W. (eds.) The Adaptive Web. LNCS, vol. 4321, pp. 291–324. Springer, Heidelberg (2007). doi:10.1007/978-3-540-72079-9_9

28. Schaller, R., Harvey, M., Elsweiler, D.: Recsys for distributed events: investigating the influence of recommendations on visitor plans. In: Proceedings of the 36th International ACM SIGIR Conference on Research and Development in Information Retrieval (SIGIR 2013). pp. 953–956. ACM, New York (2013). http://doi.acm.org/10.1145/2484028.2484119

29. Setten, M., Pokraev, S., Koolwaaij, J.: Context-aware recommendations in the mobile tourist application COMPASS. In: Bra, P.M.E., Nejdl, W. (eds.) AH 2004. LNCS, vol. 3137, pp. 235–244. Springer, Heidelberg (2004). doi:10.1007/978-3-540-27780-4_27

30. Sinha, R.R., Swearingen, K.: Comparing recommendations made by online systems and friends. In: DELOS Workshop: Personalisation and Recommender Systems in Digital Libraries (2001)

31. Smyth, B.: Case-based recommendation. In: Brusilovsky, P., Kobsa, A., Nejdl, W. (eds.) The Adaptive Web. LNCS, vol. 4321, pp. 342–376. Springer, Heidelberg (2007). doi:10.1007/978-3-540-72079-9_11

32. Sun, Y.-C., Chen, C.C.: A novel social event recommendation method based on social and collaborative friendships. In: Jatowt, A., et al. (eds.) SocInfo 2013. LNCS, vol. 8238, pp. 109–118. Springer, Cham (2013). doi:10.1007/978-3-319-03260-3_10

33. Torkington, J.: Small data: why tinder-like apps are the way of the future, März 2014. https://medium.com/@janel_az/small-data-why-tinder-like-apps-are-the-way-of-the-future-1a4d5703b4b. Accessed 13 Aug 2015

34. Vansteenwegen, P., Van Oudheusden, D.: The mobile tourist guide: an or opportunity. OR Insight **20**(3), 21–27 (2007)

35. Woerndl, W., Huebner, J., Bader, R., Gallego-Vico, D.: A model for proactivity in mobile, context-aware recommender systems. In: Proceedings of the Fifth ACM Conference on Recommender Systems (RecSys 2011), pp. 273–276. ACM, New York (2011). http://doi.acm.org/10.1145/2043932.2043981

36. Zhang, W., Wang, J., Feng, W.: Combining latent factor model with location features for event-based group recommendation. In: Proceedings of the 19th ACM SIGKDD International Conference on Knowledge Discovery and Data Mining (KDD 2013), pp. 910–918. ACM, New York (2013). http://doi.acm.org/10.1145/2487575.2487646

Enabling End-Users to Individually Share Parts of Composite Web Applications

Gregor Blichmann[✉], Carsten Radeck, Robert Starke, and Klaus Meißner

Faculty of Computer Science, Technische Universität Dresden, Dresden, Germany
{gregor.blichmann,carsten.radeck,klaus.meissner}@tu-dresden.de,
robert.starke@mailbox.tu-dresden.de

Abstract. Support for collaborative work by software or web applications is well studied for years, but yet no approach exists which allow end-users with no or limited programming skills to build custom groupware applications for individual collaboration needs. Due to an increasing number of resources, APIs, and services within the web, creating new web applications nowadays can be simplified by just combining these atomic building blocks. Meanwhile, an increasing number of mashup platforms enable non-programmers to build situational web applications by their own by facilitating recommendation techniques and visual abstraction layers. But, none of these approaches cover sufficient support for multi-user scenarios. As one major foundation for collaboratively building and using composite web application (CWAs), we propose a triple-based permission management concept in line with a target group specific UI support. Thereby, users are empowered to share either applications, components or parts of them in the form of single application features or data. Additionally, previously selected private data can be excluded from being shared. We implemented the approach within our distributed runtime environment for CWAs and proved by two user studies that the basic concepts as well as the UI guidance work as expected.

Keywords: Mashup · Groupware · End-user development · Permission management

1 Introduction

The number of different web-based applications that includes collaborative features rises almost every day. Today, end-user can choose from a variety of tools covering various application domains, like synchronous text and graphic editing or task and process management. Solutions provided for example by Google or Zoho supports user very well during the execution of collaborative workflows the tools had previously made for. Due to missing interchangeability and combinability, executing collaborative tasks, in private as well as enterprise context, often results in using different tools in parallel. Thereby, many media discontinuities and redundant task lead to an inefficient and time-consuming procedure, which could be avoided, if single groupware applications can be coupled as needed. In

© Springer International Publishing AG 2017
V. Monfort et al. (Eds.): WEBIST 2016, LNBIP 292, pp. 164–184, 2017.
DOI: 10.1007/978-3-319-66468-2_9

addition, currently available systems have to be extended to be customizable by end-users themselves to respect individual use cases which standard tools do not cover.

Considering single-user applications, existing approaches like [12] or [10] addresses the requirement for customizability by allowing non-programmers to compose heterogeneous web resources, like web services, data sources or widgets to individual applications. Thereby, these platforms hide much of the underlying complexity for their users by, for example, use graphical configuration metaphors or recommendation techniques.

However, none of this environments for composite web applications offers full support to use and reconfigure suchlike created applications synchronously in a group of users. But, combining the basic principles of CWAs created by end-users with the collaborative functionalities of groupware applications seem very promising for enabling non-programmers to build and customize collaborative web applications which support more efficient and individualized group work.

The universal composition paradigm [11] is based on the assumption that all components are consistently described as self-contained black-boxes which can exchange data by their public interface. Using this technique for collaborative applications enables an easy sharing of application parts in the form of single components. Sharing encapsulated components ensures that these parts will also correctly work when being isolated from the rest of the application. This can not be guaranteed for traditional DOM-based rich internet application (RIAs).

To empower end-users with no programming skills to create and share individually CWA, different research challenges have to be tackled first. As a foundation, a permission management system is needed, which considers the specific requirements an application built out of various black-box components poses. Also, when considering non-programmers as the target group, an adequate user interface (UI) metaphor for defining and reconfiguring permissions fo other users is needed. So-called sharing definitions allow other users to access a particular part of an application with individual access rights. Thereby, each user has to be aware of all participating partners and the permissions they have to certain parts of an application. As parts, we consider either single components or parts of them in the form of single UI elements representing application features or data. In case the UI should only partly accessible for others, a concept is needed to hide the not shared parts.

Likewise, each part of an application which is provided by a collaboration partner has to be distinguishable from parts which are private or owned by the user himself. In simple terms, users have to understand which parts of the application they can edit, only view or which parts are maybe blocked for them due to privacy requirements of others.

An evaluation of current platforms for mashup end-user development (EUD) according to the research challenges presented above revealed two relevant findings: The majority of the systems evaluated do not support synchronous collaboration at all. Solutions with a focus on synchronous or asynchronous collaborative work do not cover the handling of various access rights on different parts of a CWA as well have no adequate UI support for non-programmers. In addition, the challenge of considering privacy needs within suchlike platforms is never addressed so far.

To address these unsolved challenges, this paper introduces a permission management system for CWA in conjunction with an adequate UI metaphor for end-user with no programming skills. In detail, the contributions of this work are threefold:

1. Introduction of a generic permission management concept based on triples of subject, object, and permission which enables the sharing and collaborative usage of arbitrary parts of a CWA.
2. Presentation of a UI and interaction concept which allows regular web users without expertise about programming to share parts of their application with collaboration partners. Furthermore, it covers awareness about all parts of the application and the access rights which were shared with or received by other users.
3. Evaluation by a prototypical implemented demo system and two user studies.

Next, the underlying, briefly introduced research questions are further discussed in more detailed and illustrated by a reference scenario in Sect. 2. Section 3 describes the necessary conceptual foundation the presented concepts are based on. After Sect. 4 introduces the permission management for CWA based on triples, Sect. 5 describes details of the attached UI support for non-programmers. Section 6 presents insights of the existing demo system as well as the conducted user studies. Finally, Sect. 8 concludes the work and discusses future work.

2   Reference Scenario and Research Challenges

To illustrate the underlying research questions, a reference scenario is presented:

Peter and Mary, both scientists from Germany, plan to attend an international conference in Paris, France. Because Mary currently works at home and Peter is on a business trip in London, they decided to use a platform for creating and using collaborative CWAs. Therefore, Peter sets up an application including an event editor and a calendar to store the conference date, duration and additional dates like the return flight. A map is used to display the conference's location as well as suitable hotels around. To search for them, a hotel search component was added. After the conference date, location, and duration were stored within the calendar, it triggers the search for available hotels during the time of the conference sorted by the distance from the hotels to the conference location. All hotels within a certain radius are additionally visualized on the map.

To discuss the proposed hotels, Peter shares the hotel search and map with Mary, which accepts the invitation and joins. While Peter's application includes three components, Mary's only includes the hotel search and the map. Because Peter specified the right to edit for Alice, both can adjust the list of hotels. As soon as one of both changes the list, it is replicated to the client of the other user by the platform. Due to personal preferences, after a while, Mary exchanges the map component instantiated at her client with one from another vendor. To support a loosely coupled collaboration, this replacement does not affect Peter's client. Because of their semantic interoperability, both map components still can be synchronized. Next, Mary adds a component for public transportation as her private part to the application to ensure the hotel's reachability. Because the component was added as private, Peter neither has some information about its existence nor see some data or state changes of the components.

To ensure that only hotels with a minimum user rating of four stars are displayed, Peter adjusts the corresponding UI element and blocks it afterward for Mary. Furthermore, he adds a component for digitally approving business trip requests. After both filled in the form together, Mary likes to ask some colleagues for verification. Peter allows Mary to re-share the component with others, but first denotes his personal data, like his correspondent bank account, to be visually hidden for others. Mary creates a new group and shares the component. After one member wrote some hints for cheaper hotels, they revoke the sharing with the group and change the hotel selection.

The presented scenario reveals several research challenges, which details the problem statement introduced in Sect. 1. A suchlike platform has to face the challenge, how to provide users without an understanding of programming the possibility to share and collaboratively use individually created CWA or arbitrary parts of it during runtime. Thereby, we focus on non-programmers which regularly use the web and are familiar with the handling of for example web-based text editors or mail clients. To solve the above-mentioned challenge, there is a need for a permission management concept which is less complicated than existing solutions like in the domain of operating systems as well as considers the particular requirements of black-box-based CWA. In detail, sharing of applications has to be uniform for full applications, single components or parts of them. This especially has to be guaranteed if the components used do not offer collaborative features by themselves and have to be synchronized by their public interface. Respecting privacy needs by, e.g., blocking parts of the UI during synchronous usage is an additional challenge when using black-box components. Thereby, a platform has to ensure that components with only partly shared UI elements are still usable.

In addition, a concept has to be provided which offers awareness to all users about the access rights to certain parts of the application of all collaboration partners. This includes parts which I shared with others as well as parts I get granted access to from others. The collaborative usage of semantically compatible components from different vendors causes additional needs for a rights management in general and the UI representation in particular.

3 Foundations

Before details of the solution are presented in Sects. 4 and 5, this section introduces the necessary foundations. After providing some insights to the approach

of Composition of Rich User Interface Services for Everybody (CRUISE), the
following section shortly explains the used methodology for this work.

3.1 Composite Web Applications by CRUISE

The presented approach adheres to the universal composition approach introduced by [11]. Thereby, arbitrary web resources from all application layers,
including data, logic, and UI can be uniformly encapsulated as components.
These components can be easily combined to custom web-based applications
with the help of channels for exchanging data in a publish and subscribe manner.
A CWA, including its components, communication channels, layout, screen flows
or adaptive behavior is described by the platform and technology independent
mashup composition model (MCM). To execute them, MCMs are interpreted
by a dedicated runtime environment to, e.g., context-sensitively select suitable
components from a remote component repository.

The used components are realized as black-boxes to hide implementation
details and possible side effects. Nevertheless, to ensure a correct communication between components from different vendors, all components have to provide
a public interface comprising operations, events, and properties. Properties are
used to represent a snippet of a component's inner state, like the current position
of a map's marker and are represented as uniquely typed key value pairs. Operations can be invoked by events, which can be caused by inner state changes, by
passing a set of parameters. Currently, the component model is realized in XML
by the Semantic Mashup Component Description Language (SMCDL). It declar-
atively describes the component's metadata, like information about author or
price, the already mentioned interface, and the component's bindings. The latter
include references to all used frameworks and resources. To describe the component's provided functionality and data in more detailed, semantic information
can be annotated by referring to concepts of third-party ontologies.

Within CRUISE, the model-driven development approach has been extended
to support dynamic application reconfiguration during runtime by non-
programmers. Thereby, the semantic annotations of the SMCDL were extended
and more structured by the introduction of *capabilities* [12]. This extension is
used, for example, to establish communication channels between components
from different vendors which have non-equal but semantically compatible interfaces [13]. Capabilities can be either used to describe primary component functionalities, like the visualization of weather information or specific functionalities
of single interface elements, like operations or properties. They are represented by
a combination of *activities*, like "Display" or "Filter" and *entities*, like "Weather
Information" or "Hotels". Both have to refer concepts of third-party ontologies.
With capabilities, either user interactions or system behavior can be described.
Both can be chained by using cause and effect relations. CSS selectors are used
to establish a link between functional semantic describing capabilities and the
UI by so called *view bindings*.

The CRUISE platform is realized by a distributed client server runtime environment (CSR). It is based on a centralized architecture which enables, for example, to execute components on server and client side or coordinate multiple clients with different access permissions in multi-user and multi-device scenarios. To achieve the latter, the execution of local state changes are initially blocked and sent to the server. Afterward, they are handed over to a synchronized state change queue and then send back to each client allowed to in parallel [4]. Following the advantages of the transparent synchronization paradigm, we consider that application components are usually built for single user scenarios and therefore, do neither provide any functionality for synchronizing states, manage permissions of different users nor present awareness information. It is supposed, that all of these features are generically realized by the platform which uses the SMCDL of the components, e.g., to synchronize state changes by utilizing properties. Thereby, we only consider components based on HTML5 technologies (which are based on a DOM). Due to their vanishing relevance, plugin-based technologies, like Flash, are not in the scope of our approach.

3.2 Methodology

Because the presented solution is targeted at the characteristics of users with no or limited programming skills, we facilitated an adopted version of the user-centered design (UCD) process – for example presented in [8] – to iteratively develop the permission management in general as well as the supporting UI in particular. Thereby, we reduced software development and implementation specific activities and focused on the conceptual work. Currently, we completed two full iteration cycles of analysis, specification, prototyping, and evaluation. Within the current, third iteration, we finished the reworked specification as it is presented in this article and currently improve our prototypical solution. Within the analysis, we used personas, use cases, and scenarios as well as a context review to retrieve requirements for the system. In addition, we reviewed the current state of the art in research and industry. The specification lead to the concept presented in the next section, as well as first mockups. The latter were used as a template for our prototypical implementation (see Sect. 6.1) and were iteratively improved to be used for our user studies (see Sect. 6.2).

After briefly presenting the foundations, the next section introduces the necessary permission management system used to share different parts of a CWA during runtime.

4   Triple-Based Rights Management

This section presents details about the triple-based rights management approach for CWA. After initially defining basic terms and roles, the second subsection describes possible sharing definitions in more detail. Finally, the sharing process is explained.

4.1 Term Definitions and Roles

Before presenting details of the proposed rights management concept, first basic terms and roles have to be defined. As introduced in Sect. 1, unlike traditional CSCW tools, collaborative CWAs based on the universal composition ease the possibility to share arbitrary functional parts of an application under different permissions with various collaborative partners. In the following, such application parts are defined as *composition fragments*. They represent either a whole application, group of components, a single component or also parts of them.

Every composition fragment within an application has exactly one user as *owner*. Owners are the persons who added the fragment to the application or initialized it, in the case the fragment equals the whole composition. Self-owned fragments can repeatedly be edited, removed, or shared with other users during runtime. While an application itself is assigned to one owner, it can include smaller fragments, like a single component, which is owned by a collaborative partner. As soon as an owner creates a new sharing definition for others, the invited users can extend the received part of the application with components, to which they will be assigned as owner. Concerning the scenario presented in Sect. 2, the application owned and shared by Peter, potentially can include multiple fragments, like the public transport component, which are owned by Mary. It is important to mention, that ownership cannot be restricted by, deleted by or handed over to somebody.

4.2 Triple-Based Sharing Definitions

By default, each composition fragment is only accessible privately for their owners. They can only be seen by them no matter whether they were initially part of the composition or are added during runtime as long as they are not shared with somebody.

As pictured in Fig. 1, the sharing of composition fragments is based on an *access control list*. Thereby, a set of *sharing definitions* represents all sharings within one application. A sharing definition consists of multiple *sharing triples*. These triples comprise a number of *subjects*, a number of *objects* and one *permission*. Subjects represent a user **who** or multiple users which should be able to access an individual composition fragment of an owner. This can be distinguished in *public* sharing definitions, where every member of the collaborative group has access and definitions for dedicated *groups of users* or *single users*. **What** these users should be able to access, is specified within the object. This covers all before mentioned composition fragments, like whole applications or arbitrary parts of the composition or some components. Considering the reference scenario in Sect. 2, instead of sharing the whole component, Peter is empowered to share only the location of an event specified in the calendar or the list of selected hotels within the hotel component. Last, the permission defines **how** subjects can access the object. Either view-only or edit permissions can be assigned. While for the first, state changes are only caused by the owners and synchronized with all invitees. The second right enables even invited users to create state changes, e.g., by dragging a marker from a map component. However, the right to edit includes the right to view. The two terms were proposed by end-users during our first user study (Sect. 6) and replaced the previous, more technical names consume and contribute. Each triple includes exactly one permission.

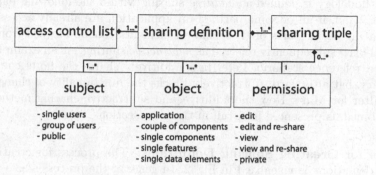

Fig. 1. Basic triple scheme.

Within the process of sharing, an *inviter* is a user who shares an object with a subject. This can be either the owner of this composition fragment or a user with the permission to *re-share* the objects he received access to. Re-share permissions can be specified for each single sharing definition independently and allows users to share received objects with the permissions the invited user got (see permission part of Fig. 1). Within one sharing definition, an *invitee* is a person who accepts a received invitation of the inviter. So an inviter which shares one component can also act as an invitee for another component within one single application instance during runtime.

Since the collaborative features are realized by a CSR environment which enables to exchange data between different components by publish-subscribe-based communication channels, sharing application parts has to consider those. The following example illustrates the proposed behavior. Peter uses and shares a component which presents the list of hotels based on the selected location of a map with Mary, but keeps the map as private. If Peter is changing the marker, his hotel component will be updated. To updated the component of Mary, the platform has to copy the event of the map and additionally invoke the corresponding operation of Mary's hotel component, even if Mary does not have a map component at her client. Consequently, users of our target group do not have to share communication channels explicitly as part of the sharing definition, because they probably do not know what they do and which data is transferred. In fact, as motivated by the example, we assume that all events on incoming or outgoing channels of a shared component will be replicated to all users who received access to the component no matter whether the channel is connected to private or shared components. To add a channel which has a shared component as subscriber or publisher, the user has to have at least the right to edit or has to be the owner of the component.

4.3 Process of Sharing

Sharing objects with collaborating partners can be realized by two contrary approaches. On the one hand, assuming objects of an application to be private per default, they can be actively shared by attaching different access rights. This methodology is defined as *additive* sharing within the following paper. On the other hand, if all or some parts of an application are already accessible for collaborating users, parts of these shared elements can be blocked from being shared. This is subsequently referred as *subtractive* sharing. As an example of the presented reference scenario, Peter first additively shares the hotel component with Mary, but afterward subtractively blocks the functionality of changing the rating filter for Mary. How the additive and subtractive sharing methodology are combined, is presented in detail in the next section.

Process for Creating Sharing Definitions. The process for creating new sharing definitions is visualized in Fig. 2. In general, the process starts with an optional pre-selection of private application data, like addresses or bank accounts ①. The fundamental purpose is to define application-wide private data which is independent of a single sharing definition. For example, users can specify that any address present in the application (which evolves over time) has to be blocked from being shared with collaborating partners. This set of private data can potentially be reused in different applications. Thereby, for example, enterprises can enforce their workers to not share any confidential data during their daily work. As soon as the user finishes a new sharing definition, the set of global defined private data gets evaluated. If one of its elements is part of an object of the sharing definition, the platform informs the user, that this element will not be able to share and excludes it from the sharing definition.

As indicated by ⑤, a sharing definition can include an arbitrary number of triples. Within each triple, first, any combination of single users and groups can be specified as subject ②. Next, as indicated in the previous section, either composition fragments, features, or data can be selected as an object. Due to interdependencies with the blocking of elements in the next step, the user can only choose an arbitrary number of objects within one of those three sharing levels to be included in the current triple ③. As the last step for each triple, either the permission to view or to edit can be assigned. While the process up to this point is based on an additive behavior, users now can either additively add further combinations of object and permission or can block some parts of the already included objects ④. Therefore, to mark parts as private, at least one object with the permission to view or edit has to exist within the current sharing definition. Additionally, the possible objects to be marked as private depends on the selected sharing level. If composition fragments are shared, like the hotel component of Peter, single features or data, like the filter functionality, can be blocked. If only features are shared, only the related data can be blocked. In the case of data, no further blocking is possible.

After finishing the current sharing definition, as indicated in the beginning, users are informed about possible conflicting application-wide settings for private data. How the platform realizes the proposed sharing definition, is described within the next section. If a proposed sharing definition was established successfully, users can add further or change arbitrary sharing definitions during runtime ⑥.

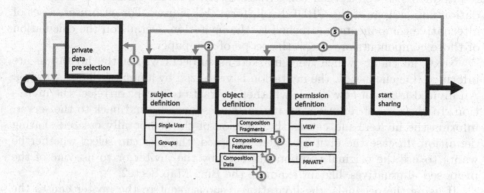

Fig. 2. Overview of the creation process for sharing definitions.

Invitation Process. To ensure that permissions are handled correctly within the CSR, synchronized ACLs are located on the client as well as on the server. On the client of each collaborating partner, only triples are stored, which mark the user as inviter or as a subject. In general, the client-side ACL serves the following purposes:

- view, edit or reconfigure all application parts the user is allowed to,
- determine the objects the user has the permission to share,
- display basic awareness information about the current permission configuration of the particular application.

The server-side ACL representation comprises the totality of all triples from all collaboration partners and serves the following purpose:

- routing of collected messages from one client to all clients that are allowed to receive the message, e.g., containing state changes of a component,
- mapping between a sender's and a receiver's component interface in the case differently implemented components have to be synchronized.

To enable users to create, reconfigure and delete triple-based sharing definitions during runtime, the platform facilitates an invitation process which is presented in more detail in the following. The creation of sharing definitions is supported by a UI dialog implemented as part of the CSR-client (see Sect. 5 for more information). During the initialization of the dialog, the platform checks the current permissions via the client-side ACL to hide all fragments which can not be shared due to missing access rights. After the valid creation of a new sharing definition, the temporal representation is send to the server as part of an *invitation* and marked on the client-side as to be approved. Afterward receiving at the server side, again all necessary permissions are checked. If the invitation was validated successfully, the server requests semantically equivalent components from the component repository for all components specified within the object. Thereby, there is a request for each subject, to consider individual user requirements as well as their context. To receive suitable results, the recommendation sub-system of the CRUISE platform [14] is used. For each user, a set of alternative components is attached to the invitation. Details on the calculation of those components are not in the scope of this paper.

Next, all clients which were marked as subjects within the invitation are informed. On client-side, the invitation is visualized by a pop-up dialog showing. An invited user can now decide whether he wants to accept or reject the invitation. In the case of rejection, an invitation response is send back to the server, informs the inviter, and causes the deletion of the temporally created sharing definition. In case the invitation gets accepted, the user can select whether he wants to use the original components used by the inviter or to use one of the proposed alternatives, like for example the Bing Map Sect. 2.

If using the originals, the invitation response sent to the inviter causes the persisting of the sharing definition within the ACL of the client of the inviter, the client of the invitee as well as on server side. After completing the invitation process, the stored triples are used for example to route state changes of the application to all clients which are allowed to receive them. If the inviter wants to stop the sharing, he either can delete the triple using the sharing dialog from the beginning, or remove the corresponding composition fragment from his application. In this case, the fragment gets removed by all invitees too as well as the related triples of the ACL. If invitees remove individual composition fragments, they only are eliminated on their client. All other clients still are able to use it.

If the invitee stops the sharing by deleting the corresponding triple, he stops the sharing of state changes. However, the inviter has to decide whether the other user is still allowed to use a local, not synchronized copy of the composition fragment.

To support non-programmers in sharing arbitrary composition fragments during runtime, an extended user guidance as well as a UI-support is needed, which is discussed in detail in the next section.

5   UI-support for the Permission Management by Non-programmers

To support users of our target group during the sharing process proposed in the last section, an adequate UI is needed. The proposed concept adheres to the triple metaphor, which promises the following advantages: First, it eases the creation of new sharing definitions while considering the challenges discussed in Sect. 2. Second, it allows an easy understanding of already defined permissions. Thereby, the UI concept follows some kind of closed world assumption, i.e. all composition fragments which are not explicitly shared by a sharing definition are private.

5.1   Triple-Based Permission Overview

Figure 3 briefly presents the proposed UI. If a user wants to review currently existing sharing definitions, the overview displayed in screen **A** can be opened as a separate window which overlays the application. The panel provides four basic functionalities: With the button in ① new sharing definitions can be created. ② presents statistical information about the currently existing sharing definitions, like the number of triples, the number of collaboration partners and groups as well as information about not yet accepted invitations. The filter and search panel ③ enables to search, sort or filter the present triples displayed in ④ by subject, object or permission. The already defined triples are shown in a grid-based overview and are clustered per default by subjects. The clustering can be changed within the filter panel. This was one of the features requested by the first user study (Sect. 6). As can be seen for example by the map and hotel component of Marry, the top-most triple summarizes the number of components and permissions assigned. Initially, the clustered triples are collapsed. Sharings which are not accepted yet, are grayed out. The size and amount of the triples displayed adapt to the dimension of the device's screen the user is currently using. The presented triples include both, the ones where the current user is the owner and the ones where the user is one of the invitees. For each object, information about the owner is attached.

To present the interaction steps necessary to create a new sharing, Fig 3 extends the reference scenario by a weather forecast component. As an extension of the reference scenario, Peter wants to share this component with Marry and Charlie. After clicking on the button of ①, the dialog presented in screen **B** overlays the current view. It allows users to create new sharing definitions by visually composing a new triple. Initially the part for the subject, indicated by **who** is activated to start with the selection of suitable collaboration partners. Furthermore, the user is guided by the message panel on the right side which includes further instructions how to create a new triple. The user can select either some single users currently registered at the platform or individually defined groups. After finishing the subject definition, the user can click on the plus symbol below **what** to start the object definition. As indicated in screen **C**, the user can choose between components, composition features and data. As soon as the user selects one item, the other both sharing levels are disabled to ensure that only elements of one level are shared within one triple (see Sect. 4.3).

Next, to specify **how** the object should be shared within screen **D**, the user first has to either select edit or view as general permission ⑤. Afterward, within ⑥, sharing-related private data can be chosen. Thereby, the set of selectable elements depends on the specified triple object, as proposed in Sect. 4.3. If any pre-selected private data elements are covered by the object(s) of the current sharing definition, they automatically are presented as blocked items.

Before finishing the sharing definition, the user can test his current sharing configuration. Thereby, a separated window can be opened which contains instantiated copies of the selected components with respect to the selected permissions. To initializing the invitation the share button on the bottom right has to be used. Additionally, users can activate the checkbox above to allow other participants to re-share the received sharing definitions. Finally, after a user clicked on the share button, screen **A** opens again and now includes the new triples marked as to be approved. In general, by hovering the mouse over an existing triple, the platform allows to delete or reconfigure it. For reconfiguration, the triple is loaded once again to the dialog presented in **B − C**.

As soon as an invitee accepts an invitation, the triple is displayed without the gray highlighting. If he rejects, the triple is removed. In both cases, a short notification is presented to the user. If the invitee selects an alternative component, again a notification is given. In addition, this is visualized by a small icon at the triple's object. If a user hovers the mouse over this icon, the alternative component replaces the object.

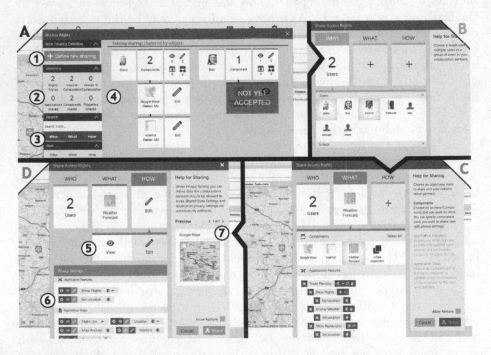

Fig. 3. Prototypically implemented UI for sharing CWAs based on triples.

5.2   Awareness and Live View Support

As a result of our user studies (Sect. 6), participants recommended to provide an easy to understand permission representation at the application's live view.

As presented in Fig. 4, the proposed support is realized by specific clickable icons at the top right corner of the components' toolbar, which provides three functionalities:

1. providing a shortcut for creating new sharing definitions with the corresponding component as an object,

2. indicating whether the component was already shared in general as well as selected details of the particular collaboration partners and their permissions,
3. providing a quick overview which components or even which parts of them were shared by other participants for the current user.

The left icon presented in ① indicates that the component can be shared by the user either because he is the owner or received the permission to re-share. This icon was suggested by the study participants, because it is established for sharing content, for example within Google's mobile platform Android[1]. If the user already shared a component, the color of this icon changes to green ②. On hovering the icon with the mouse, a small context menu visualizes all collaboration partners who received the component as part of a sharing definition and their corresponding permission ③. In this case, the first user has component-wide view rights and the second user has a very finegrained permission definition including some private data elements which are blocked for him. By using the plus icon, the user can open the share panel presented in Sect. 5.1 to create a new sharing definition. Similar to the functionality shown in ①, the same can still be achieved by directly clicking on the share icon.

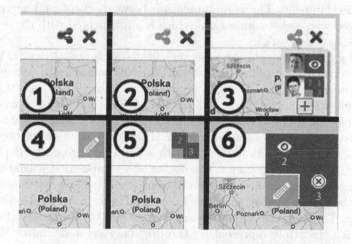

Fig. 4. Live view support for inviters and invitees.

To indicate components that were owned by others, the granted permission is represented at the top right of the component. In ④, the user received the permission to edit. If a component additionally includes parts which are blocked or are only view-able, a mixed representation is used ⑤. This can be enlarged by hovering over this icon ⑥. When hovering the indicators for, e.g., blocked parts, again, the platform highlights the corresponding UI areas. Therefore, annotated CSS selectors of the capabilities' view bindings are used. If the whole application

---

[1] https://www.android.com.

was shared, each component of the composition includes a corresponding icon. To present more detailed awareness information about, e.g., changed permissions a widget-based configurable awareness subsystem was created [3] which therefore is not part of this work.

6   Evaluation

The permission management approach for CWAs in conjunction with an adequate UI concept were evaluated by a reference implementation as part of the existing CRUISE runtime environment (Sect. 6.1) and by two user acceptance tests (Sect. 6.2).

6.1   Prototypical Implementation

The prototype is an extension of the client server runtime environment (CSR). Its server-side coordination layer is implemented by Enterprise Java Beans (EJB) and serves as a singleton for all client environments. The client-side of the CSR is realized by HTML5, CSS and JavaScript (JS) technologies. Furthermore, the implementation uses amongst others JS frameworks like Ext JS[2] and JQuery[3] to fasten development. The communication between client and server uses a channel-based web socket connection, which is implemented with the help of the Apache Apollo framework[4].

As briefly introduced, the ACL on the client-side is realized as JSON object and on the server-side as plain Java object. To synchronize both, dedicated commands and events can be exchanged between the client and the server based on the communication infrastructure of Apache Apollo. On client-side, the ACL clusters triples by users to ease the look up needed for example when creating the triple-based overview of already defined permissions. Furthermore, it was necessary to store an additional triple with a permission representing the ownership to detect whether a user is the owner of a composition fragment or not. To indicate, e.g., already accepted invitations, each triple is associated with a state. On the server-side, a mapping for semantically compatible components is necessary. Thereby, the corresponding triples will be marked as alternatives and linked to the triple representing the originally created sharing definition. If a state change occurs at a collaborating client, the server now can easily determine the components of the other participants that have to be informed to update their state. Potentially necessary data transformations are realized by the existing mediation infrastructure [13] and is implemented on the client-side.

6.2   User Acceptance

To ensure the suitability of the proposed concepts for the targeted group of users and to follow the principles of UCD, we iteratively conducted two user studies.

---

[2] https://www.sencha.com/products/extjs.

[3] https://jquery.com/.

[4] https://activemq.apache.org/apollo/.

Both was done at the end of a cycle of analysis, specification, prototype, and evaluation (see Sect. 3.2). As fundamental methodology in both we sequentially used the methods *structured interview* and *thinking aloud*. The goal of the first part was to test the general acceptance of the proposed elements. This includes among others the triple metaphor and its dimensions in the first study, and the focus on the sharing of application parts as well as the private data in the second. The goal of the thinking aloud part was to test the user acceptance and usability of the proposed UI concepts. To that end, the test was based on high fidelity mockups.

The first user study involved ten male and four female participants. The second was done with nine male and one female persons. Overall, the participants' age range from 22 to 47 with an average age of 28 years. Eight participants had no programming skills, ten considered themselves as beginner, and six were average-level programmers.

In both studies, the underlying process was three-staged: First, a video as well as a basic scenario introduced the basic concepts of CRUISE to understand what mashups are and how they potentially can ease collaborative work. Second, the participants were encouraged to discuss or solve six (first study) respectively seven (second study) use cases and tasks with increasing complexity by using paper prototypes. All tasks are based on the reference scenario presented in Sect. 2 During this session, a moderator noted all comments and thoughts as well as updated the prototype based on the desired interactions of the participants. Within the third part, the moderator explicitly checks identified misunderstandings and discussed possible alternatives with the participants. Furthermore, to get a comparable and standardized rating of the systems' usability and acceptance, the participants were asked to fill in the System Usability Scale (SUS) questionnaire – see for example [6] for details.

The overall results were very positive. Basic UI structures and metaphors of the first user study were understood correctly without further explanations by nearly all participants (12/14). Three persons explicitly mentioned the colored separation as helpful. We found that users preferred to use a share icon placed directly on top of the components instead using the icon in the main menu bar. This finding caused the extended live view support presented in Sect. 5.2. The used icons in the first study were understood by all users quite well. Within the second study, participants complain about missing icons for application features and data. 12 of 14 users from the first study were able to select multiple triple elements without help. Thereby, we found out that users, probably due to their daily usage of social networks, often thought in a group-oriented way. This underpins the necessity for specifying groups as subject, which we provide. The component icon visualizing whether a component was shared or not was instantly understood by 7 of 14 participants. All users understood the messaging symbol and menu to read and react on their invitation, the similarity to established messenger programs like Facebook was considered very positive. But, 9 of 14 users criticized the missing drag and drop support. The initially provided dedicated dialog for creating new triples was not understood by 9 of 14.

A revised version was judged to be more intuitive in the second study. Some inconsistently used icons confused the users and therefore are replaced. Surprisingly, the possibility to use an existing triple as a template for a new one was not considered as intuitive by the majority and removed from the final concept. Within the second user study, 8 of 10 participants used the newly ordered help messages, whereby some details within the texts were marked as misunderstandable. The subtractive behavior for defining private date was intuitively understood by 8 of 10 users. Nevertheless, nearly all users had problems to identify existing relations between the different sharing layers. The mockups used for the second user study intended to present the object specification with the help of an accordion layout. Thereby, only the list of components was initially extended. For this reason, nearly all user assumed that they have to select a component before they can share a specific composition feature or data. This fault was eliminated by changing the basic layout which displays all three layers equally at beginning.

The average SUS score of the first user study equals 77 with 62.5 as lowest and 98 as highest single user rating. For the second study, we received an average of 79,5. The results can be considered as a promising result in general and show, that we improved the user acceptance and usability within the second iteration. All comments of the participants showed, that the general approaches were understood and accepted very well. Suggested features or misunderstood elements of the second user study were re-worked and are already part of the presented concepts. More conceptional limitations are discussed in the next section.

6.3   Discussion

Although the concepts are already evaluated by two user studies, following the user-centered approach, further iterations are needed to continuously improve usability-related factors like self-descriptiveness or controllability to support end-users with no programming skills best. However, the basic principles of the concept as well as the majority of the UI features have successfully been proven to be acceptable. But, besides a good user acceptance, further research challenges for successfully supporting non-programmers have to be discussed. To enable users, e.g., to block single parts of the UI representing specific application features or date, quite rich component descriptions are needed. Component developers have to annotate semantic concepts in the form of capabilities and view bindings to ensure that the platform can offer the functionalities presented above. We argue that the additional effort a component developer has to invest is quite less in comparison to the benefits users can achieve by using the proposed functionalities. In addition, we support component developers by a developer guide which includes best practices for, e.g., component annotation. However, components have to be built by technologies which rely on the Document Object Model (DOM). From the authors' perspective, plugin-based technologies like Flash can be omitted due to their decreasing dissemination and importance. The technology stack of HTML5 and CSS3 offers an increasing number of functionalities and Application Programming Interface (APIs).

Managing concurrency is inevitable for collaborative systems. However, in the context of black-box-based compositions, a detailed concept is very challenging and therefore not part of this work. Due to the usage of black-box components, a local event handling after a component state change appeared can not be prevented entirely by the platform. As a result, the server is able to process and synchronize the state change with all other participants only afterward. In the case of conflicts, one of the conflicting clients have to execute a state rollback, which disturbs usability and user experience. Finally, it is still a challenging task to present a quick and easy to understand permission overview on the live view while allowing restrictions on single application features, data, and UI elements.

7 Related Work

The platform for distributed interactive workspace (DIWs) [2] allows users to synchronously use and edit component-based applications for joined learning. Thereby they can annotate, live edit or freeze parts of the application and declare theses changes as only private, public or group-width visible. In contrast to our solution, no user guidance during creating or reviewing access rights are given. In addition, no concept to block or share parts of a component's UI to respect privacy needs is presented. Collaborative sessions where participants use different components are not considered.

Tschudnowsky et al. [16] suggested an abstract architecture for mashup applications that can be used and reconfigured synchronously by multiple users. But, the authors neither present any detailed concepts for permission management nor for the user guidance which is needed when considering non-programmers as target group.

MultiMasher includes a visual tool for creating multi-device mashups by marking parts of a website's UI and afterward sharing them [9]. Due to the focus on co-located scenarios, no explicit awareness support about created right assignments or support for different components exist. It is also not possible to define single UI parts as private. Therefore, different views for the same resource can not be created. The component selection as well es interactions between components are not discussed.

The personal learning environment (PLE) Graasp [5] enables the creation and sharing of resources and widgets with participants by grouping into spaces. But, privacy settings are only maintained at space level and can not be configured more fine-grained. Additionally, the rights management is based on a dedicated set of roles which may ease the right assignment in collaborative learning scenarios, but can not be used in generic application platforms like the one we propose. Another PLE, CURE, facilitates a room key metaphor to restrict access rights [15]. CURE allows to share resources during runtime by end-users similarly to the space approach of Graasp. Access rights are defined by keys which represent access to specific spaces. This mainly focuses on sharing of documents and works fine so far. Sharing arbitrary functional parts of an application under different rights with different participants is not feasible with this metaphor.

Within social networks, the circle metaphor introduced by Google+[5] tries to enable an easy grouping of users that should receive the same content. This particular solution is quite interesting for solving sub problems but misses a strategy to represent different rights for different parts of an application efficiently.

Content or document management systems, like Typo3[6], Drupal[7] or Joomla[8], mostly facilitate the matrix metaphor to manage the user's access rights on different data objects. These approaches potentially allow for fine-grained sharing definitions with different rights on all sub parts of a mashup application. But, as the number of users and elements of the application increases, the visualization gets quite complex and hard to understand for non-programmers. In addition, highlighting dependencies between sharing definitions or respecting different used components of different users is not possible.

A number of solutions, like [1] or [7], presented UIs for defining and reviewing the consumption of private data of third party service providers in websites. These approaches work well for reviewing and configuring requested data access from, e.g., different API providers, but do not offer any possibility to generically create access right definitions for single application features or parts of the underlying data model to share them with a group of collaboration partners.

In summary, none of the examined approaches offer support for the requirements and research questions that arise when enabling non-programmers to individually share parts of a CWA.

8   Conclusion

The approach of composite web application (CWA) is promising to be used for non-programmers to individually create and adapt collaborative applications. However, current mashup platforms offer no or only limited support for synchronous collaboration. As the major contribution, this work introduces a permission management approach for collaboratively used CWA as well as an adequate UI support concept. Thereby, users can share either full applications and components, single composition features and data or block private data elements from being shared in general. After presenting the current state of the CRUISE runtime environment for CWAs based on black-box components, the basic rights management concept using triples of subject, object, and permission were introduced in Sect. 4. The permission concept includes multiple ownerships for different parts of an application. The proposed sharing process is empowered by a client- and server-side ACL. Thereby, the process differentiates between additive sharing definitions and subtractive To empower end-users with no programming skills to create and manage different permissions for CWA during runtime, we propose a triple-based overview dialog. It has two major functionalities: First, it provides a possibility to share parts of the CWA with single users or a group

---

[5] https://plus.google.com.
[6] http://typo3.org/.
[7] https://drupal.org/.
[8] http://www.joomla.de/.

of users during runtime. Second, the UI enables an easy to understand visualization of existing permission assignments where the user is either the inviter or the invitee as well as the current state of all sharings. Section 5.2 introduced a set of icons and interaction techniques which presents awareness information about currently shared components and their assigned permissions within the application's live view. Finally, the concepts were implemented within the CSR platform of CRUISE and proven by two user studies. Both showed, that the concepts are accepted by the target group of users and that the basic ideas were understood well. They also proposed some limitations within the user guidance and the interaction metaphors, which were already considered by the current state of the concept presented in the paper.

In future, the concept of sharing application and component parts in the form of features and data has to be once again improved. Currently, no concept exists which automatically identifies and prevents erroneous or meaningless sharing definitions. Thereby, the user should be supported by leveraging semantic annotations and heuristics to prevent, for example, the sharing of a map, where the zoom level and the center position is afterward marked as to be blocked. Similarly, the realization and processing of private data have to be extended. Currently, the approach misses details on the set of selectable data elements as well as a concept how blocked data elements are securely removed from a component without affecting its applicability.

Acknowledgments. The work of Carsten Radeck is funded by the European Union and the Free State of Saxony within the EFRE program. Gregor Blichmann is funded by the German Federal Ministry of Economic Affairs and Energy (ref. no. 01MU13001D).

References

1. Angulo, J., Fischer-Hübner, S., Wästl, E., Pulls, T.: Towards usable privacy policy display and management. Inform. Manage. Comput. Secur. **20**(1), 4–17 (2012)
2. Ardito, C., Bottoni, P., Costabile, M.F., Desolda, G., Matera, M., Picozzi, M.: Creation and use of service-based distributed interactive workspaces. J. Vis. Lang. Comput. **25**(6), 717–726 (2014). Distributed Multimedia Systems DMS2014 Part I
3. Blichmann, G., Radeck, C., Hahn, S., Meißner, K.: Component-based workspace awareness support for composite web applications. In: Proceedings of the 17th International Conference on Information Integration and Web-Based Applications & Services (iiWas 2015) (2015)
4. Blichmann, G., Radeck, C., Meißner, K.: Enabling end users to build situational collaborative mashups at runtime. In: Proceedings of the 8th International Conference on Internet and Web Applications and Services (ICIW2013), pp. 120–123, June 2013
5. Bogdanov, E.: Widgets and Spaces: Personal & Contextual Portability and Plasticity with OpenSocial. Theses, Ecole Polytechnique Fédérale de Lausanne (EPFL), August 2013
6. Brooke, J.: SUS: a retrospective. J. Usability Stud. **8**(2), 29–40 (2013)

7. Drogkaris, P., Gritzalis, A., Lambrinoudakis, C.: Empowering users to specify and manage their privacy preferences in e-government environments. In: Kő, A., Francesconi, E. (eds.) EGOVIS 2014. LNCS, vol. 8650, pp. 237–245. Springer, Cham (2014). doi:10.1007/978-3-319-10178-1_19

8. Gulliksen, J., Göransson, B., Boivie, I., Persson, J., Blomkvist, S., Cajander, Å.: Key principles for user-centred systems design. In: Seffah A., Gulliksen J., Desmarais M.C. (eds) Human-Centered Software Engineering – Integrating Usability in the Software Development Lifecycle. Human-Computer Interaction Series, pp. 17–36. Springer, Dordrecht (2005)

9. Husmann, M., Nebeling, M., Norrie, M.C.: MultiMasher: a visual tool for multidevice mashups. In: Sheng, Q.Z., Kjeldskov, J. (eds.) ICWE 2013. LNCS, vol. 8295, pp. 27–38. Springer, Cham (2013). doi:10.1007/978-3-319-04244-2_4

10. Picozzi, M.: End-User Development of Mashups: Models, Composition Paradigms and Tools. Ph.D. thesis, Politcnico di Milano (2013)

11. Pietschmann, S.: A model-driven development process and runtime platform for adaptive composite web applications. Technology **2**(4), 277–288 (2009)

12. Radeck, C., Blichmann, G., Meißner, K.: CapView – functionality-aware visual mashup development for non-programmers. In: Daniel, F., Dolog, P., Li, Q. (eds.) ICWE 2013. LNCS, vol. 7977, pp. 140–155. Springer, Heidelberg (2013). doi:10.1007/978-3-642-39200-9_14

13. Radeck, C., Blichmann, G., Mroß, O., Meißner, K.: Semantic mediation techniques for composite web applications. In: Casteleyn, S., Rossi, G., Winckler, M. (eds.) ICWE 2014. LNCS, vol. 8541, pp. 450–459. Springer, Cham (2014). doi:10.1007/978-3-319-08245-5_30

14. Radeck, C., Lorz, A., Blichmann, G., Meißner, K.: Hybrid recommendation of composition knowledge for end user development of mashups. In: Proceedings of the Seventh International Conference on Internet and Web Applications and Services (ICIW 2012) (2012)

15. Schümmer, T., Haake, J.M., Haake, A.: A metaphor and user interface for managing access permissions in shared workspace systems. In: Hemmje, M., Niederée, C., Risse, T. (eds.) From Integrated Publication and Information Systems to Information and Knowledge Environments. LNCS, vol. 3379, pp. 251–260. Springer, Heidelberg (2005). doi:10.1007/978-3-540-31842-2_25

16. Tschudnowsky, A., Hertel, M., Wiedemann, F., Gaedke, M.: Towards real-time collaboration in user interface mashups. In: Obaidat, M.S., Holzinger, A., van Sinderen, M., Dolog, P. (eds.) ICE-B 2014 - Proceedings of the 11th International Conference on e-Business, Vienna, Austria, 28–30 August 2014, pp. 193–200. SciTePress (2014)

Author Index

Printed in the United States
By Bookmasters